THE *Unauthorized* Jackie Chan Encyclopedia

From *Project A* to *Shanghai Noon* and Beyond

JOHN CORCORAN

Contemporary Books

Chicago   New York   San Francisco   Lisbon   London   Madrid   Mexico City
Milan   New Delhi   San Juan   Seoul   Singapore   Sydney   Toronto

Library of Congress Cataloging-in-Publication Data

Corcoran, John, 1948-
    The unauthorized Jackie Chan encyclopedia : from Project A to Shanghai
noon and beyond / John Corcoran.
        p.   cm.
    Includes bibliographical references and index.
    ISBN 0-07-138899-0
    1.   I. Title.

    PN2878.C52 C67   2002
    791.43′028′092—dc21   2002019338

Contemporary Books

A Division of The McGraw·Hill Companies

1 2 3 4 5 6 7 8 9 0   AGM/AGM   1 0 9 8 7 6 5 4 3 2

ISBN 0-07-138899-0

Cover photos courtesy of the Kobal Collection

McGraw-Hill books are available at special quantity discounts to use as premiums and
sales promotions, or for use in corporate training programs. For more information, please
write to the Director of Special Sales, Professional Publishing, McGraw-Hill, Two Penn
Plaza, New York, NY 10121-2298. Or contact your local bookstore.

This book is printed on acid-free paper.

To gorgeous Gail O'Toole, who lights up my life with love, laughter, and inspiration. You're the symphony in the soundtrack of my life.

Other books by John Corcoran

The Complete Martial Arts Catalogue

The Overlook Martial Arts Dictionary

The Martial Arts: Traditions, History, People

The Martial Arts Companion

The Original Martial Arts Encyclopedia
(an updated reprint of *The Martial Arts: Traditions, History, People*)

The Martial Arts Sourcebook

How to Become a Martial Arts Star in Your Town

The ACMA (American Council on Martial Arts) *Instructor Certification Manual*

The Ultimate Martial Arts Q&A Book: 750 Expert Answers to Your Essential Questions

Contents

Acknowledgments

I wish to wholeheartedly thank the following writers, researchers, contributors, friends, and publishing personnel for their invaluable input and/or contributions to this book.

I owe a great debt of gratitude to my literary agent, John "Lion" Monteleone, my comrade in arms who joined me in the front trenches when the going got tough and the tough got going. A special heartfelt acknowledgment pours out to Gail O'Toole of Murrysville, Pennsylvania, for her loving encouragement, moral support, and ability to cope with my mad-scientist/creative-artist alter ego throughout this project.

For physical contributions, first and foremost I want to acknowledge the superior efforts of my colleague, Los Angeles, California's Scott Rhodes, a veteran journalist, film historian, and professional stuntman. Scott wrote this book's longest entry, "Hong Kong Martial Arts Films," and also helped me find photographs of numerous actors, directors, and video and DVD box covers connected with Jackie Chan's body of film work.

No less important is the contribution by another colleague, writer and film producer Neva Friedenn of Los Angeles. Neva conducted Jackie Chan's first interview in the English language, a lengthy three-parter, back in 1981 and graciously granted me permission to use it in this book. Her classic appears in the appendix as "Jackie Chan's Lost Interview."

Two others were instrumental in the compilation of other appendices. I could not have compiled what is perhaps the best bibliography ever on Jackie Chan without the superb assistance of Kristi L. Pinkerton, M.L.S., Humanities Department, Main Branch, Carnegie Library of Pittsburgh, Pennsylvania. And super Chan fan Myra Bronstein of Bellevue, Washington, contributed the entire musicography.

Many thanks to the following folks at McGraw-Hill/Contemporary Books in Chicago. First, to my editor—and martial arts practitioner—Betsy Lancefield Lane, who championed this project from a concept to a reality. And to photo acquisitions editor Jill Birschbach, for her enthusiastic efforts to obtain dozens of official film stills and reprint permissions from official sources.

All of the other kind contributors to this work appear below, in alphabetical order by last name or corporate name. Their collective help has made this encyclopedia live up to its potential as a fine reference work on one of the world's most popular celebrities.

Avco Embassy Pictures, Los Angeles, California. CBS Television, Los Angeles, California. Jeff Chin, San Francisco, California. Columbia Pictures, Los Angeles, California. Jose Fraguas, General Manager, CFW Enterprises, Burbank, California. Stefan Hammond, author, Hollywood East, Hong Kong, China. Sang Koo Kang, taekwondo master, Miami, Florida. Linda Kay, President, National Association of Fan Clubs, Oceanside, California. Mike Leeder, editor, Impact: Action Movie Magazine, Huddersfield, England. Scott Leva, stunt coordinator, Los Angeles, California. Bey Logan, journalist and filmmaker, Hong Kong, China. Paul Maslak, author and film producer, Los Angeles, California. Miramax Films, Los Angeles, California. New Line Cinema, Los Angeles, California. See-Yuen Ng, Hong Kong, China, film producer and founder of Seasonal Films Corporation. Michiko Nishiwaki, actress and stuntwoman, Los Angeles, California. Grandmaster Jhoon Rhee, American taekwondo pioneer, Washington, D.C. Master Toddy, Muay Thai instructor, Las Vegas, Nevada. Twentieth Century Fox, Los Angeles, California. Benny "The Jet" Urquidez, fight choreographer and retired world kickboxing champion, North Hollywood, California. Keith Vitali, actor and retired karate champion, Columbia, South Carolina. Warner Bros. Studios, Burbank, California. Mike Worth, actor and black belt, Los Angeles, California.

Introduction

Veteran Hollywood stuntmen have a saying: "The ground doesn't get any softer." In other words, for professional fall guys the older you get the harder the impact of body to ground seems. When will the ground, so to speak, get too hard for the inimitable Jackie Chan?

Jackie Chan's penchant for performing his own amazing on-screen stunts has finally—after decades—made him a household name around the planet. As I write this introduction in October 2001, *Rush Hour 2* has earned a phenomenal $223 million in domestic (U.S. and Canada) ticket sales, making it this year's fourth biggest blockbuster to date. *RH2*'s amazing profit has firmly established Chan as the undisputed king of action films worldwide, and also establishes this movie as the biggest martial arts–related film hit in motion picture history.

Why is he so popular? Simply put, because Jackie Chan's martial arts and action films appeal universally to a large audience. His work is punctuated by broad humor in the tradition of the silent-movie masters like Harold Lloyd, Buster Keaton, and Charlie Chaplin.

Jackie has certainly paid a high price in his rise to global prominence. He has become the Evel Knievel of the movie business. His résumé includes a near-death accident, dozens of broken bones, and probably hundreds of minor injuries. The end credits of his films are always run over outtakes of misfired stunts and the resulting visits from paramedics.

How much more punishment can Jackie's body take before it gives out? Like all of his fans, I, too, love and admire him for what he does. But now—at age forty-eight—he cannot continue risking the consequences of a serious or fatal injury. When he hurt his back shooting *The Accidental Spy* in 2000, a doctor reportedly told him that if he sustained another injury, he might be paralyzed for life.

That he does continue pushing the stunt envelope says everything about what he does and why he does it: it's all for the audience. He feels it's both his duty and his responsibility.

Jackie's early kung-fu films as well as his more recent action movies are built around a handful of elaborate fights and stunt sequences rather than a story. The plot is merely a way to string them together. But since the fights and stunts are so inventive and original, nothing is really lost or missing. The joy of watching a Jackie Chan film is the action.

I want to make one final, significant comment about Jackie Chan, as a human being, and this is a perfect place to do it.

Success hasn't ruined him. He's down-to-earth, he makes healthy donations to charities, and he cares about other people. His Good Samaritan spirit is exemplified in the following incident that occurred in September 2000.

While driving in Hong Kong, Jackie encountered a couple pulled to the side of the road with a flat tire. He stopped—the only motorist to do so—and asked the startled couple if he could assist them. Then he dug the tools out of his trunk and proceeded to change their flat tire himself!

Reportedly, the late Elvis Presley once got out of a limousine and broke up a fight between two complete strangers. The men were so shocked by his mere presence that they immediately stopped fighting and, at Elvis's request, shook hands.

How many people, not to mention genuine superstars, would take the time to help others? No wonder Jackie is one of the world's most beloved entertainment figures.

Format

In this book, you will find just about everything that you need to know about the world's biggest action star.

Asian Names

With so many references to Jackie Chan throughout this book, the author chose to use the initials JC, without periods, when referring to him. This eliminates a massive degree of redundancy.

Asians typically use their last names first—for example, Wong Fei-Hung. This book does not. It instead uses the Western standard of placing the first name first and last name last. For example, Fei-Hung Wong.

Also, Asians who use a first and a middle name sometimes hyphenate those names and sometimes they don't. Other times, a lowercase letter is used for the middle name. For example, Fei hung Wong. For the sake of consistency, a hyphen to connect all first and middle names, and a capital letter for the middle name, are used standardly throughout this book. For example, Fei-Hung Wong.

Film Titles

To reduce confusion, all films appear under their original titles, followed by a list of all alternate titles, including those used for the U.S. releases. The alternate titles are all cross-referenced to the film's original title.

Trust me, you will not get lost, thanks to this editorial device.

Film Entries, Supplementary Information

To facilitate easy reference for most of JC's nearly ninety motion pictures, short sub-headings are used immediately following the title of each main film entry. When all the information was available, these sub-headings include Genre; Hong Kong Release Date; U.S. Release Date; Cast; Director; Other JC Credits; Location(s); Box-Office Gross; and Injuries.

Here's an example:

Accidental Spy, The

Genre: Action-Comedy
Hong Kong Release Date: January 18, 2001
Cast: JC, Min-Jeong Kim, Vivian Hsu, Eric Tsang, Hsing-Kuo Wu, Scott Adkins, Brad Allen (a.k.a. Bradley James Allen)
Director: Teddy Chen
Other JC Credits: Producer; stunt coordinator
Location: Turkey
Injuries: JC hurt his back. The doctor reportedly stated that if JC sustained another such injury, he might be paralyzed for life.

Police Story Series

This is perhaps the best place to try to summarize and clear up the most confusing element of Chan's entire body of film work.

While it comprises just four films, his *Police Story* series (1985–96) comprises a total of twenty-five titles, twenty-one of which are alternates, making it the most multi-titled—and confusing—series in motion picture history. If this summary doesn't clarify everything, I assure you that the entries themselves will.

There's yet another complication in the *Police Story* (*PS*) mixture that compounds the problem: two other Chan films, which also happen to use eleven other various titles, some of them deceptively similar to the *PS* series. One of these pictures is only semi-related; the other is totally unrelated but masquerading as a *PS*.

All told, that makes thirty-six separate titles for just six films, enough to boggle Einstein's mind.

The semi-sequel is entitled *Project S* (1993). While Michelle Yeoh reprises her role from *Police Story 3*, JC has only a cameo in this offering. It's also known as *The New Police Story* and *Police Story 3: Part 2* and *Police Story 4*.

Chan's project unrelated to the *PS* series is *Crime Story* (1993), which bears the additional titles of *Police Story 4* and *The New Police Story*.

Boldface Type

All names and places that appear in bold type *within* an entry indicate that they have a separate entry elsewhere in the book. Use them as a cross-reference for finding related information.

Bylines

Whenever a contributor has written an entry, his or her name will appear at the end of the entry between brackets, like this: [Scott Rhodes].

Jackie Chan Videos

Most Hong Kong films, even the new ones, at their best still look a little dirty and washed out on video. Reportedly, it has something to do with the film stock the Hong Kong filmmakers use.

Many problems mar Chan's collective works on video. Many—in fact, far *too* many—of his subtitled movies on video are not letterboxed. Consequently, the subtitles and even some of the action run off the screen. In too many cases as well, the subtitles blend with the background and are impossible to read.

Of course, there's also the standard use of incorrect grammar and misused words, but any veteran Hong Kong film fan will tell you that that's part of the charm and ambiance of these movies. So is the atrocious dubbing in of English in voices that many times do not fit the characters. And perhaps most common—and entertaining—of all are the wind-gushing and bamboo pole–slapping sound effects that accompany martial arts fight scenes.

So far as Jackie's pictures are concerned, reviewer and avid Chan fan Myra Bronstein writes, "Many of the early Jackie Chan movies are recorded in Extended Play (EP) mode. Some indicate it on the video box and some don't. But even if it doesn't indicate EP, you can tell because the box is suspiciously feather-light. The videotapes on EP are frequently of awful quality and flutter all over the place."

Look for videos in the SP (Standard Play) mode. As with all of Chan's films, see the widescreen version if it's at all possible, or you'll miss out on a lot. And be aware

that some video versions also contain annoying audio problems where the sound fades in and out and becomes garbled.

For the most comprehensive, up-to-date list of where in the United States and Canada to find Hong Kong movies including Chan's, consult this detailed website from the Jackie Chan Newslist: www.primenet.com/~tonylane/rent.htm.

Jackie Chan DVDs

The new DVD releases of Chan's films, thankfully, are eliminating some of the old problems connected with the videocassettes. On DVD, the picture is crisp and clean. People's faces have true color. Some shots are still overly bleached, but most scenes project pure contrast. And when the Dolby Digital sound mix is used, the soundtrack is amazingly clear and crisp.

Extra features on the DVDs of Chan's newer films can include trailers, bios, scene analysis, and talent files. But don't expect these same extras for his older movies on DVD. Hong Kong producers weren't thinking about DVD extras back in the early days. In fact, they hardly used scripts to shoot their films.

Screen Power: The Official Jackie Chan Magazine, published in England, has the best line of Chan's films on DVD available for sale internationally. Consult its excellent website: www.screen-power.com.

The Accidental Spy

Courtesy of the Everett Collection

Accidental Spy, The

Genre: Action-Comedy

Hong Kong Release Date: January 18, 2001

Cast: JC, Min-Jeong Kim, Vivian Hsu, Eric Tsang,
Hsing-Kuo Wu, Scott Adkins, Brad Allen
(a.k.a. Bradley James Allen)

Director: Teddy Chen

Other JC Credits: Producer, stunt coordinator

Location: Turkey

Injuries: JC hurt his back. The doctor reportedly
stated that if JC sustained another such
injury, he might be paralyzed for life.

The story unfolds with Bei (JC), a salesman at a workout equipment store who harbors dreams of adventures. On one normally dull day, Bei follows his instincts to trail two suspicious looking men into an alley. When he realizes that they are robbing a jewelry store, he jumps into action to foil their plans. Soon after, Bei meets Liu (Tsang), a private investigator who convinces Bei that he may be the long-lost son of a rich Korean businessman who's about to die.

His father turns out to be North Korean defector and infamous spy Won-Jung Park, now held under heavy guard in a maximum security prison in Korea. His deathbed agenda sends Bei on a mission as an "accidental spy," which fulfills Bei's dreams of adventure. As Bei is drawn deeper into a game of cat-and-mouse espionage, he realizes he has become the key to locating a lung cancer virus stolen from the U.S. Science Office. With an assortment of characters hindering his mission, Bei must succeed in finding the virus himself.

In *The Accidental Spy*, JC again displays his unequaled prowess at turning movie-set minutia into comic props. He stages a close-quarter brawl in an elevator using freight crates, his tie—and a passenger!—as fight props. In a rollicking fight against four bad guys in a public marketplace, JC uses all types of available props as fighting instruments. But what really distinguishes this sequence is that the fight begins in a Turkish bath, so all the way through it JC is buck naked and must keep his nether regions out of sight.

His major stunts include a construction crane swinging him through the side of a skyscraper, and jumping off a building using two parasols as a makeshift parachute.

The Accidental Spy is reportedly the most expensive Hong Kong film ever made, with a reputed budget of Hong Kong $170 million ($21.8 million U.S.). In late 2000, Dimension Films acquired the U.S. distribution rights.

Actress
Alternate Title: *Center Stage*
Genre: Biography

Hong Kong Release Date: February 20, 1992
Cast: Maggie Cheung, Tony Leung, Han Chin,
    Carina Lau, Lawrence Ng
Director: Stanley Kwan
JC Credit: Co–executive producer
Location: Hong Kong

JC co–executive produced this biopic based on the life of the Chinese silent movie actress Ling-Yu Ruan (Cheung), who committed suicide before she was twenty-five. Director Stanley Kwan deftly mixes his narrative with actual film clips, re-creations of lost films, interviews with survivors, and his own conversations with his cast. The result is a kaleidoscope of emotion and tragedy.

Maggie Cheung won the Best Actress Award at the Berlin Film Festival and the Hong Kong Film Awards for her portrayal of the troubled movie star.

Ads, Television. See **Commercials, Television.**

Alan Smithee Film: Burn Hollywood Burn, An
Genre: Comedy
U.S. Release Date: February 27, 1998

Cast: Eric Idle, Ryan O'Neal, Coolio, Richard Jeni, Sandra Bernhard, Cherie Lunghi
Cameos: JC, Sylvester Stallone, Whoopi Goldberg, Larry King, Billy Bob Thornton, Dominick Dunne, Robert Evans, Joe Eszterhas, Shane Black
Director: Arthur Hiller
Locations: U.S. (Los Angeles)
U.S. Box-Office Gross: $40,000

JC plays himself in a cameo role in this star-studded comedy flop about Hollywood filmmaking. The story follows a British director (Idle), whose real name is Alan Smithee, as he steals the reels of his own film when he realizes he hates the movie, but can't remove his name from it since the Directors Guild of America's official pseudonym for disputed films is "Alan Smithee." The film in question is a $250-million stinker entitled *Trio*, starring JC, Stallone, and Goldberg.

In real life, there have been over thirty films bearing the credit "Alan Smithee" in as many years, and this stab at moviemaking self-parody becomes a tedious, unfunny in-joke of little or no interest to general audiences. The proof is in its financial bath: it became one of the biggest box-office flops in decades.

All in the Family
Genre: Drama
Hong Kong Release Date: February 8, 1975
Cast: Linda Chu, Dean Shek (a.k.a. Dean Shek Tien), Sammo Hung, JC
Director: Mu Chu
Location: Hong Kong

One of JC's most embarrassing supporting roles as a rickshaw driver who seduces both a mother and her daughter. It briefly features the *only* sex scene in JC's motion picture career.

Antiques, Favorite. Ancient jade.

Armour of God
Alternate Titles: *Operation Condor 2: The Armour of the Gods* (U.S.), *Thunderarm*
Hong Kong Release Date: January 21, 1986
Cast: JC, Alan Tam, Lola Forner, Rosamund Kwan, Ken Boyle, John Ladeiski
Director: JC
Other JC Credit: Co–stunt coordinator
Location: Yugoslavia
Box-Office Gross: $35.4 million (Hong Kong)
Injuries: JC was nearly killed when a tree limb broke during a leap from a high castle wall to the tree. He plunged twenty feet and landed

A promotional flyer for *Armour of God*   Courtesy of Scott Rhodes   JC in action   Courtesy of the Everett Collection

on his head, suffering a brain hemorrhage and a cracked skull. Even today, long after the surgery, he can manually twist his scalp back and forth a few inches. The fall also left him hard of hearing in one ear.

JC plays "Asian Hawk," an Indiana Jones–style character who finds pieces of ancient armor that is known as the "Armour of God," which he sells at an auction. But when his ex-girlfriend has been kidnapped by a religious cult, he has to ask for the armor's return to use as ransom. In the end, he rescues his ex-girlfriend and returns the armor along with related pieces owned by the cult.

Armour of God is a slight take-off on the Indiana Jones pictures, in which JC's humor and affable personality carry most of the show. The film's downside is its slow pace. There are some spectacular action sequences, but save for one in the beginning they don't start until late in the movie. In one grand fight scene, three vampire women clad in black leather attack JC.

Armour of God is the movie in which JC was nearly killed when a dangerous stunt backfired in Yugoslavia. The accident appears in the end credits.

As a whole, however, this picture is nowhere near as good as its sequel, ***Armour of God II: Operation Condor***. Nevertheless, it became Hong Kong's third-highest grossing film of the 1980s.

Armour of God, released in the United States on video under the title *Operation Condor 2: The Armour of the Gods*, is not the second but the first in the series. The "real" English-language title is *Armour of God*. Its sequel, *Armour of God II: Operation Condor*, was released in the United States as just *Operation Condor*.

Armour of God II. See ***Armour of God II: Operation Condor***.

Armour of God II: Operation Condor
Alternate Titles: *Armour of God II, Desert Meltdown, Operation Condor* (U.S.), *Operation Eagle, Project Eagle*

Armour of God II: Operation Condor (DVD). Dimension Home Video: 92 minutes/rated PG-13. In English.

Courtesy of Scott Rhodes

Genre: Period Action-Comedy
Hong Kong Release Date: March 22, 1990
U.S. Release Date: July 18, 1997

Cast: JC, Carol Cheng, Eva Cobo De Garcia, Shoko Ikeda, Ken Lo, Vincent Lin, Ken Goodman
Director: JC
Other JC Credits: Producer, coscreenwriter, stunt coordinator
Location: Spain, Morocco, Hong Kong
Box-Office Gross: $39 million (Hong Kong); $10.4 million (U.S.)
Injuries: JC dislocated his sternum (breastbone) when he fell from a hanging chain, and sustained a puncture wound in his leg.

Reprising his "Asian Hawk" role as an Indiana Jones–style character, JC is hired in post–World War II by a European count on behalf of the United Nations to find gold reputedly stolen and hidden by Nazis. Joining him are an archaeologist (Cheng) and the daughter of one of the dead Nazis (Cobo). A parade of mercenaries and Palestinians impedes their quest all the way to their discovery of the hidden gold in an underground complex in the Sahara Desert.

This was JC's biggest film to date, a lavish production costing $115 million Hong Kong dollars ($15 million U.S.), making it the most expensive in Hong Kong history, and taking one full year to shoot. *Armour of God II* has exceptional production values, plenty of action and broad humor, and one of the greatest car chases on film. It by far eclipses the slower-paced original, *Armour of God*.

JC's speed and agility in stunts and combat is once again mind-boggling. In one stunt, JC is hanging from a beam near the roof of a warehouse. A car catapults through the air, straight at him. He swings up out of the way and the car misses him—barely. In another stunt, he leaps from a motorcycle speeding off a pier, and grabs a safe hold on a fisherman's net. And there's a wonderfully choreographed fight above flat, moving steel platforms high above a hangar floor.

The finale is an amazing airborne fight in a wind tunnel with huge fans blowing JC and his adversaries bodily all over the place while they engage in combat.

In 1997, this picture was painstakingly transformed into an English-language version entitled just *Operation Condor*. Trimmed by thirteen minutes and fitted with a dynamic new score and sound design, the new version of the film is far more accessible to JC's American fans.

Armour of the Gods. See *Armour of God*.

Art of Influence, The
Genre: Documentary
Year of Release: 1997
Cast: JC (in Part 2)
Director: Deborah Dickson, Roberto Guerra

Divided in five parts, *The Art of Influence* registers fifteen artists' impressions on the life and work of other artists that influenced them. In Part 2, "Ways of Seeing," JC discusses Bruce Lee's films, Buster Keaton's stunts, Charlie Chaplin's humor, Fred Astaire's and Gene Kelly's dancing, and Sylvester Stallone's action films.

Asian Hawk, The. JC's character name in *Armour of God* and *Armour of God II: Operation Condor.*

Asian Cult Cinema. See Appendix 3: Jackie Chan Bibliography.

Attack of the Kung Fu Girls. See *The Heroine.*

Australia. Where JC's father, Charles Chan, found a job as the head cook for the American embassy in 1961. Before leaving Hong Kong for this job, he enrolled JC in the **China Drama Academy** and temporarily left his wife Lee-Lee behind.

Awards. See Appendix 4: Jackie Chan's Awards, Honors, and Offices Held.

Bao, Sammo Hong Jin. See **Sammo Hung.**

Basic Operation. See *Police Story 4: First Strike.*

Battle Creek. See *The Big Brawl.*

Battle Creek Brawl. See *The Big Brawl.*

Bei. JC's character in *The Accidental Spy.*

Bellboy, The. At press time, JC was finalizing a deal with MGM Studios to star in the remake of this 1960 Jerry Lewis comedy of the same title. Actor Ivory Wayans was also in negotiations to costar and direct. Lewis, who owns the remake rights, would also costar and coproduce. The remake report-

The Big Brawl   Courtesy of the Kobal Collection

edly would be shot at the MGM Grand Hotel in Las Vegas.

Best of the Martial Arts Films, The

Alternate Titles: *The Best of the Martial Arts Movies, Deadliest Art: The Best of the Martial Arts Films*
Genre: Documentary

Year of Release: 1990
Cast: JC, Bruce Lee, Sammo Hung, Yuen Biao, Cynthia Rothrock, Kareem Abdul-Jabbar, Sho Kosugi, Karen Shepard, Richard Norton, Keith Cook (a.k.a. Keith Hirabayashi)

A fascinating American-made genre documentary/overview narrated by *Enter the Dragon* costar John Saxon and featuring a

"THE BIG BRAWL"

800125

JC and Mako in
The Big Brawl

Courtesy of the
Everett Collection

parade of prominent martial arts film stars. It was coproduced by **Fred Weintraub** and his daughter, Sandra.

Best of the Martial Arts Movies, The. See ***The Best of the Martial Arts Films***.

Bibliography. See Appendix 3: Jackie Chan Bibliography.

Big and Little Wong Tin Bar. A 1962 drama that marked JC's first role as a child actor, with Taiwanese star Li-Hua Li.

Big Brawl, The

Alternate Titles: *Battle Creek, Battle Creek Brawl*
Genre: Period Martial Arts Comedy
Year of Release: 1980
Cast: JC, Jose Ferrer, Kristine Debell, Mako, The
    Great John L.
Director: Robert Clouse
Other JC Credit: Stunt coordinator
Location: United States (San Antonio, Texas)

JC is a Chinese immigrant in Chicago during the 1930s who's forced to compete in the Battle Creek Brawl in Texas in order to free his sister-in-law, who's been kidnapped by one of the mobsters. He must defeat the opposing mob's fighter in order to win.

   The Big Brawl, JC's first American film, is generally regarded as a disaster. One critic called it "The Big Bore." It failed to establish him in the West and it didn't entertain his fans in Asia, either. JC had no control over his own destiny in this important transition, but should have. His flamboyant style of fighting was severely restricted by director Robert Clouse and fight choreographer Pat Johnson. All of JC's inventive suggestions were typically shot down, paralyzing his natural showmanship and making him little more than an actor.

   On the positive side, JC was paid $1 million for his role, at that time making him the highest paid Asian star ever to make an American movie. He spent two years in the United States, most of the time learning English from a Beverly Hills language coach and from watching American television. He also learned many hard lessons about the nature of the American film business through his *Big Brawl* failure.

Big Drunk Hero. See Come Drink with Me.

Birthdate.
JC was born on April 7, 1954, the Year of the Horse in the Chinese calendar.

Black Dragon. See Miracles: Mr. Canton and Lady Rose.

Blockbuster Presents Jackie Chan: From Stuntman to Superstar

Alternate Title: *Jackie Chan*
Genre: Documentary
Year of Release: 1997

This retitled documentary is actually the American-produced A&E biography entitled "Jackie Chan," which originally aired as a one-hour TV show in 1996. The Blockbuster version has lost host Peter Graves's brief prologue and epilogue and made a few editing changes, but it does, of course, retain JC's personal comments.

It is this documentary in which JC made his now famous self-evaluation statement: "Bruce Lee number one. John Wayne number two. Jackie Chan number three. That's the way I would like to be remembered in the history books."

Overall, it's an interesting overview of JC's career, and a perfect introduction for those new to the action master and his work.

Blood Pact. See *The 36 Crazy Fists*.

Book, Favorite. Comics.

Bo, Sammo Hung Kam. See **Sammo Hung**.

Brother vs. Brother. See *Twin Dragons*.

Bruce vs. Snake in Eagle's Shadow. See *Snake in the Eagle's Shadow*.

Burning Island. See *Island of Fire*.

Cannonball Run
Genre: Action-Comedy
Year of Release: 1981
Cast: Burt Reynolds, Farrah Fawcett, Roger Moore, Dom DeLuise, Dean Martin, Sammy Davis Jr., JC
Director: Hal Needham
Locations: United States (various)
Box-Office Gross: $59.9 million (U.S.)

JC plays a small role as a Japanese Subaru driver in this American-produced, star-studded account of a group of drivers competing in a cross-country race named the "Cannonball Run," after which this movie takes its title. JC does engage in a short, flamboyant fight, but it's too abbreviated to appease any of his fans.

But one aspect of *Cannonball Run* did impact JC's career to this day. The use of outtakes in the end credits, which has become a JC trademark, was an idea he adapted from this film.

Cannonball Run II
Year of Release: 1983

Cast: Burt Reynolds, Dean Martin, Sammy
    Davis Jr., Dom DeLuise, Susan Anton, JC,
    Richard Kiel
Director: Hal Needham
Locations: United States (various)
Box-Office Gross: $28.1 million (U.S.)

JC again plays a small role as an Asian driver whose copilot is played by Richard Kiel ("Jaws" in the James Bond film *Moonraker*), in this American-produced sequel. In a basic repeat of the original formula and plot, a star-studded cast competes in a mindless cross-country race named the "Cannonball Run," only this time they're pursued by the Mafia.

JC was bound by contract to work on this picture or he would have otherwise passed it up. He was already Hong Kong's foremost star.

Canton Godfather, The. See *Miracles: Mr. Canton and Lady Rose*.

Center Stage. See *Actress*.

Challenge. See *Drunken Master*.

Chan, Charles. JC's father. See **Family**.

Chan, Cho-Ming. See **Jason Chan**.

Chan, C. N. JC's character name in *Gorgeous*.

Chan, Inspector. JC's character name in *Project S*.

Chan, Inspector Eddie. JC's character name in *Crime Story*.

Chan, Jackie. JC is the only actor in the film business who uses his real name for the fictional characters he portrays in his movies. Sometimes this is by his own design, but mainly it is the device used by his films' distributors to capitalize on his stardom.

To date, JC's real name has been used as a character name in *Little Tiger from Canton* (1978), *Police Story* (1985), *Armour of God* (1986), *Police Story II* (1988), *Armour of God II: Operation Condor* (1990), *Thunderbolt* (1995), and *Police Story 4: First Strike* (1996).

Chan, Jason. Born in 1982 to JC and his former wife, **Feng-Chiao Lin**, Jason (a.k.a. Cho-Ming Chan) is JC's only son.

Chan, Kevin. JC's character name in *Police Story 3: Supercop*.

Chan, Lee-Lee. JC's mother. See **Family**.

Chan, Lung. JC's character name in *Fearless Hyena II*.

Chan, Willie. JC's flamboyant, longtime manager, friend, and business partner. Chan (a.k.a. Willie Chan Chi-Keung, no relation to JC) was a production assistant for **Wei Lo** in 1973 when he befriended JC and recognized in him the potential for stardom. Upon JC's signing with **Golden Harvest Studios** in 1980, the pair formed Jackie & Willie Productions, with Willie as managing director, to focus on JC's career outside of the studio's agreement, and the two have enjoyed a long, prosperous business relationship ever since.

JC is the only actor who plays fictional characters named "Jackie Chan."

Charlie's Angels. See **Wirework**.

Cheng, Pei-Pei. See *Come Drink with Me*; **Hong Kong Martial Arts Films**.

Chen, Yuen-Lung. One of JC's alternate screen names. He is credited in this name in the casts of *Little Tiger of Canton* (1971), *The Heroine* (1971), *Police Woman* (1972), and *Not Scared to Die* (1973).

Cheung, Maggie. One of JC's favorite leading ladies, she's costarred with JC in five of his films: the first three *Police Story* actioners (1985, 1988, 1992), *Project A II* (1987), and *Twin Dragons* (1992). She's also won Best Actress at the Hong Kong Film Awards a record four times.

Born in Hong Kong on September 20, 1964, Cheung immigrated to England when she was eight. She returned to Hong Kong after completing her education, where she began a modeling career and was a runner-up in the 1983 Miss Hong Kong Pageant.

As required by the Miss Hong Kong contract, two years of television work followed, coupled with appearances in numerous low-budget comedies. In 1985, she appeared opposite JC as his girlfriend, May, in *Police Story*, which launched her to stardom, and later drew critical attention in Kar Wai Wong's debut feature, *As Tears Go By* (1988), the same year she again appeared with JC in *Police Story 2*.

Her versatility, paired with a flair for comedy, gained Cheung myriad roles

Maggie Cheung with JC in *Twin Dragons*
Courtesy of the Kobal Collection

throughout the nineties in what amounts to a massive body of work. Western audiences have seen her in the upgraded U.S. versions of JC's *Police Story 3: Supercop* (1992) and *Twin Dragons* (1992). In 1992, she won the Berlin Silver Bear Award for her performance in Stanley Kwan's *Actress*, which JC produced. She continued to draw acclaim for her dramatic work and on the art house circuit with **Hark Tsui's** romantic fantasy *Green Snake* (1993).

Cheung continued her serious dramatic work in Kar Wai Wong's *Ashes of Time* (1994), *The Soong Sisters* (1996) with **Michelle Yeoh**, and the French art house film *Irma Vep* (1996).

Cheung sustained a serious injury in *Police Story 2* when a falling metal frame struck her on the head, which appears in the film's outtakes.

See also: **Hong Kong Martial Arts Films**.

Chiang, David. See **Hong Kong Martial Arts Films**.

China Drama Academy. The Peking Opera school in Kowloon where JC spent a full decade, the longest term permissible, as a youth, from age seven to seventeen (1961–71).

The academy assumed complete responsibility for all its students. In return, it kept all the money earned by students from public performances. An alarming clause in the legal contract with the parents permitted the academy's master, **Jim-Yuen Yu**, to discipline the students, even "to death." Essentially, it was a form of indentured servitude.

All the students, who ranged in age from toddlers to teenagers, assumed the last name of "Yuen," after the academy master's middle name. JC was named Lo Yuen.

Life at the academy was decidedly brutal. Through ten years of nineteen-hour days, punctuated with the traditional canings for any indiscretions, JC learned the rigorous discipline of the **Peking Opera**. Peking Opera training encompasses acting, singing, dance, mime, acrobatics, and a variety of martial arts. The hardships were many and varied. Students seldom were fed enough food to sustain their tremendous physical expenditures. They slept on a hardwood floor in ragged blankets and used outdoor showers and toilets.

But because of the grueling training, JC developed an awesome level of physical skill and bodily control as well as an ability to excel even in difficult circumstances.

It was here that JC met two other pupils with whom he would forge lifelong relationships. The first, Lung Yuen (a.k.a. **Sammo Hung**), the senior student at the academy, was JC's boyhood nemesis. All the students addressed him as "Big Brother." The other was **Biao Yuen**. The three were members of the academy's performing troupe called the **Seven Little Fortunes**. The film *Painted Faces* (1988) was based on the Peking Opera training of JC and his classmates.

JC left the China Drama Academy in 1971 and became a freelance stuntman, working on numerous kung-fu films for **Shaw Brothers Studios**.

Chinese Connection, The. See *Fist of Fury*.

Chinese Godfather, The. See *Miracles: Mr. Canton and Lady Rose*.

"Chop-Sockies." See **Hong Kong Martial Arts Films**.

Chow, Raymond. The visionary chairman of **Golden Harvest Studios** who signed JC to a multipicture contract in 1980 and catapulted his leap to superstardom.

Chow was the head of production at Shaw Brothers for eleven years, until he decided to produce independent films on his own. With partner **Leonard Ho**, he founded **Golden Harvest Studios** in 1970. Chow made a brilliant business move by signing American martial arts sensation **Bruce Lee** to a multipicture contract.

Chow shrewdly made distribution deals for Lee's films throughout the world. Lee became a worldwide phenomenon and the fledgling studio an overnight powerhouse.

Chow followed up on these successes with the Michael Hui films, which were the vanguard of Hong Kong films flowing into the Japanese market, followed by those of JC and **Sammo Hung**. Each of JC's many Golden Harvest–produced pictures, starting with *The Young Master* (1980), was in most cases more successful than its predecessors.

Today, Chow's Golden Harvest Entertainment conglomerate has produced more than five hundred films, many of which have won awards and critical acclaim at the world's most prestigious international festivals such as Cannes, Berlin, Edinburgh, London, New York, Chicago, San Francisco, and many others. Its films are seen by millions of people in most countries throughout the world and in many formats: cinemas, television cable networks, videocassettes, laser discs, and satellite.

Chow, Yun-Fat. See **Hong Kong Martial Arts Films**.

CID 07. JC's character name in *Winners and Sinners*.

Cinematheque Francaise, The. See Appendix 4: Jackie Chan's Awards, Honors, and Offices Held.

Cinema of Vengeance

Genre: Documentary
Year of Release: 1994
Cast: JC, Bruce Lee, Don "The Dragon" Wilson, John Woo, Jimmy Wang Yu, Sammo Hung, Cynthia Rothrock, Sophia Crawford, Woo-Ping Yuen, Tak-Hing Kwan, Gary Daniels, Donnie Yen
Director: Toby Russell

Cinema of Vengeance was produced, written and directed by England's Toby Russell, an expert on Hong Kong cinema. His knowledge is put to great use in this in-depth look at Hong Kong films, with an emphasis on the martial arts genre.

Although fairly cheaply budgeted, *Cinema of Vengeance* contains many interesting action clips and interviews with the stars from the famous to the not-so-famous. One of its highlights is an exclusive interview with the late Bruce Lee, who explains his perspective on the Chinese martial art of kung-fu.

Overall, *Cinema of Vengeance* is a fine introduction for those new to the genre.

Cirque du Soleil. According to the *New Times Los Angeles*, when JC once attended a performance by this internationally renowned acrobatic troupe, two of the female performers spotted him in the audience. Awestricken, they reportedly stopped in mid-performance and exclaimed, "Jackie!"

City Hunter

Genre: Action-Comedy
Hong Kong Release Date: January 16, 1993
Cast: JC, Richard Norton, Gary Daniels, Chingmy Yau, Joey Wong, Kumiko Goto, Leon Lai, Michael Wong
Director: Jing Wong
Locations: Japan, Hong Kong
Box-Office Gross: $30.7 million (Hong Kong)
Injuries: JC broke the instep on his foot, dislocated his shoulder, and suffered his worst knee injury to date during the skateboarding scenes.

JC plays the high-tech, girl-chasing detective character Ryu Saeba, originally created for the Japanese comic and animation series *City Hunter*. With his bumbling assistant Kaori (Wong), Ryu is asked by newspaper tycoon Imamura to return his beautiful runaway daughter, Shizuko (Japanese supermodel Goto). Ryu and Kaori make their way onto a cruise ship, whose guests include Shizuko and a ruthless gang of international terrorists, led by McDonald

(Norton), attempting to kidnap the luxury liner's prominent passengers for ransom.

City Hunter, strangely, hits and misses. Although it's packed to the brim with stunt sequences and fight routines, the characters strain for laughs throughout the picture, and the good-natured cartoon elements are mixed with occasional detracting scenes of brutal violence and sexist gags. Conversely, the film boasts some classic sequences that are pure JC.

In one inventive scene, JC and Goto enter the ship's movie theater, which is showing **Bruce Lee's** *Game of Death*. While losing a fight against two giant opponents, JC gets inspiration from Lee's on-screen battle with towering basketball star Kareem Abdul-Jabbar and defeats the two giants.

Another wildly creative highlight comes in the form of a dream sequence where the characters from the popular *Streetfighter II* Nintendo video game come to life and engage in combat. This inspired live-action sequence expertly emulates the persona, wardrobe, movements, and sound effects of the game and its characters.

To add to *City Hunter*'s comic-book quality, the entire movie is shot very bright and colorful in cartoon style.

City Hunter (DVD). Mega Star Video: 95 minutes/unrated. In Cantonese and Mandarin with English subtitles.

Courtesy of Scott Rhodes

Clinton, President Bill. A known JC fan, the former U.S. president extended an open invitation to JC to visit the White House after viewing a private screening of **Shanghai Noon**. JC, however, was unable to take him up on his offer before Clinton left office in January 2001. So he sent an autographed *Shanghai Noon* T-shirt to First Daughter Chelsea Clinton.

Clouse, Robert. The American director of JC's *The Big Brawl*. See **Fred Weintraub**.

Colors, Favorite. Blue, white, black, and beige.

Come Drink with Me
Alternate Titles: *Big Drunk Hero* (U.S.), *The Girl with the Thunderbolt Kick*
Genre: Docudrama
Year of Release: 1965

JC has a child role in this groundbreaking kung-fu picture starring Pei-Pei Cheng. Helmed by legendary Hong Kong director King Hu, *Come Drink with Me* was the first martial arts film to feature a female lead. The movie made a star of Cheng, who came to be nicknamed "the Queen of Martial Arts," and paved the way for scores of other Hong Kong movies starring women.

According to some sources, JC's role in this film is uncredited.

Comedy Kung-Fu. A genre created in 1978–79 by JC, which transformed the Hong Kong film industry. His talents as a physical comedian were first introduced in two films, ***Snake in the Eagle's Shadow*** (1978) and ***Drunken Master*** (1978). These were the first films to effectively fuse kung-fu and comedy, and they collectively rocketed JC to stardom.

See also: **Hong Kong Martial Arts Films**.

Commercials, Television. JC has done hundreds of commercials endorsing various products in just Hong Kong alone, as well as ads for products in numerous other countries. This is a selective list since, due to volume, a full and complete list is impossible.

JC's American ads have been action-oriented. They include one for Mountain Dew soda pop in 1997, in which he escapes from a gang of attackers, and a milk commercial for the American Milk Advisory Board, which features him hanging from a rope ladder à la *Police Story 3: Supercop*.

In Asia, JC has done commercial endorsements for American Express (1998) and a 1998 public service announcement shown in Asia that highlighted the dwin-

Comedy Kung-Fu, as portrayed in *Drunken Master*

Courtesy of Seasonal Films Corporation

dling numbers of tigers due to "bone tonic" products.

In Taiwan in the early 1990s, he endorsed his own health drink, Bo Bo Tea.

In Japan, starting in the mid-1980s he's been a commercial spokesman for Mitsubishi motors, as well as Cannon cameras in 1997 (appearing in a traditional white karate gi).

Among his many Hong Kong commercials was one for "Hong Kong City of Life" (1999) for the HK Tourist Association, and one for his own Foodland (2000) website.

Cooper, Richard. British publisher-editor of *Screen Power* magazine and president of the official United Kingdom branch of Jackie Chan's International Fan Club.

Born in 1974 in Bath, England, Cooper watched his first JC movie, ***Drunken Master*** (1978), at age eleven and has been hooked ever since. He graduated from the City of Bath College after two years, at the age of twenty, gaining top honors in Business and Finance.

Cooper ventured to Hong Kong in December 1994 to approach JC's management about launching an official United Kingdom–based fan club, and eight months later received their full approval and support.

In late 1997, he developed an interest in the publishing business and received approval from The Jackie Chan Group to publish *Screen Power*, a fully-endorsed, official bimonthly magazine focused entirely on JC and his films. Since its debut the glossy magazine has grown in distribution and status and is well received by readers all over the world.

Cooper continues to hold his office as president of the U.K. branch of Jackie Chan's International Fan Club, and maintains a strong working relationship with JC and his Hong Kong headquarters. In September 2001, he launched a second publication, *Jade Screen Magazine*, a glossy bimonthly periodical covering the entire Hong Kong movie industry. Author of the book *The Best of Jackie Chan's Screen Power*, he is currently developing other books and video documentaries in conjunction with the magazines.

See also: Appendix 5: Jackie Chan Official Fan Clubs.

Countdown in Death; Countdown in Kung Fu.
See *Hand of Death*.

Crime Story
Alternate Titles: *Hard To Die, The New Police Story, Police Dragon, Police Story IV, Serious Crimes Squad*
Genre: Action
Hong Kong Release Date: June 24, 1993
Cast: JC, Kent Cheng, Ling-Ling Poon, Wing-Nie Ng, Blackie Ko, Stephan Chan, Wai-Kwang Lo, Fa Chung, Mars, Ken Lo, Yeung Pooi Saan Ang, Christine Ng, Ling Ling Poon
Director: Kirk Wong
Other JC Credit: Stunt coordinator
Locations: Hong Kong, Taiwan
Box-Office Gross: $27.4 million (Hong Kong)
Injuries: JC injured both legs when they were pinned between two moving cars.

First, to clear the confusion, *Crime Story* is in no way related to the **Police Story** series, in spite of the fact that occasionally it is found under the titles *New Police Story* and *Police Story IV*.

In *Crime Story*, JC does play a cop, but unlike the adventure-laden martial arts action films of the *Police Story* series, *Crime Story* is a realistic, gritty drama based on the real-life kidnapping of Hong Kong real-estate magnate Tak-Fai Wong. Consequently, it may not be quite what fans have come to expect from one of his films, since JC's usual stunning athleticism and comic personality are mostly absent despite the film's escapist elements.

Corrupt Hong Kong police detective Hung joins several powerful magnates from Hong Kong, China, and Taiwan in a plot to kidnap Hong Kong billionaire real estate mogul Yat-Fei Wong. But Inspector Eddie Chan (JC), known for his loyalty and brilliance, is assigned the case. Hung volunteers to be his partner in order to lead the investigation astray. The case takes the pair to Taiwan, and JC begins to suspect his partner may be one of the kidnappers. As JC continues to hunt down suspects and gets closer to solving the case, Hung tries to kill him and is instead apprehended.

In an explosive climax in a burning building, Hung unsuccessfully tries to escape from JC. Before he dies, Hung tells him where Wong is being hidden. Wong is rescued by the police, and begins a new life in a foreign country.

Crouching Tiger, Hidden Dragon. See **Hong Kong Martial Arts Films**; **Wirework**.

Cub Tiger from Canton. See *Little Tiger from Canton*.

Cyclone Z. See *Dragons Forever*.

Dance of Death
Alternate Title: *The Eternal Conflict*
Year of Release: 1976
Cast: Angela Mao Ying, Dean Shek (a.k.a. Shek Kin), Pei Chin

Director: Chi-Hwa Chen
JC Credit: Stunt coordinator
Location: Hong Kong

JC served as stunt coordinator and does not appear in this conventional kung-fu story about a woman who learns the martial arts from two rival masters to enable her to take revenge on those responsible for killing her clan members.

Dance of Death is also an alternative title for ***The Odd Couple*** (1979), a completely different film.

Dead Heat. See *Thunderbolt*.

Deadliest Art: The Best of the Martial Arts Films. See *The Best of the Martial Arts Films*.

Deadly Three, The. See *Enter the Dragon*.

Delicacy, JC's Favorite. Cracked crab.

Desert Meltdown. See *Armour of God II: Operation Condor*.

Dey, Tom. The director of JC's *Shanghai Noon* (2000). Born in New England, he was graduated from Brown University. In 1987, he studied film in Paris, France, at the Centre des Etudes Critiques. In 1990, he moved to Los Angeles and attended the American Film Institute (AFI) and became a writer for *American Cinematographer* magazine.

Dey was graduated from AFI in 1993, and made commercials for Ridley Scott Associates. *Shanghai Noon* was his feature film directorial debut.

Diet, JC's Favorite. Vegetables.

Double Dragon. See **Twin Dragons**.

Dragon. JC's character name in *Dragon Lord* and *The Young Master*.

Dragon Attack, The. See **Fantasy Mission Force**.

Dragon Fist
Alternate Title: *In Eagle Dragon Fist*
Genre: Period Martial Arts

Hong Kong Release Date: April 21, 1979
Cast: JC, Nora Miao, James Tien
Director: Wei Lo
Location: Korea
Injuries: JC suffered a broken nose.

How-Yuen Tang (JC) helps his master's widow (Miao) seek revenge for the needless death of his master at the hands of another fighter. But when they find the perpetrator, he is repentant and has cut off his leg to demonstrate his sorrow. An evil lord then poisons the widow, and JC and the one-legged master dispense kung-fu justice.

Dragon Fist is one of the worst films JC made before his breakthrough hit **Snake in the Eagle's Shadow** (1978). It decidedly lacks the enjoyable feel exhibited in **Half a Loaf of Kung Fu** and **Spiritual Kung Fu**, all of which were shot in the same year, 1978.

This film is not to be confused with **Dragon Lord**, whose alternate title is also *Dragon Fist*.

Dragon Lord
Alternate Titles: *Dragon Fist, Dragon Strike, Young Master in Love*
Genre: Martial Arts

(Both photos) *Dragon Fist*

Year of Release: 1982
Cast: JC, Mars, Inn-Sik Whang, Wai-Man Chan,
     Fun Tien
Director: JC
Other JC Credit: Fight choreographer
Location: Hong Kong
Box-Office Gross: $10.9 million (Hong Kong)
Injuries: JC injured his chin so badly that he
     couldn't speak.

JC plays a girl-chasing youth called Dragon, who accidentally stumbles across a gang of thieves who are planning to sell off the country's national treasure.

Dragon Lord is a fun romp coupling JC's trademark comedy with straightforward but frenetic fight action. Plenty of set pieces will entertain the viewer. One, a bizarre form of rugby, features a scene that entered the **Guinness Book of World Records** for the highest number of takes—over fourteen hundred.

Dragon Lord was originally intended to be a sequel to JC's **The Young Master** (1980), thus the alternate title, *Young Master in Love*. But the story link between the two films disappeared in editing.

Dragons Forever

Alternate Titles: *Cyclone Z, 3 Brothers, Three
     Brothers*
Hong Kong Release Date: February 11, 1987
Cast: JC, Sammo Hung, Biao Yuen, Wah Yuen,
     Benny "The Jet" Urquidez, Deannie Yip,
     Pauline Yeung, Billy Chow, Dick Wei

Director: Sammo Hung
Location: Hong Kong
Box-Office Gross: $33.5 million (Hong Kong)
Injuries: JC badly impacted his ankle.

JC plays a somewhat sleazy attorney hired to defend a fish-processing factory owner accused of dumping toxic waste into fish-ponds owned by a beautiful woman. JC enlists the help of a weapons dealer (Hung) and a scientist (Yuen) to investigate the claim. Things go awry when JC and Hung fall in love with the leading lady and her cousin. JC's investigation ultimately uncovers the fact that his client's company is a front for an illegal drug operation.

 Dragons Forever is the last movie featuring JC and his two Peking Opera school colleagues, Sammo Hung and Biao Yuen—the so-called "**Three Brothers**." The beginning of the movie places JC in a neat little fight in a restaurant with some flips, kicks, and a cute gag with a ceiling fan. In fact, since there are three stars, the film is packed with fights: When JC's not fighting, the other two are. When they all fight together, sometimes against each other, you get a sense of the amazing skill and grace they developed together at the **China Drama Academy**. There's also plenty of slapstick physical comedy that works even

Dragons Forever (VHS). Tai Seng Video Marketing: 93 minutes/unrated. In Cantonese and Mandarin with English subtitles.

Courtesy of Scott Rhodes

if you don't read the subtitles, like JC's attempt to stuff the hefty Sammo into a small closet.

(Both photos) *Drunken Master*   Courtesy of Seasonal Films Corporation

The sensational American kickboxing champion **Benny "The Jet" Urquidez** plays the main villain in the frenetic climactic fight, battling JC for the third time in as many films. The pair pulls out all the stops in this grand finale, which some fans maintain is almost as satisfying as their showstopper in *Wheels on Meals* (1984).

Dragon Strike. See *Dragon Lord*.

Dragon Tamers. A 1975 kung-fu picture about which little is known other than JC's role as its stunt coordinator.

Drink, Favorite. Ice water.

Drunken Fist II. See *Drunken Master II*.

Drunken Master
Alternate Titles: *Challenge; Drunken Monkey; Drunken Monkey in the Tiger's Eye; Eagle Claw; Snake Fist; Cat's Paw, Part 2; The Story of Drunken Master*
Genre: Comedy Kung-Fu
Hong Kong Release Date: November 5, 1978
Cast: JC, Simon Yuen, Jang-Lee Hwang, Dean Shek (a.k.a. Dean Shek Tien)
Director: Woo-Ping Yuen
Location: Hong Kong

(Both photos) *Drunken Master* Courtesy of Seasonal Films Corporation

Injuries: JC suffered a concussion, injured the bone under his eyebrow, and almost lost an eye.

Fei-Hung Wong (JC), is the lazy, rambunctious son of a staid master who isn't conscientious enough to learn his father's style properly. After getting trounced a few times, JC is sent to train with a brutal, alcoholic uncle, Sam Seed (Yuen)—a master of the drunken style of kung-fu. In the meantime, it's revealed that villains are trying push JC's father off his coal-rich land.

After undergoing considerable pain and humiliation, JC escapes the uncle's clutches, only to humbly return after being defeated by a martial arts bully (**Jang-Lee Hwang**).

Now his training escalates. In the prolonged climactic fight, JC uses the long-range fighting strategies of the mythical "Eight Drunken Fairies." Seven of these eight lurching, off-center styles are beautifully demonstrated in the climactic scene, and Chan fake-fights the eighth style to defeat Hwang.

JC, who exercised almost complete creative control of this film, is spectacular in this witty, fast-paced assemblage of fight scenes profusely layered with humor and deftly directed by **Woo-Ping Yuen**. Blaring music, "chop-socky" sound effects (wind gushes when an arm or leg is swung!), and sensational martial arts scenes make this an experience not to be missed. JC is simply

Drunken Master   Courtesy of Seasonal Films Corporation

brilliant in the rugged training sequences, demonstrating superior athleticism and physical conditioning.

Drunken Master was JC's second film with Seasonal Films producer **See-Yuen Ng** and his second big hit—the first was ***Snake in the Eagle's Shadow*** (1978). *Drunken Master*'s box-office success was, by Hong Kong standards, phenomenal: $8 million (Hong Kong) in its first run, and by 1979 it broke the box-office record previously set by **Bruce Lee**. The **comedy kung-fu** genre had arrived, with JC its sole superstar.

A sequel, ***Drunken Master II*** (1994), was shot many years after this original.

Drunken Master II (a.k.a. *The Legend of Drunken Master*) (DVD). Dimension Home Video: 102 minutes/rated R. In English. Courtesy of Scott Rhodes

Drunken Master II

Alternate Titles: *Drunken Fist II, Drunken Monkey II, The Legend of Drunken Master* (U.S.), *Legend of the Drunken Master*

Genre: Period Martial Arts Action-Comedy

Hong Kong Release Date: March 2, 1994

U.S. Release Date: October 20, 2000 (upgraded version)

Cast: JC, Ti Lung, Anita Mui, Ken Lo, Long Di, Felix Wong, Chia-Liang Liu, Wing-Fong Hiu, Chi-Gwong Cheung, Ken Andy Lau

Director: Kar-Leung Lau

Other JC Credits: Stunt coordinator

Locations: Shanghai, northern China

Box-Office Grosses: $40.9 million (Hong Kong); $11.4 million (U.S.)

Injuries: JC suffered burns on his arm during the firefight scene.

JC stars in this nominal sequel to his first big box-office hit *Drunken Master* (1978), once again playing legendary Chinese folk hero **Fei-Hung Wong**. As he and his father head home on a train in 1915, they accidentally grab an invaluable national treasure that's about to be smuggled out of China to the West. A sinister profiteer (Lau) is illegally exporting Chinese treasures overseas, and it's up to JC to put a stop to it. This ignites an escalating series of exuberant fight scenes that alternate with broad slapstick. Most of the fights involve the drunken style of kung-fu, which, in this film, actually requires Wong to get drunk! In using it, Chan lurches and leans at impossible angles during combat, as if inebriated, almost defying the laws of gravity.

Drunken Master II emphasizes fighting more than death-defying stunts. This amazing film, which boasts lavish production values, single-handedly revitalized the conventional kung-fu genre in Hong Kong. It's a throwback to the old **Shaw Brothers Studios'** period costume pictures and is helmed by one of the studio's best directors, Kar-Leung Lau, who also plays a Chinese missionary working for the government. Anita Mui, who plays Madame Wong, JC's conniving, gambling-addicted stepmother, is riotously funny and steals the spotlight in just about every scene she appears in.

The fight scenes in a marketplace and a tea shop are impressive, but it's only a warm-up to the punishment JC endures in the exhausting, twenty-minute climactic battle at a foundry. His fight with relentless kicking expert Ken Lo (JC's bodyguard in real life), who plays the film's main villain, is a scorcher—literally. JC gives new meaning to the term "fire-breathing dragon" when he swigs grain alcohol and actually blows fire flamethrower-style at his opponent, and at one point, even drags himself

Drunken Master II   Courtesy of the Kobal Collection

Drunken Master II   Courtesy of the Everett Collection

through real burning coals. Coming at the end of a film filled with jaw-dropping action scenes, this extended virtuoso effort, which alone took four months to shoot, sets some kind of milestone: it may not be possible to film a better fight scene.

Drunken Master II set a new Hong Kong box-office record and won an award for action design. Some Western movie critics consider it one of the two or three best films of JC's career. It was reportedly made to raise money for a new headquarters for the Hong Kong Stuntman's Association.

Drunken Monkey; Drunken Monkey in the Tiger's Eye. See *Drunken Master*.

Drunken Monkey II. See *Drunken Master II*.

Duel of Dragons. See *Twin Dragons*.

Dying for Action: The Life and Films of Jackie Chan. See Appendix 3: Jackie Chan Bibliography.

Eagle Claw, Snake Fist, Cat's Paw, Part 2. See *Drunken Master*.

Eagle Shadow Fist. See *Not Scared to Die*.

Eagle's Shadow, The. See *Snake in the Eagle's Shadow*.

Encyclopedia of Martial Arts Movies. See Appendix 3: Jackie Chan Bibliography.

Enter the Dragon
Alternate Titles: *The Deadly Three, Operation Dragon* (Europe)
Genre: Martial Arts
Hong Kong Release Date: November 18, 1973
Cast: Bruce Lee, John Saxon, Jim Kelly, Shek Kin, Yang Tse, Angela Mao, Bob Wall, Peter Archer, Bolo Yeung, Sammo Hung
Director: Robert Clouse
Location: Hong Kong

Mr. Han (Kin), an evil drug lord, stages an underground martial arts tournament on his island fortress. Lee plays an undercover agent sent to gather evidence against him, while also avenging his sister's death by Han's henchmen.

Enter the Dragon is the first modern masterpiece of the martial arts movie genre, and the film that made Bruce Lee a worldwide phenomenon.

JC plays an uncredited stuntman and appears four different times in the underground finale, where the dynamic Lee defeats an army of attacking guards, using, alternately, empty hands, the staff, the nunchaku, and two sticks. In one of the film's most dramatic moments, JC gets his neck snapped by Lee, immediately after which the camera zooms in to catch Lee's furious facial expression.

In a 2001 poll of Hollywood stuntmen, compiled for *Inside Kung Fu* magazine by stuntman/martial arts film historian Scott Rhodes, Lee's underground battle in *Enter the Dragon* was voted the single best fight sequence ever filmed.

Escape from the KGB. See *Police Story 4: First Strike*.

Essential Guide to Hong Kong Movies, The. See Appendix 3: Jackie Chan Bibliography.

Essential Jackie Chan Sourcebook, The. See Appendix 3: Jackie Chan Bibliography.

Bruce Lee grabs young stuntman JC by the hair during the underground battle with the guards in *Enter the Dragon*.

Courtesy of Jeff Chinn

Eternal Conflict, The. See **Dance of Death**.

Family. JC was born after a remarkable twelve-month pregnancy, three months longer than normal, and he weighed twelve pounds at birth. He is the only son of Charles and Lee-Lee Chan. His parents were destitute refugees who fled mainland China during the Communist Revolution and settled in Hong Kong. Both parents found work with the French ambassador to Hong Kong and lived in the cramped servant's quarters of the ambassador's man-

sion on Victoria Peak. JC remained there for six years.

JC wasn't told until much later in life that he had three half brothers and one half sister from his parents' former marriages.

Fan Clubs, JC Official. See Appendix 5: Jackie Chan Official Fan Clubs.

Fantasy Mission Force

Alternate Titles: *The Dragon Attack*, *Mini Special Force*
Genre: Action-Comedy
Year of Release: 1982
Cast: Jimmy Wang Yu, Brigitte Lin, Sun Yuen, JC, Adam Cheng, David Tao, Pearl Cheung, Bat-Liu Hui, Ching Fong, Kwan Lee
Director: Yen-Ping Chu
Location: Taiwan

Despite his top billing, JC appears in just a few stunt scenes in this saga of a military expert (Yu) hired to assemble a commando team to rescue four army generals who've been captured by the Japanese. The team consists of crooks, gamblers, and con artists, and the outrageous characters they fight include vampires, Amazons, Nazis, and zombies!

JC reportedly only worked on this picture as a favor to Jimmy Wang Yu, who had earlier helped his career, and it is definitely *not* a "Jackie Chan movie."

Fearless Hyena, The

Genre: Comedy Kung-Fu
Hong Kong Release Date: February 17, 1979
Cast: JC, Shi-Kwan Yen, Kuan Li, James Tien,
    Shih Tien (a.k.a. Shek Kin)
Director: JC
Other JC Credits: Screenwriter, stunt coordinator
Location: Hong Kong
Box-Office Gross: $5.4 million (Hong Kong)

JC stars as Lung Shing, a fighting clown/con artist paid to attract students to a bogus kung-fu school. His irresponsible actions result in his grandfather's death, and he is trained for vengeance by a long-lost clan uncle who teaches him "emotional kung-fu."

Wei Lo, who had JC on exclusive contract, finally caved in and let him do a picture *his* way. As writer-choreographer-star, JC couldn't miss with the kung-fu in this picture. The training and fighting sequences are truly astonishing. The film is crammed with scenes in which he fights for morsels of food with chopsticks and fights as a silent comedy mime, as a cross-eyed buffoon, or disguised as a girl.

The prolonged but terrific climactic fight is based on the esoteric "wire technique," a series of exercises accompanied by uttering cries that JC converts to fighting. He translates the cries into "four emotions" to confound his adversary. This was JC's invention, and it was a brilliant device to use in a fight scene. It's never been duplicated since.

Fearless Hyena emerged as the second-highest grossing film in Hong Kong history, proving that JC knew how to appeal to the taste of his audience. This was JC's last complete picture under Lo's contract. A semi-sequel, *Fearless Hyena II*, followed, but was completed with a JC look-alike.

Fearless Hyena II

Genre: Martial Arts
Year of Release: Filmed in 1980, but only
    released in 1983
Cast: JC, Shih Tien (a.k.a. Shek Kin)
Director: Wei Lo
Location: Hong Kong
Box-Office Gross: $1.9 million (Hong Kong)

Despite his starring credit, JC appears in only a few scenes of this story about two brothers avenging their father's murder. He left this picture unfinished when he left **Wei Lo**'s company. Lo completed it with a look-alike and stored footage from the original *Fearless Hyena*, which does feature JC as its prominent star.

Fighting Stars. A U.S.-based martial arts entertainment magazine founded by publisher Mito Uyehara in 1973. *Fighting Stars* flourished until the late 1980s and featured a number of cover stories, features, and news pieces about JC and his film work.

Figures, JC Action. In early February 2000, Marco Polo, a leading distributor of high-quality model kits, replicas, and action figures, announced the release of a series of twelve-inch action figures based on JC. The first in the series was the **Jackie Chan: My Story** figures, shortly followed by the **Dragon Lord** figure. More figures are expected to be released in the near future.

JC worked very closely on the overall design, personally overseeing and approving the final production of the figures. Each figure has over thirty points of articulation at the neck, shoulders (ball joints), waist, hips, thighs, knees, ankles, wrists, and fully posable fingers. They stand approximately twelve inches tall and come complete with accessories like wraparound sunglasses, movie clapper board, and stunt team uniform.

The *My Story* figure was the first to reach retail stores and hobby shops throughout the United States in April 2000. Figures are available for purchase online at www.screen-power.com.

Filmography, JC. See Appendix 2: Jackie Chan Filmography.

First Mission. See **Heart of Dragon**.

First Strike. See **Police Story 4: First Strike**.

Fist of Anger. See **Not Scared to Die**.

Fist of Fury
Alternate Titles: *The Chinese Connection* (U.S.), *The Iron Hand*
Genre: Period Martial Arts
Hong Kong Release Date: March 22, 1972
U.S. Release Date: 1973

Fighting Stars magazine

Courtesy of Neva Friedenn

Cast: Bruce Lee, Nora Miao, Feng Tien, James Tien, Robert Baker, Wei Lo

Director: Wei Lo

Location: Hong Kong

Set in Shanghai in 1908, a Japanese-led gang murders Lee's kung-fu master and terrorizes his former school. Lee brings swift and terrible justice to the wrongdoers, but sacrifices his life to save his friends.

Asian history fuels the scenes of this period-piece film, which some consider the greatest of all Bruce Lee films. The story plays on themes that are extremely emotive for a Chinese audience only a quarter of a century after World War II, during which China had suffered terribly at the hands of the Japanese. The film is set in the Japanese-occupied sector of Shanghai, when it was divided among a number of major powers including the British. It boasts the classic scene in which Lee uses a flying kick to shatter a Japanese sign reading "No Chinese or Dogs Allowed," which forever endeared Lee to the Chinese people.

One scene features Lee's now-legendary nunchaku fight, the first time these weapons had ever been seen in a film. The film was also the first to use a Western martial artist as a villain, Bob Baker playing the Russian fighter Petrov, who is hired by the Japanese to fight Lee.

JC stunt-doubles for the Suzuki character, the main villain, whom Lee kicks through a wall panel in the terrific final showdown. This scene is famous for its intentional humor. Lee kicks the villain so hard that the perfect outline of his body is left in the panel after he flies through it.

As the actor's stunt double, JC was yanked back on a wire some fifteen feet from Lee's kick before hitting the ground, without the benefit of any safety devices—a Hong Kong stunt record for its time. JC was the only stuntman who volunteered to do it and, after successfully completing the stunt, his profile as a stuntman was greatly improved. JC also appears briefly as an extra in an early scene sparring at a kung-fu school, right before the Japanese trash it.

Fists to Fight. See *New Fist of Fury*.

5 Lucky Stars; Five Lucky Stars. See *Winners and Sinners*.

Food. Self-admittedly, one of JC's greatest pleasures is eating a good meal. This is undoubtedly due to the fact that throughout his youth he seldom had enough food to eat to fully satisfy his hunger.

From Bruce Lee to the Ninjas: Martial Arts Movies. See Appendix 3: Jackie Chan Bibliography.

Fruit, JC's Favorite. Young coconut.

Fu, Chien. JC's character name in *Snake in the Eagle's Shadow*.

Fung, Tat. JC's character name in *Heart of Dragon*.

Genre, Classical Kung-Fu. See **Hong Kong Martial Arts Films**.

Gen-X Cops
Genre: Action
Hong Kong Release Date: June 17, 1999
Cast: Stephen Fung, Nicholas Tse, Sam Lee, Grace Yip, Eric Tsang, Daniel Wu, Jaymee Ong, Bey Logan
Director: Benny Chan
JC Credits: Co—executive producer, cameo
Location: Hong Kong

JC makes a brief cameo appearance as a fisherman.

Benny Chan, who helmed JC's *Who Am I?* (1998), directs this saga of three off-beat young cops (Tse, Fung, and Lee) who oppose a sinister alliance of Hong Kong Triads and members of the Japanese Yakuza.

Girl with the Thunderbolt Kick, The. See *Come Drink with Me*.

Glass Bottle. See *Gorgeous*.

Glickenhaus, James. See *The Protector*.

Godenzi, Joyce. See **Hong Kong Martial Arts Films**.

Golden Dragons. See *Police Story 4: First Strike*.

Golden Harvest Studios. The motion picture company, founded in 1970 by **Raymond Chow** and **Leonard Ho**, that in 1979 offered JC a $4.2 million (HK) multipicture contract and vaulted his career into the major leagues. Through its business interests to both JC and **Bruce Lee**, Golden Harvest became the biggest motion picture studio in the history of Hong Kong.

Chow was the head of production at Shaw Brothers for eleven years, until he decided to produce independent films on his own. Soon after establishing Golden Harvest, he signed American martial arts sensation Bruce Lee to a multipicture deal. This resulted in four completed films before Lee's untimely death, each one a bigger success than the last: *The Big Boss*

(1972), **Fist of Fury** (1972), *Way of the Dragon* (1972), and **Enter the Dragon** (1973). Partial footage of Lee was shot in 1972 for *Game of Death* (1979), which Golden Harvest completed later with doubles and look-alikes.

The savvy Chow compounded the profits dramatically for all these movies by selling distribution rights to international markets throughout the entire world. Thus, Hong Kong–based Golden Harvest became a global enterprise.

Chow's first Golden Harvest production with JC, **The Young Master** (1980), broke box-office records previously set by Lee's films and rocketed JC to overnight stardom. This led JC to roles in several U.S. films produced by Golden Harvest, **The Big Brawl** (1980), **Cannonball Run** (1981), and **Cannonball Run II** (1983). While the *Cannonball* films were popular at the box office, they failed to make JC the Hollywood star he had hoped to become.

Back in Hong Kong again, JC and Golden Harvest hit pay dirt with a virtual parade of record-breaking hit films starting with **Winners and Sinners** (1983). Much of the success of these films was due to JC's having been given complete creative control by Golden Harvest. His genius was then forever evident to the world as each of his films superseded the last in concept, budget, production values, creativity, and profits.

Today, under the umbrella title Golden Harvest Entertainment, the company is Asia's premier Chinese entertainment conglomerate and engages in a wide range of activities including film production, talent management, film distribution, cinema exhibition, and print processing. It has, together with its partners, successfully brought the multiplex theater concept to Asia, operating a network of 283 theaters in Hong Kong, Singapore, Malaysia, Thailand, Korea, and mainland China. It also distributes Chinese-language films globally throughout the Far East and to Australia, New Zealand, Europe, and the Americas.

Golden Horse Awards. See Appendix 4: Jackie Chan's Awards, Honors, and Offices Held.

Golden Lotus. A 1974 forgettable kung-fu film in which JC had only a small supporting role.

Gorgeous
Alternate Title: *Glass Bottle*

Genre: Romantic Comedy

Hong Kong Release Date: February 13, 1999

Cast: JC, Tony Leung (a.k.a. Tony Leung Chiu Wai), Hsu Qi, Emil Chau, Brad Allen, Stephan Chow

Director: Vincent Kok

Other JC Credits: Producer, coscreenwriter, stunt coordinator

Location: Hong Kong

Box-Office Gross: $27.4 million (Hong Kong)

Gorgeous (DVD). Columbia/Tri Star Home Video: 99 minutes/unrated. In English and Cantonese.

Courtesy of Scott Rhodes

JC softens up considerably in this offbeat—for him—PG-rated romantic comedy about a young Taiwanese woman (Qi) from a small fighting village who finds love and adventure in Hong Kong after meeting a lonely playboy (JC).

There are slapstick comedy elements and some fights mixed into the plot including two lengthy unarmed, one-on-one battles between JC and Brad Allen.

Guinness Book of World Records. JC holds two different *Guinness Book* records and participated in a third. The first is for the highest number of takes for a single movie scene, over fourteen hundred for his bizarre form of rugby in ***Dragon Lord*** (1982). JC's second record is more serious. He made it into the 2001 edition of the *Guinness Book* for being uninsurable due to his personal performance of dangerous stunts.

JC took part in a third Guinness record in 2000. Since 2000 was the Year of the Dragon on the Chinese calendar, Hong Kong, in association with China, planned the largest ever Dragon Dance staged on

Gorgeous

Courtesy of the Everett Collection

the Great Wall of China. JC had the honor of leading the dance with the dragon's head.

Half a Loaf of Kung Fu

Genre: Comedy Kung-Fu
Year of Release: Filmed in 1978, but only
    released in 1980
Cast: JC, James Tien, Chung-Erh Lung, Kan Kam
Director: Chi-Hwa Chen

Other JC Credit: Stunt coordinator
Location: Hong Kong

Essentially a slapstick send-up of martial arts movies, *Half a Loaf of Kung Fu* has JC playing a hapless martial arts student who teams with a father and daughter to help them protect a sacred relic from bandits.

JC's character is a wandering klutz who reads fighting instruction books upside down and stumbles when surrounded by crazed killers. His character wins fights by accident and the martial arts action is almost pure parody. For example, pinned to a wall by the throwing stars of twenty pursuers, he hangs with his arms outstretched to the strains of "Jesus Christ, Superstar." Or, in need of quick energy to rescue a damsel in distress, he eats spinach while the soundtrack delivers the "Popeye the Sailor Man" theme song. In another scene, he uses his female costar as a fight prop, whipping her around his body while she fires kicks and punches at the bad guys.

Half a Loaf of Kung Fu is JC's first attempt at comedy and contains the elements that would later make him a comedy superstar in Hong Kong. **Wei Lo**, whose company financed the picture, was so upset he shelved it for two years before releasing it in June 1980, when JC had become an established star. It then grossed $1 million Hong Kong in its first two months.

Hand of Death

Alternate Titles: *Countdown in Death, Countdown in Kung Fu, Shaolin Men, Strike of Death*
Genre: Period Kung-Fu
Hong Kong Release Date: July 15, 1976
Cast: Dorian Tan, James Tien, Chang Chung, JC, Sammo Hung, John Woo, Biao Yuen
Director: John Woo
Location: Hong Kong
Injuries: JC sustained a concussion.

An unexceptional directorial debut for the now legendary **John Woo**, *Hand of Death* also has the distinction of featuring JC, **Sammo Hung**, and **Biao Yuen** in small roles—the first time the **"Three Brothers"** from the **China Drama Academy** appear together in one film. Woo also wrote the script.

JC is a spear-fighting expert and the sidekick of superkicker Dorian Tan, a Shaolin student who must find a Manchu traitor named Shih responsible for the murder of his abbot.

Yuen is unrecognizable, while Hung, the film's stunt coordinator, portrays a henchman whose bucked teeth and makeup make him appear more absurd than threatening.

Hapkido

Alternate Title: *Lady Kung Fu*
Genre: Martial Arts
Hong Kong Release Date: October 12, 1972
Cast: Sammo Hung, Carter Wong, Angela Mao Ying, Inn-Sik Whang, Ying Pai, JC
Director: Feng Huang
Location: Hong Kong

JC has a small cameo as a student in a crowd scene. *Hapkido* marks Sammo Hung's debut in a leading role. After studying hapkido, a Korean martial art, in Korea, Hung and two friends return to China to open a martial arts school. One of the friends is slain by a rival Japanese school, so the remaining two seek revenge. Costar **Angela Mao Ying**, a genuine black belt in hapkido, was the biggest female martial arts star in Hong Kong at the time.

Hard to Die. See *Crime Story*.

Heart of Dragon
Alternate Titles: *First Mission, Heart of the Dragon*
Genre: Drama
Hong Kong Release Date: October 16, 1985
Cast: JC, Sammo Hung, Melvin Wong, Emily Chu, Heoi Mang, Chia-Yung Liu, May Wu, Wei Dick
Director: Sammo Hung
Location: Hong Kong
Box-Office Gross: $20.3 million (Hong Kong)

Concept: Martial arts meets *Rain Man*. JC is a cop who forsakes his dream of sailing around the world so that he can care for his gullible, mentally disabled brother (Hung). Innocently caught up in a gangland fight over some stolen jewels, Sammo is kidnapped to force Jackie to hand over a police informant.

Heart of Dragon is not a conventional JC film but a heartwarming drama of filial love and devotion. The film is fundamentally a drama about the relationship between the two brothers and the tension between family responsibility and dreams. Significant portions of *Heart of Dragon* even qualify it to be called JC and Hung's first tearjerker-type sentimental film.

The one attempt to make it something else, via the stolen jewels device, distracts from—if not hurts—the core movie. The film, in fact, is nearly ruined by a gratuitous and formulaic fight scene at the end, but a brilliant and moving summary montage—the bookend to an earlier montage in the film—saves everything.

Although JC was nominated for a Best Actor award, *Heart of Dragon* was a box-office disappointment and sent the clear signal to JC that his audience demands action, not sentiment, from him.

Heart of the Dragon. See *Heart of Dragon*.

Height. JC is five feet, six inches tall.

Heroine, The

Alternate Titles: *Attack of the Kung Fu Girls, Kung Fu Girl* (U.K.)
Genre: Period Martial Arts
Hong Kong Release Date: April 26, 1971
Cast: Pei-Pei Cheng, JC (a.k.a. Yuen-Lung Chen), James Tien, Jo Shishido
Director: Wei Lo
Location: Hong Kong
Other JC Credit: Stunt coordinator

A female martial arts expert assists the Chinese resistance movement against the Japanese.

The Heroine marked two firsts for JC: his first adult role on screen (he plays a Japanese villain) and his first shot at stunt coordinating.

Highbinders

Genre: Action-Comedy
Year of Release: 2002
Cast: JC, Lee Evans
Director: Gordon Chan
Locations: Ireland, Thailand, Hong Kong

JC plays Eddie Yang, an indomitable Hong Kong cop who's on the trail of a ruthless modern day slave-trader. He finds himself teamed with eccentric British agent Arthur Watson (Evans). Both men are killed in the line of duty, but each finds himself reanimated as a supernaturally enhanced hero, a "Highbinder."

Just as the pair get a handle on their new abilities, they learn that their foe has some unexpected powers of his own.

Highbinders was cowritten by **Bey Logan**, with **Sammo Hung** as stunt coordinator. U.S. director Reginald Hudlin will helm the film, which points to the increasing attempts by the Asian film industry to become more competitive internationally. The budget for *Highbinders* is reportedly $35 million (U.S.), making it the largest ever for a Hong Kong film. [Bey Logan]

Himalayan, The

Genre: Martial Arts
Year of Release: 1975
Cast: Angelo Mao Ying, Sing Chen, Tao-Liang Tan, Sammo Hung
Director: Feng Huang
Location: Hong Kong

JC has a small role and works as a stuntman in this routine martial arts story about a woman who studies kung-fu with a holy lama in Nepal, then uses it to exact revenge against a villainous town leader back in her native village.

Ho, Leonard. JC's filmmaking "godfather." The late cofounder and president of Hong Kong's enormously successful **Golden Harvest Studios**, one of the most influential and prolific movie empires in Asia. Ho produced over five hundred films in his illustrious career.

Before creating the studio in 1971 with partner **Raymond Chow**, Ho spent eleven years heading the Shaw Brothers studio. When not working, Ho was a generous contributor to and worker for charities in Hong Kong and the United States.

When Golden Harvest placed JC on contract in 1979, the savvy executive took the young star under his wing and, using Golden Harvest's financial muscle, gave him complete creative control over his own destiny. It was the major turning point in JC's professional career.

Before his death in 1997, Ho produced many of JC's biggest and best motion pictures. They are ***Winners and Sinners*** (1983), ***Project A*** (1983), ***Wheels on Meals*** (1984), ***My Lucky Stars*** (1985), ***Armour of God*** (1986), ***Project A 2*** (1987), ***Dragons Forever*** (1987), ***Police Story 2*** (1988), ***Miracles: Mr. Canton and Lady Rose*** (1989), ***Drunken Master II*** (1994), ***Thunderbolt*** (1995), and ***Mr. Nice Guy*** (1997).

Hollywood East: Hong Kong Movies and the People Who Make Them. See Appendix 3: Jackie Chan Bibliography.

Home, Beverly Hills. According to the *Los Angeles Times*, JC purchased a four-bedroom house for $3 million here in spring 1998. Built in the 1980s, the gated, 7,000-square-feet house reportedly has four fireplaces, a pool, a five-car garage, and a motor court.

Hong Kong Action Cinema. See Appendix 3: Jackie Chan Bibliography.

Hong Kong Film Awards. See Appendix 4: Jackie Chan's Awards, Honors, and Offices Held.

Hong Kong Martial Arts Films. Some of the earliest Chinese martial arts movies were black-and-white silent films produced in Shanghai and Hong Kong. These included *Thief in the Car* (1920), *Monkey Fights Golden Leopard* (1926), and *The Burning of the Red Lotus Temple* (1929). During the 1930s, 1940s, and 1950s, Shanghai was considered to be *the* Hollywood of China, as well as the motion picture capital of Asia. It produced lavish, high quality Mandarin-language films, which were also popular in Hong Kong. Among these were many musicals.

Hong Kong, on the other hand, produced Cantonese-language films, which were considered low-budget "B" pictures with very low production values. It was Hong Kong cinema, however, that gave birth to the modern martial arts movie with the Yong Yao Film Company production of *The True Story of Wong Fei-hung* (1949), starring former Peking Opera star **Tak-Hing Kwan** in the title role.

Kwan (1905–1996) was Hong Kong's first true martial arts action star and played the true-life Chinese folk hero **Fei-Hung Wong** in nearly one hundred films over the next twenty years. (JC and Jet Li are just two of the other stars who have played

A rare promotional shot of Bruce Lee from *Enter the Dragon*
Courtesy of Warner Bros. Studios

Wong, who is perhaps the most famous character in Hong Kong cinema.)

Kwan's excellent performances and the accuracy and intricacies of the films' kung-fu sequences helped elevate and popularize Hong Kong cinema throughout Asia. Until the Fei-Hung Wong series, many of the martial arts sequences in Chinese films were not terribly accurate or exciting. They consisted of magic, swordplay, **wirework**, and a number of untrained actors flailing their arms wildly about. Kwan was a real kung-fu master and performer and the action in his films raised these sequences and films to a new, higher standard.

The Big Boss (DVD). Universe Laser and Video Co.: 95 minutes/unrated. In Cantonese and Mandarin with English subtitles. Courtesy of Scott Rhodes

Authentic kung-fu was now in demand in Chinese cinema.

Classical Kung-Fu Genre

From the early 1960s to the early 1980s, **Shaw Brothers Studios** was the biggest film studio in Hong Kong. It was responsible for countless martial arts movies, many of which were lavish costume epics and period films set in the late Ching dynasty of the late 1800s to early 1900s. These came to be known as the classical kung-fu genre. Shaw Brothers also launched the careers of many famous Hong Kong stars such as Jimmy Wang Yu, **Ti Lung**, David Chiang, **Alexander Fu Sheng**, **Lo Lieh**, and **Gordon Liu** as well as respected directors such as Chia Liang Liu (a.k.a. Kar Leung Lau) and Cheh Chang.

The Shaws, Run Run and Run Me, were originally from Shanghai, where they produced and distributed films throughout China during the 1920s. In 1958, studio head Run Run Shaw moved the company to Hong Kong's Clearwater Bay, where he built the largest motion picture production facility in Asia, a studio lot in the grand Hollywood tradition called "Movie Town."

Over the next twenty-five years, the studio turned out a number of classic martial arts films, including *One Armed Swordsman* (1967), *Vengeance* (1970), *King Boxer* (1972), *Shaolin Martial Arts* (1974), *Five Masters of Death* (1975), *Flying Guillotine* (1976), *Chinatown Kid* (1977), *Shaolin Challenges Ninja* (1978), *Five Deadly Venoms* (1978), *The Master Killer* (1978), *Kid with the Golden Arm* (1979), *Dirty Ho* (1979), *Legendary Weapons of Kung-Fu* (1982), and *8 Diagram Pole Fighter* (1984).

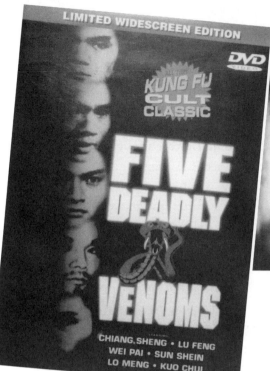

When 1972's *King Boxer* was widely released in the United States the following year as *5 Fingers of Death*, it was a huge box-office success and is credited with helping to usher in the first martial arts movie boom in the United States. Courtesy of Scott Rhodes

Five Deadly Venoms (DVD). Steeplechase: 95 minutes/ unrated. In English. Courtesy of Scott Rhodes

1972's *King Boxer* had a totally unexpected impact on the history of Hong Kong films. Bought by Warner Bros. and widely released in the United States in 1973 as *5 Fingers of Death*, it was a huge box-office success and is credited with helping to usher in the first martial arts movie boom in the United States.

The Shaw Brothers' pictures also introduced wirework to the martial arts genre, which today is influencing fight action in big-budget Hollywood films.

The Bruce Lee Era

During the 1970s and 1980s, Shaw Brothers Studios' main competition was **Golden Harvest Studios**, a company founded in 1970 by **Raymond Chow** and **Leonard Ho**. Chow was the head of production at Shaw

Kid with the Golden Arm (DVD). NS Video: Approximately 75 minutes/unrated. In English.

Courtesy of Scott Rhodes

Brothers for eleven years, until he decided to produce independent films on his own.

After seeing **Bruce Lee** performing a martial arts demonstration on Hong Kong television, Chow contacted Lee and offered the rising star a multipicture contract. Lee was originally contacted by the Shaw Brothers, but was not satisfied with their meager financial offer. Lee had already been a moderate success in Hollywood, having won some fame for his work on the TV shows "The Green Hornet," which was also popular in Hong Kong, and "Longstreet," but he had lost the role of "Caine" to David Carradine in the American hit series "Kung Fu."

This was Lee's opportunity to finally star in feature films and show the world what his unique martial arts and philosophy were all about. His first three films, *The Big Boss* (1971), **Fist of Fury** (1972), and *Way of the Dragon* (1972), were produced on low budgets, but became some of the biggest hits in Hong Kong history. Bruce Lee became a superstar in Asia, and his films were soon taking America and the rest of the Western world by storm.

In 1973, Warner Bros. and Golden Harvest collaborated on what would become Bruce Lee's biggest production, **Enter the Dragon**. Unfortunately, Lee died on July 20, 1973, before the movie opened. The film was a huge international success and Bruce rocketed to superstardom in the West. Although Bruce Lee's Hong Kong career was relatively short, the quality of his work raised the standard of martial arts films and helped bring Hong Kong films to worldwide attention.

The Chop-Sockies

A number of producers tried to exploit Bruce Lee's international fame by producing numerous "Chop-Sockey" pictures (a.k.a. "Chop-Sockies") and Bruce Lee–imitator films. These starred a host of Bruce Lee look-alikes with sound-alike names such as Bruce Li, Bruce Le, Dragon Lee, Tang Lung, Bruce Leung, Bruce Liang, etc. They were usually low budget, low quality productions that capitalized on Bruce's fame and made some fast money for the producers. Try as they might, however, not one of the clones could duplicate Lee's magnetic screen presence and performance.

The term "Chop-Sockies" soon became synonymous with cheap, poorly made, and badly dubbed Hong Kong martial arts movies. Since the Bruce Lee–imitator craze was relatively short-lived, Hong Kong producers began to search for other stars to fill the late Dragon's shoes.

Jackie Chan in an early kung-fu role

Kung-Fu Comedy

Like many other former Peking Opera performers, JC entered the Hong Kong film industry and put his considerable skills to work as an extra and stuntman in many films, including the Bruce Lee films *Fist of Fury* and *Enter the Dragon*. He eventually worked his way up to the position of stunt coordinator and moved on to win supporting and starring roles in several kung-fu dramas that included *Little Tiger from Canton* (1973) and *New Fist of Fury* (1976). The films met with very little success and JC saw little future in being groomed as the next Bruce Lee.

JC realized that in order to be successful, he had to be different. Consequently, he combined his martial arts and acrobatic skills with comedy and a likeable "everyman" heroic character who often wins fights purely by accident. He found success with his unique approach in the films *Snake in the Eagle's Shadow* (1978) and *Drunken Master* (1978), the picture that broke all existing Hong Kong box-office records and made Jackie Chan a new star on his own terms.

JC's success with his new formula also gave birth to the popular comedy kung-fu genre. JC joined Raymond Chow and Golden Harvest in 1979, and he soon became the number-one box-office draw in Asia with the hits *Fearless Hyena* (1979) and *The Young Master* (1980). His growing status also led to roles in several U.S. films produced by Golden Harvest, *The Big Brawl* (1980), *Cannonball Run* (1981), and *Cannonball Run II* (1983). While the Cannonball films were popular at the box office, they failed to make JC the Hollywood star he had hoped to become.

"New Wave" Action Films

JC returned to Hong Kong and put his time spent in Hollywood and the knowledge he gained there to very good use. He had seen firsthand how large Hollywood films were produced and he had worked with some of the best stuntmen in the industry. So once again, he reinvented himself and his films.

JC chose to steer away from the popular traditional period costume pieces and began to do large-scale contemporary action films integrating Hong Kong fights, Hollywood stunts, and his own unique brand of comedy. This formula quickly propelled him to superstardom in Asia with big hit films such as *Project A* (1983), *Wheels on Meals* (1984), *Police Story* (1985), *Armour of God* (1986), and *Dragons Forever* (1987).

The rest of the Hong Kong film industry soon followed suit and began to produce contemporary action films using JC's successful formula of martial arts fights and large-scale, dangerous stunts. This period in Hong Kong cinema has often been referred to as the "New Wave" Era. In it, larger, more ambitious productions were made by a group of multitalented filmmakers, who got their starts in the 1970s' film and TV production studios. These filmmakers include JC, **Sammo Hung**, **John Woo**, **Hark Tsui**, **Stanley Tong**, and **Ringo Lam**, to name a few.

Chop-Sockey pictures now fell from popularity as JC and the rest of the New-

Wave talent raised the bar for quality and action in Hong Kong films. The 1980s also gave rise to epic fantasy/horror films such as *Encounters of the Spooky Kind* (1980), *Zu, Warriors from the Magic Mountain* (1983), and *A Chinese Ghost Story* (1987), as well as the gangster genre with such gun-blazing hits as *A Better Tomorrow* (1986), *City on Fire* (1987), *The Killer* (1989), *A Bullet in the Head* (1990), and *Hard Boiled* (1992).

The late 1980s and 1990s found more changes and successes in the Hong Kong film industry. JC finally became a star in the United States with the upgraded version of **Rumble in the Bronx** (1996) and reached superstardom with the blockbuster **Rush Hour** (1998).

Back in Hong Kong, classical kung-fu period dramas reemerged in popularity with the *Once Upon a Time in China* film series (launched in 1991), starring the sensational Jet Li. JC even climbed on board with the period sequel *Drunken Master II* (1994). Hong Kong stars such as Li, **Michelle Yeoh**, **Sammo Hung**, and **Yun-Fat Chow** have all found successful careers in Hollywood, while Asian directors like Woo, Lam, Tsui, Ang Lee, and **Woo-Ping Yuen** have brought their unique visions to both Eastern and Western screens.

During this period, women also made big strides in the Hong Kong action arena. Following on the heels of 1960s' and 1970s' stars **Pei-Pei Cheng** and Angela Mao (a.k.a. **Angela Mao Ying**), actresses such as **Michelle Yeoh**, **Joyce Godenzi**, **Cynthia Khan**, **Moon Lee**, **Anita Mui**, **Maggie Cheung**, and **Yukari Oshima** found themselves dishing out martial mayhem with the best of the male action stars.

Even the descriptive term "Hong Kong action" has found its way into U.S. filmmaking terminology with the success of JC; television shows like "*Buffy the Vampire Slayer*," "*Martial Law*," "*Angel*," and "*Dark Angel*"; and films such as *The Matrix* (1999), *Charlie's Angels* (2000), the critically acclaimed and Oscar-winning action-romance *Crouching Tiger, Hidden Dragon* (2000), and *Lara Croft: Tomb Raider* (2001).

From its colorful cultural sets and costumes to its uniquely stylized violence-turned-art form, Hong Kong martial arts/action films have grown from a regionalized cottage industry into a worldwide phenomenon. Bolstered by the recent success of Taiwan's global blockbuster *Crouching Tiger*, the Hong Kong film industry is more vibrant and productive than it has been in years. [Scott Rhodes]

Horse. JC's birthday animal in the Chinese calendar.

Hsu, Yin-Fung. JC's character name in *Snake and Crane Arts of Shaolin*.

Hung, Sammo. JC's lifelong friend, rival, and collaborator, he has worked closely with JC on many motion pictures, starting in the early 1970s. Hung (a.k.a. Samo Hung, Sammo Hung Kam Bo, Sammo Hong Jin Bao), whose massive body of work includes acting, producing, directing, and stunt coordinating, is one of Hong Kong's most prolific and famous modern filmmakers. His stellar career spans three decades.

Born in 1950 in Hong Kong, Hung joined the **China Drama Academy**, overseen by the stern master **Jim-Yuen Yu**, at the age of ten. At the academy he was given the name Lung Yuen. Tutored in acting and the martial arts, he became the academy's "Biggest Brother," and instructed classmates JC and **Biao Yuen**, among others. He became a nemesis to JC, and the two have since held a professional rivalry all their lives.

Hung was a member of the academy's famed **Seven Little Fortunes** performing troupe. Upon leaving the academy, he rapidly rose to prominence as a martial arts choreographer after being hired by the **Shaw Brothers Studios** in 1970, and continued in this capacity throughout the decade-long kung-fu movie craze of the 1970s.

As well as appearing opposite JC in director **John Woo**'s early kung-fu film *Hand of Death* (1975), Hung choreographed legendary 1970s kung-fu icon **Angela Mao Ying** during her active years with the Shaw Brothers. He made his directorial debut and starred in the **Bruce Lee** parody *Enter the Fat Dragon* (1978).

Hung's fascination with the wing chun style of kung-fu led to what are generally accepted as two of his finest films, *Warriors Two* (1978) and *Prodigal Son* (1981). Within the confines of his own production companies, Bo Ho Films and Bo Jon Films,

Sammo Hung, as he appeared in his American TV series "Martial Law." Courtesy of CBS Television

Hung was instrumental in initiating the flood of Chinese horror-comedies in the early eighties with *Encounters of the Spooky Kind* (1980) and *Mr. Vampire* (1985). Throughout the 1980s, he worked with JC on a host of highly successful, dynamic action pictures, among them *Project A* (1983), *Winners and Sinners* (1983), *Wheels on Meals* (1984), *My Lucky Stars* (1985), *Twinkle, Twinkle, Lucky Stars*

(1985), **Heart of Dragon** (1985), and **Dragons Forever** (1987).

Perhaps Hung's best work came with his ballistic Vietnam epic *Eastern Condors* (1987), a film often acknowledged as one of the finest Hong Kong actioners of all time. Sammo ushered in the new decade by surviving near fatal injuries on the shoot of *Pantyhose Hero* (1990). He recouped with a score of acting roles, new productions, and a renaissance period as a director. His directorial work on *Moon Warriors* (1992), *Blade of Fury* (1993), and *Kung Fu Cult Master* (1993) saw the inception of a new era in high-wire, powerhouse martial arts cinema.

Hung resumed his work with JC as co-stunt coordinator for **Rumble in the Bronx** (1995) and **Thunderbolt** (1995), and he directed JC in **Mr. Nice Guy** (1997). He finally saw long overdue Western recognition when director **Hark Tsui** called upon his martial arts prowess as fight choreographer on both *Double Team* (1997) and *Knock Off* (1998), both starring Jean-Claude Van Damme. Hung then reached Western audiences en masse with his U.S. debut in director **Stanley Tong**'s 1998 TV series "*Martial Law*," a short-lived kung-fu action-comedy that still plays in syndication today.

Hung's unusual first name, Sammo, which, literally translated, means "Three Hairs," was self-adopted from a popular cartoon character.

Hwang, Jang-Lee. A Korean-born tae-kwondo master who made his cinematic debut as the main villain in JC's *Snake in the Eagle's Shadow* (1978). He immediately reprised a similar bad guy role in JC's *Drunken Master* (1978).

Cashing in on his fast notoriety, Hwang was immediately hired to play both heroic and villainous roles without changing his Drunken Master persona. His most notable performances were as the hero in *Game of Death 2* (a.k.a. *Tower of Death*) (1980) and as a hit man in *Hand of Buddha* (1981).

I Am Jackie Chan: My Life in Action. The only authorized life story of JC in book form, which he coauthored with journalist **Jeff Yang**. It traces JC's rags-to-riches rise from his harrowing ordeals as a rebellious child at the **China Drama Academy** to his ultimate triumph of cracking the Hollywood big time.

Published by Random House, the book became a New York Times bestseller upon

Jang-Lee Hwang
Courtesy of Seasonal Films Corporation

Ice Cream, JC's Favorite. Chocolate.

Impact: The Ultimate Action Magazine. Founded by Roy Jessop and MAI (*Martial Arts Illustrated*) Publications in January 1992, this English-language, United Kingdom–based periodical covers the entire universe of action films and stars. Each issue consists of two separate sections. The first, entitled "Impact," is devoted to Western movies, the second, entitled "Impact East: China Beat," covers Hong Kong films. JC is frequently featured in articles, columns, and news pieces.

 Impact is distributed in Europe, Asia, Australia/New Zealand, and, to a limited degree, in the United States. [Mike Leeder]

In Eagle Dragon Fist. See *Dragon Fist.*

In Eagle Shadow Fist; In the Eagle's Shadow Fist. See *Not Scared to Die.*

its original hardcover release in 1998. In 1999, Ballantine released the book in paperback.

I Am Sorry. JC coproduced and does not appear in this 1989 story about two women and their relationships with men.

Inside Kung-Fu. A U.S.-based martial arts magazine founded by publisher **Curtis Wong** in 1973. Wong and JC are longtime

Impact: The Ultimate Action Magazine Courtesy of Mike Leeder

Inspectors Wear Skirts. See *Inspector Wears Skirts*.

Inspector Wears a Skirt. See *Inspector Wears Skirts*.

Inspector Wears Skirts

Alternate Titles: *Inspectors Wear Skirts, Inspector Wears a Skirt, Lady Enforcers, Top Squad*
Genre: Martial Arts-Action
Hong Kong Release Date: June 3, 1988
Cast: Cynthia Rothrock, Sibelle Hu, Jeff Falcon, Billy Lau, Kara Hui, Bill Tung
Director: Wilson Chin
JC Credits: Producer, stunt coordinator
Location: Hong Kong
Box-Office Gross: $15.5 million (Hong Kong)

friends. Throughout its history, *Inside Kung Fu* has published countless cover stories, features, and news pieces about JC and has been instrumental in introducing his work to Western audiences. The magazine is considered the world's leading publication on the Chinese martial arts.

Policewoman Rothrock and tough drill instructor Hu are assigned to form a "Top Squad" of women cadets in the RHKP academy, which they will lead in an effort to round up a gang of notorious thieves. Meanwhile, the male SWAT trainees at the neighboring police academy take notice of their female counterparts. A martial arts tournament is staged between the two

Inside Kung Fu magazine   Courtesy of Neva Friedenn

groups, with the women coming out victorious. The initial conflicts are eventually resolved as the Top Squad and the SWAT team join forces to catch the villains. Meanwhile, inevitable romances develop.

Produced by JC, *Inspector Wears Skirts* is an amusing, fast-paced comedy mixing elements of the *Police Academy* series, *Private School for Girls*, and the Hong Kong "Girls-with-Guns" police genre. **Cynthia Rothrock**, one of the greatest female forms and weapons champions in U.S. history, was the first Caucasian superstar in Hong Kong.

A sequel, ***Inspector Wears Skirts II*** (1989), followed sans Rothrock.

Courtesy of Neva Friedenn

JC and veteran martial arts journalist Jose Fraguas (left), General Manager of CFW Enterprises, publishers of *Inside Kung Fu* and other major industry magazines

Courtesy of Jose Fraguas

Hu assumes **Cynthia Rothrock**'s role as head of the female Top Squad in the original film. She, her squad, and her love interest (Lau) pursue the villains from the first movie when they break out of jail.

Inspector Wears Skirts II

Alternate Title: *Top Squad II*
Genre: Martial Arts-Action
Hong Kong Release Date: January 28, 1989
Cast: Sibelle Hu, Billy Lau, Jeff Falcon
Director: Wilson Chin
JC Credits: Producer, stunt coordinator
Location: Hong Kong
Box-Office Gross: $18.1 million (Hong Kong)

Iron Fisted Monk

Genre: Martial Arts
Year of Release: 1977
Cast: Sammo Hung, Sing Chan, James Tien
Director: Sammo Hung
JC Credit: Co–stunt coordinator
Location: Hong Kong

JC was only the co–stunt coordinator for this picture, which stars first-time director, co–stunt coordinator, and cowriter Sammo Hung. In a beaten-to-death plot used prolifically in hundreds of kung-fu films, Hung's character learns martial arts at the Shaolin Temple to avenge a family member's death.

This film is not recommended for children due to its two sex/rape scenes, both featuring topless women and some discreet full frontal nudity.

Iron Hand, The. See *Fist of Fury*.

Island of Fire
Alternate Titles: *Burning Island, Island on Fire, The Prisoner*
Year of Release: 1991
Cast: Tony Leung, Sammo Hung, Andy Lau, Jimmy Wang Yu, JC
Director: Yen-Ping Chu

Despite his billing as star, JC has only a small role in this picture. The story is a standard treatment about an undercover cop trying to expose prison corruption. JC appears for a few scenes twenty minutes in and does some decent action in a pool hall and poker club, using props and working around the scenery. He's back for the last twenty minutes in a prison fight that has some decent acrobatics, but absolutely no humor.

This is another film in which JC appeared only as a favor to his old friend Jimmy Wang Yu. It is definitely *not* a JC movie, and is nothing more than a shameless attempt to capitalize on his star power.

Island on Fire. See *Island of Fire*.

Jackie. JC's character name in *Armour of God*, *Armour of God II: Operation Condor*, *Cannonball Run II*, and *Mr. Nice Guy*.

Jackie Chan. See Appendix 3: Jackie Chan Bibliography.

Jackie Chan Adventures
Genre: Animation
Debut Year: 2000
Cast: JC (himself), Adam Baldwin (Finn), Clancy Brown (Captain Black/Ratso), Stacie Chan (Jade), Noah Nelson (Tohru), Julian Sands (Valmont), Sab Shimono (Uncle), James Sie (JC/Shendu/Chow)

Island of Fire (a.k.a. *The Prisoner*) (DVD). Columbia/Tri Star Home Video: 96 minutes/rated R. In English.

Courtesy of Scott Rhodes

An animated weekly cartoon produced in the United States in English starring JC. The show has been rated the number-one cartoon in its Saturday morning time period.

In it, JC, an amateur archaeologist, would prefer to quietly do his work for the local university, but fate has dealt him another hand. That happens when he finds a shield containing a talisman and becomes the first of a dozen people pursued by a criminal organization called The Dark Hand, led by a villain called Valmont and guided by a spirit called Shendu.

JC and his eleven-year-old tomboy niece and apprentice Jade must cooperate with the secret law enforcement organization Section 13 to oppose this threat. Along the way, the heroes must face wild dangers that will demand all of JC's daring and skill in the martial arts to overcome.

JC served as the live model for the animators and uses his own voice to add authenticity to his cartoon character. Because his films are restricted to certain age groups, he felt that this animated TV series would be a suitable alternative for young kids.

Jackie Chan Connection. See *To Kill with Intrigue*.

Jackie Chan: Inside the Dragon. See Appendix 3: Jackie Chan Bibliography.

Jackie Chan: The Most Dangerous Hands in Hollywood. See Appendix 3: Jackie Chan Bibliography.

Jackie Chan: The Invincible Fighter
Year of Release: 1999

Jackie Chan: The Invincible Fighter is a documentary spanning JC's rise in the Hong Kong film industry. Included are some of his greatest fights and stunts from ten of his classic Hong Kong films.

JC promotes his new animated TV series by posing with his poster from "Jackie Chan Adventures."

Courtesy of Reuters NewMedia Inc./Corbis

Jackie Chan: My Story
Genre: Documentary
Year of Release: 1998
Cast: JC, Charles Chan (JC's father), Willie Chan, Michelle Yeoh, Chuck D., Bruce Willis, Sylvester Stallone, Bruce Lee, Wesley Snipes, John Woo, Biao Yuen, Jay Leno, David Letterman, Joe Eszterhas, Whoopie Goldberg, Arthur Hiller, Sammo Hung, Martin Lawrence, Sir David-Akers Jones, Quentin Tarantino, Stanley Tong, Michael Warrington
Director: JC

Produced by **Bey Logan**, *Jackie Chan: My Story* is the definitive video biography of one of the world's favorite action stars, as told by the man himself. A combination of exclusive interviews, rare behind-the-scenes footage, and vintage movie clips describe the many facets of JC's remarkable life. [Bey Logan]

Jackie Chan: My Stunts
Genre: Documentary
Year of Release: 1999
Cast: JC and the Jackie Chan Stunt Team: Ken Lo, Mars, James Allan Bradley, Anthony Carpio, Chi-Li Chung, Rocky Cheung, Andy Cheng
Director: JC
Other JC Credits: Coproducer

Locations: Various in Australia and the
United States

Written by **Bey Logan**, *Jackie Chan: My Stunts* combines live demonstrations with classic movie clips as JC and his action team take the viewer on a unique behind-the-scenes journey into the amazing world of Hong Kong action cinema. JC himself describes the transition from the kung-fu movie era to his current high-octane actioners.

The documentary features exclusive behind-the-scenes footage from the films *Rush Hour* and *Who Am I?* [Bey Logan]

Jackie Chan's Action Kung-Fu

Year of Release: 1992
Genre: Video Game
Producer: Nintendo

JC and his twin sister, Josephine, were two of China's best kung-fu fighters. Trained together from birth, they were a formidable team. All was fine until their Master's arch enemy, the Sorcerer, returned from behind the Great Wall to seize power and rule China. The Sorcerer put a spell on Josephine and made her disappear, believ-

Jackie Chan: My Stunts (DVD). Mega Star Video: Approximately 180 minutes/unrated. In English.
Courtesy of Scott Rhodes

ing that neither twin would be strong enough to defeat him without the other.

Along the way, the Sorcerer sends his henchmen to try to destroy JC. He must now rescue his sister and save China by defeating the Sorcerer and the evil monsters created by the Sorcerer's magic. His master guides and instructs him through the action-packed ordeal.

This side-scrolling fight game with 16-bit graphics boasts large characters and amusing sound effects. Special power-ups allow players to use different styles of kung-fu moves as well as a power punch. It is set for a single player, ages eight to adult, and features five stages, five bonus stages, and five special attacks.

Jackie Chan's Bloodpact. See *The 36 Crazy Fists*.

Jackie Chan's First Strike. See *Police Story 4: First Strike*.

Jackie Chan's Police Force; Jackie Chan's Police Story. See *Police Story*.

Jackie Chan's Project A. See *Project A*.

Jackie Chan's Stuntman Association. A professional stunt team (a.k.a. the JC Stunt-men's Club or the *Sing Ga Ban*, meaning the Sing Lung Family Team in Cantonese) founded by JC in 1983 during the filming of *Project A*.

Starting with just six members, the group grew progressively larger as JC made more and more movies. By the time *Project A II* (1987) was in production, the team had reportedly grown to more than three times its original size, boasting nearly twenty members.

Until August 1990, JC's Stuntman Association members received a monthly salary and worked on every JC picture. After that, each member was contracted on a film-by-film basis as needed and did not necessarily work on every JC movie. Today each team member is basically a specialist who knows perfectly how to handle JC's specific type of stylized action, from cinematic fighting to stunts.

Prominent members of JC's Stuntman Association include his three bodyguards: Ken Lo, Brad Allen (a.k.a. Bradley James Allen), and William Tuan (a.k.a. Ah Tuan). Lo and Allen have played major villains for key fight scenes in numerous JC films. Lo is memorable as JC's nemesis in the twenty-minute climactic battle of *Drunken Master II* (1994).

Chan is known for paying all the expenses of any stuntman injured on one of his pictures, whether or not the injured person is a member of his stunt team.

Jackie Chan Stuntmaster

Year of Release: 2000
Genre: Video Game
Producer: PlayStation
Director: JC

JC lends his voice, English, and his direction to this arcade-style game, which rates very high in player satisfaction due to its quality graphics and sound. JC himself was motion-captured for this game and the likeness and attitude is unmistakably his. He also did the corny but endearing voiceovers, in broken English, which are scattered profusely throughout the game. For instance, when the player falls into the water on the Waterfront level, JC's voice remarks, "I've got a sinking feeling."

Jackie Chan's Stuntmaster's plot is simple. Our hero plays a delivery boy for his grandfather's New York City company. Grandpa sends him on assignment to take a package to the "Temple of the Shaolin." While having dinner at a cafe, JC's grand-

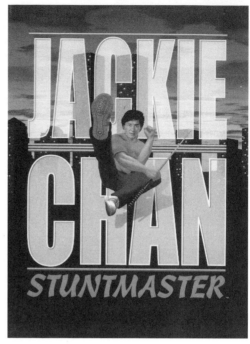

The *Jackie Chan Stuntmaster* video game
Courtesy of Midway Games

father is kidnapped along with the package by henchmen working for an unknown boss. JC tries to chase them down, but loses them. Now he has to journey to areas of the city to find his grandfather and the package before it's too late.

The game levels include a variety of urban settings: Chinatown, Waterfront, Sewer, Rooftops, and Factory. They are all

Jackie Chan Stuntmaster Courtesy of Midway Games

designed to allow JC to show off his fanciest stunts—running from trains and trucks, balancing on top of a variety of moving and stationary objects, running up walls, and so on. As the player takes JC through these levels, he meets a constant barrage of villains trying to hinder his progress.

With a simple control system (punch, kick, grapple, block), the player can pull off some classic JC fighting combinations at blazing speed. Environmental objects, like a broom or even a fish, also come into play as fighting implements. The game even features JC's trademark outtakes.

As for the difficulty level, there are enough obstacles and enemies to keep the player on his or her toes, but not so many as to be frustrating. The game is for all age groups and the violence is not excessive.

Jackie Chan's Who Am I? See ***Who Am I?***.

Jackie Chan vs. Wang Yu. See ***Killer Meteor***.

Jiang. JC's character name in ***Half a Loaf of Kung Fu***.

Johnny. JC's character name in ***Dragons Forever***.

Karate Bomber; Karate Ghostbuster. See
  Spiritual Kung Fu.

Keung, Ah. JC's character name in *Rumble in the Bronx.*

Khan, Cynthia. See **Hong Kong Martial Arts Films.**

Khan, Michelle. See **Michelle Yeoh.**

Kid from Tibet, A. JC has only a small cameo appearance in this 1991 picture starring his friend Biao Yuen, who also made his directorial debut. Yuen plays a monk gifted with mystical powers who must overthrow a sinister sorcerer.

Killer Meteor
Alternate Titles: *Jackie Chan versus Wang Wu,*
  The Killer Meteors
Genre: Period Martial Arts
Year of Release: Produced in 1977, released in
  1979
Cast: Jimmy Wang Yu, JC, Feng Chu

Director: Jimmy Wang Yu
Other JC Credit: Stunt coordinator
Location: Hong Kong

A villain named "Immortal Meteor" (JC, in a rare role as a bad guy), terrorizes a small town until he faces final justice from a heroic character named "Killer Weapon" (Yu).

Beware: The cover of more than one video version of this film prominently displays JC, but it is unmistakably a standard **Jimmy Wang Yu** vehicle. JC appears in it for only about ten minutes, and much of that time he spends lying down!

Overall, there's less action here than in many of Yu's other films, but the sheer number of fight scenes help disguise this deficiency.

Killer Meteor is weighed down by the combination of a complex, convoluted plot and a parade of duplicitous characters. You never know whether characters who die or kill themselves are actually dead and if they'll come back to fight again.

Killer Meteors, The. See **Killer Meteor.**

King of Comedy, The

Genre: Comedy
Year of Release: 1999
JC Credit: Extra

JC appears only as an extra in this comedy starring his friend Stephen Chow, who also wrote and directed it. The film is a variation on Chow's earlier film themes of a guy who's good at one thing, but utterly incompetent in life. Watch for the side-splitting spoof of Hong Kong action films. A wing chun kung-fu stylist in real life, Chow was also an actor in JC's *Gorgeous* (1999).

Kin, Shek. See **Dean Shek**.

Kowloon's Eye. See *Police Story 2*.

Kung-Fu Chic. See **Wirework**.

Kung-Fu Comedy. See **Comedy Kung-Fu**.

Kung Fu Girl. See *The Heroine*.

Kwan, Jerry. JC's character name in *The Big Brawl*.

Kwan, Tak-Hing. See **Hong Kong Martial Arts Films**.

Lady Enforcers. See *Inspector Wears Skirts*.

Lady Kung Fu. See *Hapkido*.

Lam, Ringo. With colleague **Hark Tsui**, he codirected *Twin Dragons* (1992), starring JC, in a unique collaboration of Hong Kong filmmakers for a charitable cause. He's recognized as one of the greatest action directors to come out of Hong Kong in modern times.

Ringo Lam (a.k.a. Ringo Lam Ling Tung) was born in Hong Kong in 1955 and enrolled in the TVB actors' training program before relocating to Canada, where he studied film at York University. On his return, he began working for Cinema City, directing a number of romantic comedies before casting superstar Chow Yun Fat in the explosive heist thriller *City on Fire* (1987). A huge box-office hit, the film firmly established Lam, winning him the Best Director Award at the 1986 Hong Kong Film Awards and later proving a seminal influence on American director Quentin Tarantino's *Reservoir Dogs* (1992).

Two sequels followed: *Prison on Fire* (1987), which starred Tony Leung and Yun-Fat Chow, and the bleak and widely banned *School on Fire* (1988). *Wild Search* (1989), once again starring Chow, was released to resounding critical and popular acclaim.

Lam reached a new peak three years later with his sumptuous *Full Contact* (1992), a graphic and controversial radical overhaul of the then-stagnant contemporary gangster thriller genre that reunited him with Chow. This picture introduced the so-called bullet point-of-view style, which has become Lam's trademark. Lam followed with the violent martial arts epic *Burning Paradise: Rape of the Red Temple* (1994).

Lam made his Hollywood directorial debut with *Maximum Risk* (1996), starring Jean-Claude Van Damme. After returning to Hong Kong for three films, he reunited with Van Damme to direct the sci-fi thriller *Replicant* (2001). He's reportedly set to

Director Ringo Lam

team with Van Damme for the third time in late November 2001 for *The Monk*, a $25 million budgeted saga of a Shaolin who journeys to America in search of his father and finds himself in a battle with an evil crime lord.

Languages. JC is fluent in five languages: Chinese—Cantonese (native) and Mandarin—Japanese, Korean, and English.

Lau, Kar-Leung. The veteran Hong Kong director who helmed JC's *Drunken Master II* (1994) and a master of Hung Gar kung-fu. He also duels with JC underneath a train car in this same picture.

Lau is best known for having helmed dozens of violent kung-fu pictures for the **Shaw Brothers Studios** during its heyday in the 1960s and 1970s. He also gave **Stanley Tong**, one of JC's modern action directors, his start as a stuntman in 1980.

Lee, Ang. See **Hong Kong Martial Arts Films**.

Lee, Bruce. The cinema icon with whom JC worked as a stuntman in two films, *Fist of Fury* (1972) and *Enter the Dragon* (1973).

Bruce Lee was born in San Francisco, California, on November 27, 1940. His father was a member of the Cantonese Opera Company, which was on tour in the United States. After the tour Lee's family returned to Asia and settled in Hong Kong.

There the young Lee appeared in over twenty films as a child actor.

In 1959, Lee returned to America. In Seattle, Washington, he earned a high school diploma and studied philosophy at the University of Washington. Also in Seattle, he met and later married Linda Emery.

After moving to Oakland, California, Lee put on a dazzling kung-fu demonstration at a Los Angeles karate tournament, which brought him to the attention of a Hollywood producer, who cast him in the role of Kato in the short-lived television series "The Green Hornet" (1966). Although Lee's portrayal of Kato made him popular with the American audience, he still faced a lot of adversity earning acting roles in Hollywood. At the time, it was very rare for Asians to appear on screen except in clearly defined stereotypical roles.

Lee was written into several roles by Oscar-winning screenwriter Stirling Silliphant (*In the Heat of the Night*, 1968), one of his private martial arts students. These were *Marlowe* (1969) and the TV series "Longstreet" (1971).

After losing the lead role to David Carradine in TV's "Kung Fu" series (1971), Lee returned to Hong Kong, where he was known for his "Green Hornet" role. This

The late, great Bruce Lee

popularity led producer **Raymond Chow** to offer Lee the chance to play the lead in a movie for Chow's studio, **Golden Harvest Studios**. He starred in three groundbreaking films for Chow's company, *The Big Boss* (1972), *Fist of Fury* (1972), and *Return of the Dragon* (1972). These pictures broke and reset every box-office record in Hong Kong history and rocketed Lee to superstardom.

Lee's martial arts masterpiece came with *Enter the Dragon* (1973), the first coproduction between Hollywood and Asian filmmakers (Golden Harvest and Warner Bros.). Although Lee died tragically at age thirty-two on July 20, 1973, shortly before the classic film was released, *Enter*

the Dragon became an international blockbuster and secured his place in cinematic history as an immortal star.

See also: **Hong Kong Martial Arts Films**.

Lee, Detective Inspector. JC's character in *Rush Hour* and *Rush Hour 2*.

Lee, Moon. See *Hong Kong Martial Arts Films*.

Legend of Drunken Master, The; Legend of the Drunken Master. See Drunken Master II.

Lieh, Lo. See **Hong Kong Martial Arts Films**.

Li, Jet. See **Hong Kong Martial Arts Films**; **Hark Tsui**; **Fei-Hung Wong**; **Woo-Ping Yuen**.

Lin, Feng-Chiao. JC's first wife (a.k.a. Fung-Yu Lung), a Taiwanese actress, whom he married in the 1970s. They are separated and have a son, **Jason Chan** (a.k.a. Cho-Ming Chan), born in 1982.

Liquors, Favorite. Australian red wine, Kahlua.

This rare collector's item is a photo novella in Chinese of the story line from *Little Tiger from Canton*, the film in which JC made his starring-role debut. It was issued under one of the film's alternate titles, *Master with Crack Fingers*.

Courtesy of the Everett Collection

Little Tiger from Canton

Alternate Titles: *Cub Tiger from Canton*, *Little Tiger of Guandong*, *Little Tiger of Kwantung*, *Master with Crack Fingers*, *Master with Cracked Fingers*, *Snake Fist Fighter* (U.S.), *Son of Master with Cracked Fingers*, *Stranger in Hong Kong*, *Ten Fingers of Death*, *Young Tiger of Canton*

Genre: Martial Arts

Year of Release: Filmed in 1971, but only released in 1978

Cast: JC (a.k.a. Yuen-Lung Chen), Juan Hsao Ten, Shih Tien (a.k.a. Shek Kin), Kuo Tse Han, Bill Yuen, Chin Chang, Yung-Man Juen

Director: Hsin Chin

Location: Hong Kong

JC's father is killed in a feud between rival Triad gangs. JC learns how to fight from a mysterious martial arts master who lives in a forest. After he grows up, he returns to avenge his father's death.

Little Tiger from Canton marks JC's starring-role debut. This early vehicle was produced before he refined the personal style that launched him to stardom. It's a poorly made, low-budget formula picture whose storyline makes very little sense.

An unscrupulous producer released this movie as *Master with Cracked Fingers* in 1978, after JC had become a box-office star.

JC performing a snake-fist maneuver in *Little Tiger from Canton.* Courtesy of the Everett Collection

A JC look-alike was hired to enhance JC's role in the film, and the main character's name was even changed to "Jackie Chan." This type of repackaging, sans the look-alike, once a bit player becomes a star is a universal pattern throughout the motion picture business and has been done in Hollywood with stars like Kevin Costner and many others.

Little Tiger of Guandong; Little Tiger of Kwantung. See **Little Tiger from Canton**.

Liu, Gordon. See **Hong Kong Martial Arts Films**.

Liu, Lucy. See *Shanghai Noon*; Wirework.

Lo, Wei. The pompous millionaire Hong Kong director (1918–96) who signed JC to an exclusive multipicture contract in 1976 and propelled him to his first starring roles. Lo is also linked to **Bruce Lee**, but his contribution to the careers of the two biggest stars in Hong Kong history was minimal, and in JC's case, as detrimental as it was helpful.

In 1965, Lo joined **Shaw Brothers Studios** and directed a string of undistinguished films. He moved on to **Golden Harvest Studios**, where cofounder Raymond Chow gave Lo the opportunity to helm Bruce Lee's first two pictures, *The Big Boss* (1972) and *Fist of Fury* (1972). Lo reportedly acted like a buffoon, not a director, on the set. Many times, reputedly, he would place all his attention on radio reports of horse races and was completely oblivious to what was being filmed a few feet away. Other times, he reportedly slept through films that he was supposedly directing.

This gross negligence didn't hinder his claiming credit for making Lee, and later, JC, big stars. In truth, Lee, like JC, was a creative genius way ahead of his time and

Director/producer Wei Lo

JC made thirteen pictures with Lo's company over the next five years: ***Not Scared to Die*** (1973), ***Heroine*** (1973), ***All in the Family*** (1975), ***Hand of Death*** (1976), ***New Fist of Fury*** (1976), ***Shaolin Wooden Men*** (1976), ***To Kill with Intrigue*** (1977), ***Spiritual Kung Fu*** (1978), ***Killer Meteor*** (1977), ***Snake and Crane Arts of Shaolin*** (1978), ***Dragon Fist*** (1979), ***Magnificent Bodyguards*** (1978), and ***Half a Loaf of Kung Fu*** (1978).

Except for JC's wildly parodic *Half a Loaf of Kung Fu* (made in 1978, but only released in 1980), his work for Lo either fell into the costume-epic genre or, alternately, emulated Bruce Lee's style of serious combat films. JC was restrained by what can be called the "Post–Bruce Lee Syndrome." Lee's international impact was so far beyond anything Hong Kong cinema had previously experienced that the industry, not unreasonably, spent years trying to unsuccessfully duplicate it.

It was only when Lo loaned JC out to Seasonal Films' founder **See-Yuen Ng** for ***Snake in the Eagle's Shadow*** (1978) that JC blossomed. In this film and its successor, ***Drunken Master*** (1978), JC and director **Woo-Ping Yuen** forged a comedy style that incorporated traditional Chinese fighting arts, much as American actor Buster

he and Lo were embroiled in constant arguments over Lo's lack of it.

Lo's reputation suffered and he left Golden Harvest in 1975 to form the Lo Wei Company and become an independent producer-director. Seeking to find the new Bruce Lee after Lee died suddenly, Lo brought JC back to Hong Kong from a lengthy visit with his parents in Australia.

Keaton, one of JC's idols, had incorporated acrobatic action into his silent comedies of the 1920s.

Like Lee before him, JC severed his professional relationship with Lo when Golden Harvest bought JC's contract, for an unprecedented $4.2 million. Another asset to JC's rise to stardom was the relationship he built with **Willie Chan**, Lo's assistant who became JC's lifelong manager and close friend. Perhaps the best thing Lo did for JC was to arrange for and pay to have JC's teeth fixed and for an operation to cut his eyelids, to give him a "wide-eyed" look that's more appealing to international audiences.

Although he directed over sixty-five films in his lifetime, Lo generated so much inferior work that both he and his films have fallen into cinematic oblivion.

Logan, Bey. A Hong Kong–based filmmaker and JC documentarian. Born in Stamford, England, he was educated at Uppingham Public School, Rutland. A professional writer, he served as the editor of *Combat* magazine, one of the most popular martial arts periodicals in the United Kingdom, from 1985 to 1990, before leaving to found *Impact: The Ultimate Action Magazine*, a publication devoted to action cinema.

Logan relocated to Hong Kong in 1995 to write the film *Tiger Storm*, eventually released as *White Tiger*, and the book *Hong Kong Action Cinema* (Titan Books, UK/ Overlook Press, U.S., 1996).

He subsequently joined the Media Asia Group, for whom he wrote and produced two documentaries, *Jackie Chan: My Story* (1998) and *Jackie Chan: My Stunts* (1999). Logan wrote the English dialogue for, and appeared in, the JC-produced actioner *Gen-X Cops* (1999), and cowrote its sequel, *Gen-Y Cops* (2001). In 2001, he left Media Asia to join Emperor Multimedia Group, for whom he cowrote the JC action film *Highbinders* (2002).

"Lost Interview." See Appendix 1: Jackie Chan's "Lost Interview."

Love Eternal, The. See *Love Eterne.*

Love Eterne. JC's second role as a child actor, again with Taiwanese star Li-Hua Li. A love story released in 1963, it's also entitled *The Love Eternal.*

Lucky Stars, The. See *My Lucky Stars*.

Lung. JC's character name in *Island of Fire*.

Lung, A. JC's character name in *New Fist of Fury*.

Lung, Fung-Yu. See **Feng-Chiao Lin**.

Lung, Ti. See **Hong Kong Martial Arts Films**.

Ma, Dragon. JC's character name in *Project A* and *Project A II*.

Magnificent Bodyguards

Alternate Title: *Magnificent Guardsmen* (U.S.)
Genre: Period Martial Arts
Hong Kong Release Date: April 27, 1978
U.S. Release Date: 1983
Cast: JC, James Tien, Bruce Leung
Director: Wei Lo
Location: Hong Kong
Injuries: JC broke his hip.

Magnificent Bodyguards (JC, right)

JC agrees to escort a dying brother and his sister through the Stormy Hills in order to save his life. They join a band of fighters and set off. On their travels, JC and his cohorts face numerous dangers and engage in combat with many unsavory characters.

Magnificent Bodyguards is an experimental film shot in 3-D, the first in Hong Kong cinema history, in which encounters with snakes and other dangers exploit the potential of three-dimensional effects. The martial arts action in this period costume-drama is similarly played for shock, realism, and speed, especially the sword fights.

Some of it makes no sense at all. For example, music from the *Star Wars* soundtrack plays at random! The final fight scene, however, is impressive.

Magnificent Guardsmen. See **Magnificent Bodyguards**.

Ma, John/Ma, Yau. JC's character name in *Twin Dragons*.

Making of 36 Crazy Fists, The. See **The 36 Crazy Fists**.

Mako. The veteran Japanese-American actor who played JC's mentor in **The Big Brawl** and who has played the sensei role to more martial arts stars than any other actor in Hollywood. His career now spans some forty years with credits in films, television, and on stage.

Mako (whose real name is Makoto Iwamatsu) launched his acting career on stage after joining the Pasadena (Calif.) Playhouse. In his second film, *The Sand Pebbles* (1966), Mako's portrayal of the tragic engine-room coolie, Po-han, opposite Steve McQueen, earned him award nominations for both the Oscar and the Golden Globe.

In 1965, Mako cofounded and became the artistic director of the East West Players, the critically acclaimed Asian-American Theater in Los Angeles. Mako and the East West Players have been honored with the Margaret Harford Award, the Los Angeles Drama Critics Circle's most prestigious award. He made his Broadway debut in 1976, starring in Steven Sondheim's *Pacific Overtures*, for which he received a Tony nomination.

Mako's martial-arts roles include an episode of the TV series "The Green Hornet" (1966), in which he fought **Bruce Lee** in a kung-fu duel, and the following films: *The Killer Elite* (1975), *The Big Brawl* (1980), *An Eye for an Eye* (with Chuck Norris, 1981), *Conan the Barbarian* (with Arnold Schwarzenegger, 1982), *Conan the Destroyer* (again with Arnold, 1984), *Kung*

Mako, the veteran actor who's played more mentor/sensei roles than anyone in Hollywood. He plays JC's mentor in *The Big Brawl.* Courtesy of Avco Embassy Pictures

Fu: The Movie (with David Carradine and Brandon Lee, 1986), *Armed Response* (again with Carradine, 1986), *My Samurai* (1992), *Sidekicks* (again with Norris, 1993), *Red Sun Rising* (with Don "The Dragon" Wilson, 1994), *Highlander: The Final Dimension* (with Christopher Lambert, 1994), *A Dangerous Place* (with T.J. Roberts, 1994), *Blood for Blood* (with Lorenzo Lamas,

1995), and *Balance of Power* (with Billy Blanks, 1996).

Mann's Chinese Theater. On January 5, 1997, before hundreds of screaming fans, JC placed his hands, feet, and nose in cement at the famed courtyard, where major Hollywood movies stars' images have been immortalized since the 1940s. The ceremony was held in conjunction with the U.S. release of *First Strike* (a.k.a. **Police Story 4: First Strike**).

JC's inscription reads—in four languages: English, Chinese, Japanese, and Korean—"My Dream Come True! Love, Jackie Chan." JC rates this event as the accomplishment of one of his two biggest goals in his life. The courtyard of Mann's Chinese Theater reached full capacity for these star imprints many years ago. Therefore, new ones, like JC's, cannot be exhibited to the public. All the more recent imprint events, although conducted in the courtyard, are mainly ceremonial occasions to generate publicity. The cement blocks upon which new imprints appear are lifted from their frames and given to the star who made them. JC took his cement imprint home to Hong Kong after the ceremony.

Mao, Angela. See Angela Mao Ying.

Martial Arts. See Training, Martial Arts.

Martial Arts Illustrated. The flagship magazine of MAI Publications in Huddersfield, England. *Martial Arts Illustrated*, one of the United Kingdom's foremost periodicals on the subject, is the sister publication of **Impact: The Ultimate Action Magazine**, *Combat and Survival*, and *M.A.I. Video.* [Mike Leeder]

Martial Arts Movies. A U.S.-based magazine founded by publisher **Curtis Wong** in 1980. Its inaugural edition, edited by John Corcoran, this book's author, featured JC as its cover story. Throughout its history and especially in the 1980s, *Martial Arts Movies* published more cover stories, features, and news pieces about JC than any other U.S. periodical and has been instrumental in introducing his work to Western audiences.

Martial Arts Illustrated

Courtesy of Mike Leeder

Martial Arts Sourcebook, The. See Appendix 3: Jackie Chan Bibliography.

Ma, Sargeant. Dragon. See *Project A; Project A II.*

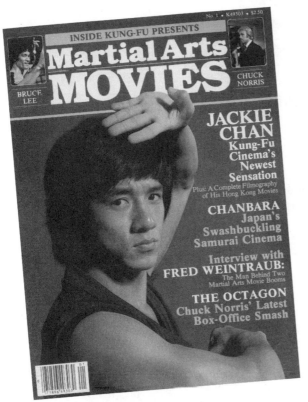

Martial Arts Movies was the first U.S.-based publication to feature JC on its cover, in its inaugural edition in 1980.
Courtesy of John Corcoran

Master and the Boxer. See *The 36 Crazy Fists*.

Master with Cracked Fingers. See *Little Tiger from Canton*.

Ma, Yue-Lung. JC's character name in *Project A*.

Meals on Wheels. See *Wheels on Meals*.

Mei, Yan-Fang. See Anita Mui.

Million Dollar Heiress. See *Wheels on Meals*.

Mini Special Force. See *Fantasy Mission Force*.

Miracles: Mr. Canton and Lady Rose
Alternate Titles: *Black Dragon, The Canton Godfather, The Chinese Godfather, The Miracle, Miracles, Miracles: The Canton Godfather* (U.K.), *Mr. Canton and Lady Rose*
Genre: Period Action
Hong Kong Release Date: June 15, 1989
Cast: JC, Anita Mui, Gloria Yip, Jackie Cheung, Billy Chow, Bill Tung
Director: JC
Other JC Credits: Screenwriter and stunt coordinator
Location: Hong Kong
Box-Office Gross: $34 million (Hong Kong)

JC was a favored cover personality, as demonstrated in these *Martial Arts Movies* covers from 1981, 1982, and 1996.

Courtesy of Michael Worth

A derivative tale set in the 1930s, based on the Hollywood classic *Pocketful of Miracles* (1961), where JC plays a naive but good-hearted country boy who comes to the big city penniless. After buying a rose from an old lady, he unwittingly gets involved in a gangland shootout between two mob bosses. As one of the bosses dies, with his last breath he names JC as his successor. JC accepts and, after proving himself worthy, uses his basic decency to lead the gang to prosperity while swaying them away from crime and into more charitable pursuits. He and his gang execute an elaborate deception and occasional flashes of humor. Since he focused more on story content than action, however, the film is not packed with as much bone-crunching action as usual. There are two outstanding fight scenes, one in a restaurant and an amazing confrontation in a rope factory that defies appropriate description.

Miracles is also populated by many star cameos and guest appearances including one by **Biao Yuen**, who pops up briefly as a beggar.

Courtesy of Neva Friedenn

that allows a simple flower seller to fulfill her dreams. As his power grows, he also inevitably heads for the final conflict with the rival gangster who murdered this predecessor.

The most elegantly executed of JC's films, *Miracles* combines superb camerawork with his trademark fast-paced antics

Miracle, The; Miracles; Miracles: The Canton Godfather. See *Miracles: Mr. Canton and Lady Rose*.

Movie Town. See **Shaw Brothers Studios**.

Mr. Canton and Lady Rose. See *Miracles: Mr. Canton and Lady Rose*.

Mr. Nice Guy
Alternate Titles: *A Nice Guy, The Nice Guy, No More Mr. Nice Guy* (U.S.), *One Good Man, Superchef*

Miracles: Mr. Canton and Lady Rose (DVD). Mega Star Video: 122 minutes/unrated. In Cantonese and Mandarin with English subtitles.

Courtesy of Scott Rhodes

Genre: Action-Comedy
Hong Kong Release Date: January 31, 1997
U.S. Release Date: March 20, 1998 (upgrade version)
Cast: JC, Richard Norton, Gabrielle Fitzpatrick, Miki Lee, Karen McLymont, Vince Poletto, Barry Otto, Sammo Hung, Emil Chow, Joyce Godenzi
Director: Sammo Hung
Location: Australia (Melbourne)
Box-Office Gross: $45.4 million (Hong Kong), $12.6 million (U.S.)
Injuries: JC injured his neck bone during a throw gone awry and broke his nose for the third time.

Ambitious Australian reporter Diana (Fitzpatrick) secretly videotapes a drug deal and the murder of a local mob boss by henchmen of Giancarlo's (Norton), who orders the retrieval of the incriminating tape. But the video accidentally falls into the hands of a mild-mannered celebrity TV chef (JC), who now gets embroiled in the gang's murderous recovery efforts. As events unfold, the chef cooks up his own recipe for justice.

The big action sequences in *Mr. Nice Guy* involve runaway horses, a chase through a shopping center, the use of a crane, and an escape across a steel beam high in the air, and some of the stunts are simply amazing.

There's also an eye-popping fight scene set on a construction site. In the climax, JC "infiltrates" the villain's mostly glass house by means of a monster earthmoving vehicle, completely demolishing it!

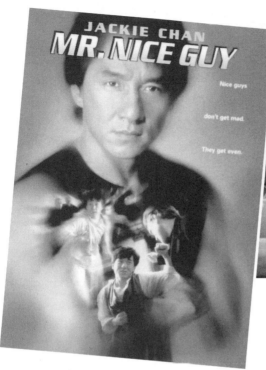

Mr. Nice Guy (DVD). New Line Video: 87 minutes/rated PG-13. In English. *Courtesy of Scott Rhodes*

Mr. Nice Guy. Courtesy of the Kobal Collection

It might be equally astounding just how far JC can go on the thinnest of plots. Even the greatest performers can sink in bad material, but JC movies aren't about such trifling details as plot and character. They're about ingenuity, self-effacing humor, and clever, lightning-fast fight choreography. The formula is delightful, and *Mr. Nice Guy* is a fine reworking of it, packed with action, fun, and laughs.

This was JC's first movie filmed mainly in English, even though it was produced in Hong Kong.

MTV Movie Awards. See Appendix 4: Jackie Chan's Awards, Honors, and Offices Held.

Mui, Anita. The singer-actress who worked with JC in *Rouge* (1987), *Miracles: Mr.*

龍

Mr. Nice Guy

Courtesy of the Kobal Collection

Canton and Lady Rose (1989), *Drunken Master II* (1994), and *Rumble in the Bronx* (1995). A veteran of over forty Hong Kong films, she's also known as the former queen of the Hong Kong pop-music industry.

After winning a singing contest in 1983 at age twenty-three, Anita Mui (a.k.a. Yan-Fang Mei) launched a career as a professional singer. In the early stages, she projected a sexy image, which led to her label as the "Madonna of Hong Kong." She won a couple of "Best Female Singer" awards in the mid-1980s.

Mui initiated her acting career in 1983 and reached her pinnacle as an actress by winning "Best Actress" awards in Hong Kong and Taiwan for her performance in 1987's *Rouge*, produced by JC. She also won acclaim for her hysterically funny role as JC's conniving mother in *Drunken Master II*. She later partnered with JC and other investors to establish the Orient Star restaurant, a copycat of Planet Hollywood.

Muscles. JC's character name in *My Lucky Stars* and *Twinkle, Twinkle, Lucky Stars*.

Mr. Nice Guy

Courtesy of the Kobal Collection

Musicography, JC. See Appendix 6: Jackie Chan Musicography.

My Lucky Stars

Alternate Titles: *The Lucky Stars*; *Twinkle, Twinkle, Little Stars*
Genre: Comedy
Hong Kong Release Date: February 10, 1985
Cast: JC, Sammo Hung, Biao Yuen, Charlie Chin, Eric Tsang, Shui-Fan Fung, Richard Ng, Sibelle Hu, Michiko Nishiwaki, Dick Wei

Director: Sammo Hung
Locations: Hong Kong, Tokyo, Japan
Box-Office Gross: $30.7 million (Hong Kong)

My Lucky Stars begins with two Hong Kong cops, Muscles (JC) and Ricky (Biao Yuen), chasing after an ex-cop that stole millions of dollars worth of diamonds. They chase him into a Japanese theme park, where they are unexpectedly ambushed by ninjas, and an approximately ten-minute fight sequence ensues, ending with Ricky's capture. JC can't return to rescue him because he'd be recognized, so his boss recruits JC's childhood friends from an orphanage he grew up in. The group, called the "Lucky Stars," consists of five misfits, including their apparent leader, Kidstuff (Hung), who has to first be paroled from jail. At face value, this wild bunch doesn't appear to be much help since they have very little skill in kung-fu. So they engage in numerous absurd antics on their way to helping JC save his partner and capture the main villain.

Fightwise, *My Lucky Stars* improves drastically toward the end, when JC occupies more screen time. Back in the Japanese amusement park, JC has to penetrate a haunted house featuring different "theme" rooms, each of which presents a challenge

My Lucky Stars (DVD). Universe Laser & Video Company Ltd.: 96 minutes/unrated. In Chinese and Mandarin with multiple choices of subtitles including English. Courtesy of Scott Rhodes

fights JC for the third time in *My Lucky Stars*. Japanese actress/bodybuilding champion Michiko Nishiwaki makes an impressive film debut as a Yakuza hitwoman, pitted in a rough-and-tumble brawl with Sibelle Hu as a female cop. A professional stuntwoman with many motion picture credits who's now based in Hollywood, Nishiwaki has since appeared in JC's **Rush Hour 2** (2001).

My Lucky Stars is another masterpiece of action-comedy. Asian audiences must have thought so, too. The picture earned a record-breaking $30.7 million (Hong Kong).

Due to its vast array of alternate titles, the Lucky Stars trilogy is the second most confusing in all of JC's body of work (**Police Story** (1985–96) is by far the *most* confusing). To clarify, *My Lucky Stars* is the second entry—in other words, the first sequel—in the Lucky Stars trilogy. The first entry in this series is **Winners and Sinners** (1983) and the final entry is **Twinkle, Twinkle, Lucky Stars** (1985). In this trilogy, JC is part of an ensemble cast and has only a supporting role.

of its own, and within each he engages in a remarkable and unique action sequence against the villains.

Look for some other noteworthy fights, too. American World Kickboxing Champion **Benny Urquidez**, in a cameo role,

My Lucky Stars II: The Target. See *Twinkle, Twinkle, Lucky Stars*.

Names. Born Kong-Sang Chan, which translates as "Born in Hong Kong," later in life, JC found out that he had another birth name, Si-Lung Fong. JC is also known as Sing Lung or Shing Lung (Cantonese) and Long Cheng (Mandarin). His Peking Opera stage name was Lau Yuen. His film credits sometimes use the name Yuen-Lung Chen.

JC's nicknames throughout his life include "Pao-Pao" ("Cannonball"), a name his mother Lee-Lee gave him because of his unusual size at birth. "Western boy" was a name given to him by students at the **China Drama Academy** because, upon his first visit, he wore a Western cowboy outfit complete with hat and plastic guns. Later, they called him "Big Nose" for obvious reasons.

The name Jackie Chan is a stage name.

Nan-Hua School. The only academic school that JC attended. A poor student, he found academic studies tortuous. He never did homework, and he often engaged in fights with other students. He lasted there only one year, flunking his first year in school before his parents removed him. This represented the only formal education that JC ever received.

Through a friend's introduction, JC's father then enrolled him at the **China Drama Academy**.

Naughty Boys
Year of Release: 1986
Cast: Kara Hui, Carina Lau, Clarence Ford, Mars, Ken Lo, Mang Lo
Director: Wilson Chin
JC Credits: Producer, stunt coordinator, cameo role
Location: Hong Kong

JC only has a small cameo role and appears in the outtakes of this account of an ex-convict searching for the money he stashed before his prison term. His former gang members are after the hidden loot, too.

Of further interest to JC's fans is Ken Lo, who would later join JC's stunt team, play one of his on-screen adversaries, and, finally, become his personal bodyguard.

New Fist of Fury
Alternate Titles: *Fists to Fight, Red Dragon*
Genre: Period Martial Arts
Hong Kong Release Date: July 8, 1976
Cast: JC, Nora Miao, Sing Chang, Ying-Chieh Han

Director: Wei Lo
Location: Hong Kong

A tedious straight kung-fu picture set during World War II that's ineptly directed by **Wei Lo**. The plot involves rival Chinese and Japanese karate schools in Taiwan. Overall, the fighting bears only a slight resemblance to Lee's, but with some of JC's acrobatics thrown in. Except for the climactic fights at the end, which are entertaining enough—though they don't compare to the kind of amazing athletics JC would perform later—this is a plodding, interminable picture. JC does, however, display some sensational handling of the complex three-sectional staff in one fight scene.

The worst scene in the entire movie is its horrible ending. After defeating the Japanese, JC and his cohorts remove the defeated out of a building, where everyone, including JC, is shot to death!

New Fist of Fury, starring JC in his first major role for Lo's company, is the wannabe sequel to **Bruce Lee**'s *Fist of Fury*. This was an early role for JC, too soon for kung-fu films to be free of the highly successful Lee formula for JC's charismatic style to have emerged.

Historically speaking, the only advantage to this picture was Lo's effort to bring JC back to Hong Kong from a lengthy visit to his parents in Australia and putting him in a starring role.

New Police Story, The. See *Crime Story*.

New Wave Era. See **Hong Kong Martial Arts Films**.

Ng, See-Yuen. The visionary Hong Kong producer who gave JC his first major break by putting him in starring roles with uncharacteristic creative freedom. This resulted in the creation of the **comedy kung-fu** genre through two influential JC films, *Drunken Master* (1978) and *Snake in the Eagle's Shadow* (1978). Ng is recognized as a "starmaker."

A former executive at **Shaw Brothers Studios**, See-Yuen Ng (pronounced "eng") left in the early 1970s and became a director for independent film companies. In 1975, he founded Seasonal Films Corporation, a production company known today for quality films starring unknowns.

Ng's eye for raw talent that he could shape into stars also led to his discovery of Jean-Claude Van Damme, whose career Ng launched with *No Retreat, No Surrender* (1985), Van Damme's first starring role. Other lesser-known stars whose careers Ng has helped include Americans Loren Avedon in *No Retreat, No Surrender II* (1989) and Gary Daniels in *Bloodmoon* (1997).

Ng has also directed nineteen motion pictures and written five screenplays.

Nice Guy, A; *Nice Guy, The*; *No More Mr. Nice Guy*. See *Mr. Nice Guy*.

Ninja Wars
Genre: Martial Arts
Year of Release: 1982
Cast: Henry Sanada, Noriko Watanabe, Sonny Chiba, JC
Director: Masao Sato
Location: Japan

JC only has a cameo role in this Japanese production about a man who avenges his girlfriend's death. Known for his ultraviolent *Street Fighter* films (1975–79), costar Sonny Chiba was a big star in Japan.

Nishiwaki, Michiko. The U.S.-based Japanese actress and stuntwoman who has worked in four JC films: ***My Lucky Stars*** (1985), ***Drunken Master II*** (1994), ***Mr. Nice Guy*** (1997), and ***Rush Hour 2*** (2001).

Professional stuntwoman Michiko Nishiwaki is also an actress, a black belt in Goju-ryu, a fight choreographer, and Japan's first woman's bodybuilding and power-lifting champion. Her success launched a female bodybuilding and workout boom all over Japan. She is fluent in four languages: English, Japanese, and the Cantonese and Mandarin Chinese dialects. Her work has attracted an international cult following all over the world.

Nishiwaki has worked with some of the best talent in Asia. Besides JC, she has worked in films starring **Sammo Hung** and Yun-Fat Chow. Since moving to the United States in the 1990s, she has worked in a martial arts and stunt capacity in pictures starring Jim Carrey, Wesley Snipes, and **Cynthia Rothrock**, as well as in the film *Charlie's Angels* (2000) and TV's "Buffy the Vampire Slayer."

Norton, Richard. The U.S.-based Australian actor who costarred in two JC pictures: ***Mr. Nice Guy*** (1997) and ***City Hunter*** (1993).

Norton has starred in about thirty martial arts films since he made his debut as a

Michiko Nishiwaki with JC on the set of *Rush Hour 2*

Courtesy of Michiko Nishiwaki

centers on a window washer (JC) at the World Trade Center in New York City, who takes a fancy to a waitress working at the Windows of the World restaurant atop the building. The pair becomes embroiled in a plot to bomb the twin towers.

This setting, of course, was prior to the terrorist attacks of September 11, 2001, that demolished the two main World Trade Center towers. Since the attack, Hollywood is reluctant to release pictures with terrorist plots. Consequently, the script will probably be rewritten.

villain opposite Chuck Norris in *The Octagon* (1980). Over the years, he's acted with some of the best martial arts stars including Joe Lewis in *Force: Five* (1980), **Sammo Hung** in *Shanghai Express* (1987), and **Cynthia Rothrock**, a close friend with whom he's worked in numerous pictures starting with *China O'Brien* (1988).

Nosebleed. The working title for one of JC's planned films that was in development at MGM Studios as this book was being completed. The script, for which the two original screenwriters were paid $600,000,

Not Scared to Die

Alternate Titles: *Eagle Shadow Fist, In Eagle Shadow Fist, In the Eagle's Shadow Fist, Fist of Anger*

Genre: Period Martial Arts

Hong Kong Release Date: January 12, 1973; rereleased in 1978

Cast: Qing Wang, Xiu Lin, JC (a.k.a. Yuen-Lung Chen)

Director: Wu Zhu (a.k.a. Tsu Heng)

Other JC Credits: Stunt coordinator

Location: Hong Kong

Based on a true story, *Not Scared to Die* is the saga of a group of patriotic Chinese performers who become resistance fighters against the oppressive Japanese. JC appears in the opening scene in full **Peking Opera** costume and makeup, and also has a small supporting role, playing a character that gets killed.

Following the resounding success of JC's *Snake in the Eagle's Shadow*, this film was released in 1978 as *Eagle's Shadow Fist*.

Sword, respectively, who ultimately join forces against the bad guys.

Packed with duels and laced with comedy, *The Odd Couple* helped usher in the golden age of kung-fu films with a new sophistication that showcased a dynamic realism in speed, agility, movement, and editing that was a departure from the stagy martial arts choreography of earlier films.

Number, Favorite. Seven.

Odd Couple, The
Genre: Martial Arts
Alternate Title: *Dance of Death*
Year of Release: 1979
Cast: Sammo Hung, Chia-Yung Liu, Shih Tien
    (a.k.a. Shek Kin)
Director: Chia-Yung Liu
JC Credit: Stunt coordinator

JC was stunt coordinator for this film and doesn't appear in it, but his fight choreography is top notch. *The Odd Couple* is a lighthearted classical kung-fu movie featuring **Sammo Hung** and Chia-Yung Liu (who also directed) as rival masters, the King of the Spear and the King of the

Offices. See Appendix 4: Jackie Chan's Awards, Honors, and Offices Held.

Official Karate. A U.S.-based martial arts magazine founded by publisher Al Weiss in 1968. *Official Karate* flourished until the late 1980s and featured a number of cover stories and features about JC and his film work.

Once a Cop. See **Project S**.

One Armed Swordsman. See **Yu, Jimmy Wang**.

One Good Man. See **Mr. Nice Guy**.

Official Karate magazine. Most of the early JC interviews and stories in this New York–based publication were written by Neva Friedenn, who did a prolific amount of literary work on JC during his budding career. Courtesy of Neva Friedenn

Operation Condor. See *Armour of God II: Operation Condor*.

Operation Condor 2: The Armour of Gods. See *Armour of God*.

Operation Dragon. See *Enter the Dragon*.

Operation Eagle. See *Armour of God II: Operation Condor*.

Oshima, Yukari. See **Hong Kong Martial Arts Films**.

Outlaw Brothers. JC was stunt coordinator only for this 1989 film, which mixes car racing and fights, as a favor to his friend, director Frankie Chan.

Painted Faces
Genre: Docudrama
Year of Release: 1988

Cast: Sammo Hung, Ching-Ying Lam, and Pei-
  Pei Cheng
Director: Alex Kai-Yui
Location: Hong Kong

A docudrama that follows the highly disci-
plined training and progress of the **Peking
Opera** troupe called the **Seven Little Fortunes**, of which JC was a childhood member. Although JC does not appear in, nor
did he work on this project, his troupe
comember **Sammo Hung** does.

Hung plays the venerable and strong-
armed instructor Master Yu, who puts the
students through their paces. We follow the
students' trials and tribulations all the way
through the closing of the school to when
they get their first taste of movie work as
underpaid stuntmen.

Painted Faces is a classic look at the traditional institution that produced Hung,
JC, and **Biao Yuen**, who became three of
the hottest stars in Hong Kong cinema.

Peking Opera. The venerable, highly disci-
plined stage art that JC learned as a youth
at the **China Drama Academy**.

China's Peking Opera is considered a
national treasure with a history of two
hundred years. From approximately 1790

Peking Opera performers from *Farewell My Concubine*

Courtesy of Miramax Films

to 1840, an integration of various types of
opera took place and eventually evolved
into the present form of Peking Opera,
whose richness of repertoire is striking.

Peking Opera is a synthesis of stylized
action, singing, dialogue, mime, acrobatic
fighting, and dancing to represent a story
or depict different characters and their feelings of happiness, anger, sorrow, surprise,
fear, and sadness. In Peking Opera there
are four main types of roles: *sheng* (male),
dan (young female), *jing* (painted face,
male), and *chou* (clown, male or female).
The characters may be loyal or treacherous,
beautiful or ugly, good or bad, their corre-
sponding images being vividly manifested.

The costumes in Peking Opera are elegant and magnificent. Most of them are made in handicraft embroidery. The types of facial makeup are rich and various, depicting different characters and remarkable images.

The repertoire of Peking Opera is mainly engaged in fairy tales of preceding dynasties, important historical events, emperors, ministers and generals, geniuses and great beauties, from ancient times to more recent dynasties. The music of Peking Opera is that of the "plate and cavity style." Its melody with harmonious rhythms is graceful and pleasing to the ears. The performance is accompanied by a tune played on three types of instruments, wind, percussion, and stringed.

Pirate Patrol. See **Project A**.

Police Dragon. See **Crime Story**.

Police Force. See **Police Story**.

Police Force II. See **Police Story 2**.

Police Story

Alternate Titles: *Jackie Chan's Police Force*, *Jackie Chan's Police Story*, *Police Force*
Genre: Action
Hong Kong Release Date: December 14, 1985
Cast: JC, Chu Yuen, Brigitte Lin, Maggie Cheung, Bill Tung, Kenneth Tong
Director: JC
Other JC Credits: Coscreenwriter
Locations: Hong Kong
Box-Office Gross: $26.6 million (Hong Kong)
Injuries: During the seventy-foot pole-slide plunge, JC dislocated his pelvis and severely injured the seventh and eighth bones of his vertebrae, which nearly paralyzed him. He also seriously scraped his skin in that same stunt.

Kevin (JC), a member of an elite Hong Kong squad fighting organized crime, is assigned to protect a star witness—a crime boss's girlfriend (Lin)—in a drug case. He not only loses the witness, but is framed for the murder of a fellow cop and ends up on the run from his own comrades. Further, in attempting to right all the wrongs, he jeopardizes the relationship with his girlfriend (Cheung).

Police Story, the first in a confusingly named series of JC films (see this book's Introduction), has a surprisingly solid

Police Story
Courtesy of the Kobal Collection

wrapped in Christmas lights—both are superb and rank among JC's finest work on film. In fact, they defy the imagination: you wonder how JC's still living, or stays in one bodily piece.

Of his entire body of work, the award-winning *Police Story* is self-admittedly JC's favorite action film. It's a high-octane actioner that actually changed how Hong Kong movies would be made from that point onward.

Three sequels followed: ***Police Story 2*** (1988), ***Police Story 3: Supercop*** (1992), and ***Police Story 4: First Strike*** (1996).

story. Normally, the fun of JC movies is to marvel at his lightning-fast fight scenes and spectacular stunts, all of which he performs himself, and laugh at his unpretentious, self-effacing humor. *Police Story* certainly has these elements, but here the story propels the action, rather than vice-versa.

Police Story's jaw-dropping opening grabber that ended with villains being flung through the front of a bus window was duplicated almost shot for shot in Sylvester Stallone's *Tango and Cash* (1990). The extravagant set pieces of a hillside car chase that demolishes a shantytown, and the grand finale in a shopping mall—capped by a slide down a seventy-foot pole

Police Story 2
Alternate Titles: *Kowloon's Eye, Police Force II*
Genre: Action
Hong Kong Release Date: August 20, 1988
Cast: JC, Maggie Cheung, Gok-Hung Lam, Crystal Kwok, Yuen Choh, Angile Leung, Kenny Ho, Bill Tung, Sing Feng, Ma Wu, Saan Gwaan, Siu Ming Lau, Gaau Chiu
Director: JC
Other JC Credits: Coscreenwriter, stunt coordinator
Location: Hong Kong
Box-Office Gross: $34.1 million (Hong Kong)
Injuries: JC sustained lacerations to his head crashing through a glass window.

JC and Michelle Yeoh in *Police Story 3*

Courtesy of the Everett Collection

Sylvester Stallone raises JC's hand in celebration during the U.S. film premiere party for *Supercop* at Planet Hollywood in New York City. Courtesy of Mitchell Gerber/Corbis

JC reprises his role as the fearless Hong Kong cop Ka-Kui Chan in this sequel to his hit. Now demoted to a mere traffic cop because of the trouble he caused in the first film, he's out to apprehend some terrorists who randomly bomb buildings. At the same time, Chu Tao, the criminal boss he nabbed in the first film, threatens him and his girlfriend (Maggie Cheung, also reprising her original role). The final fight in a fireworks factory is another spectacular JC action sequence.

Although *Police Story 2* has a lot more humor than its predecessor, it is literally packed with action and fight sequences, including a raucous fight in a playground where JC converts his environment into weapons. In two totally different and very dangerous scenes, he gives new meaning to the once simple act of "crossing the street."

Police Story 3. See *Police Story 3: Supercop*.

Police Story 3: Supercop

Alternate Titles: *Police Story 3* (U.K.),
　　　　　Supercop (U.S.)
Genre: Action
Hong Kong Release Date: April 7, 1992
U.S. Release Date: July 26, 1996 (upgraded
　　version)

Cast: JC, Michelle Khan (a.k.a. Michelle Yeoh),
   Maggie Cheung, Kenneth Tsang, Wah Yuen,
   Bill Tung, Josephine Koo, Siu Wong, Wai-Lum
   Tuan, Phillip Chan
Director: Stanley Tong
Other JC Credit: Co–executive producer
Locations: Hong Kong, China, Kuala Lumpur
Box-Office Gross: $32.6 million (Hong Kong);
   $16.2 million (U.S.)
Injuries: JC dislocated his cheek bone, broke his
   shoulder, and badly bruised his back.

JC plays Kevin Chan, a Hong Kong "supercop" who goes undercover in mainland
China in order to bust a drug cartel. In the
People's Republic, he hooks up with a no-
nonsense PRC soldier (Khan), whose physical competence matches Chan's.

   One of JC's best films, this is the third
installment of the hit **Police Story** series,
which was upgraded and released as *Supercop* in the United States in 1996. A dizzy-
ingly fast actioner with over-the-top stunts,
JC pursues—or is chased by—bad guys by
means of cycle, train, and, astonishingly, by
hanging from the rope ladder of a speeding, high-flying helicopter with no safety
devices in sight! He actually risked his life
to jump from a tall building to that copter's
rope ladder to launch the sequence.

Police Story 3: Supercop (a.k.a. *Supercop*) (DVD). Dimension
Home Video: 91 minutes/rated R. In English.
Courtesy of Scott Rhodes

Police Story 3: Supercop, in fact, provides a double dose of stunts and martial
arts. JC's costar, **Michelle Yeoh** (billed as
Michelle Khan), matches JC's antics one-
for-one and, like him, also performs her
own stunts. Her big moment was a motorcycle jump onto the top of a moving train.

Yeoh became the highest-paid female star in Hong Kong after this hit film, and it led to her casting as the lead Bond Girl opposite Pierce Brosnan in *Tomorrow Never Dies* (1997).

Like most JC films, the slight plot is good enough to stitch the movie together and add a little tension, but is purposefully secondary to the JC's derring-do and, in this case, that of his worthy female costar.

Police Story 3: Part 2. See ***Project S.***

Police Story 4. See ***Project S*** and ***Police Story 4: First Strike.***

Police Story IV. See ***Crime Story.***

Police Story 4: First Strike

Alternate Titles: *Basic Operation, Escape from the KGB, First Strike, Golden Dragons, Jackie Chan's First Strike* (U.S.), *Police Story 4, Police Story 4: Piece of Cake, Police Story 4: Simple Mission, Police Story 4: Story of the CIA, Simple Mission, Story of the CIA*
Genre: Action-Comedy
Year of U.S. Release: 1997 (upgraded version)

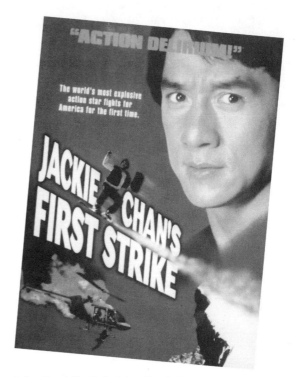

Police Story 4: First Strike (a.k.a. *First Strike*) (DVD). New Line Video: 85 minutes/rated PG-13. In English.

Courtesy of Scott Rhodes

Hong Kong Release Date: March 4, 1996
Cast: JC, Jackson Lou, Chen-Chen Wu, Bill Tung, Jouri Petrov, Grishajeva Nonna, Hok-Yin Lau, San-Gwan Neung
Director: Stanley Tong
Other JC Credit: Co–stunt coordinator
Locations: Ukraine, Australia
Box-Office Gross: $57.5 million (Hong Kong)

Novelty items: two Egyptian movie posters promoting JC's *Police Story 4: First Strike* (a.k.a. *Escape from the KGB*) and *Master with Cracked Fingers*. Courtesy of Reuters NewMedia Inc./Corbis

Injuries: JC sustained another concussion and injured his nose.

In this slick, entertaining tribute to the James Bond films, JC plays a Hong Kong cop working for the CIA in a plan to coordinate intelligence with the new KGB to stamp out a duplicitous group of Russian mobsters. Everyone's objective is to steal a nuclear detonator held by a Chinese /Russian double agent and spymaster, Lui, whose deft disguises include a couple of blonde wigs and some sunglasses. Lui's duplicity runs even deeper: He's supposedly attached to a Triad family—the Hong Kong crime organization—that resides in Australia!

It becomes increasingly clear that the film's distinction lies not with the plot, but rather a handful of great fight scenes and

(Both photos) *Police Story 4*   Courtesy of the Everett Collection

龍

superstunts. These include JC's sparring match with seven-foot-tall Russian toughs, and a dazzling ladder-fighting sequence that represents JC at his athletic, prop-converting best. Bond-style spectacle fills in the rest of the movie, including JC snowboarding down mountains ending with a heart-stopping leap onto the runners of an airborne helicopter, engaging in a surprisingly agile underwater fight, and escaping from live—not prop—sharks in an oceanarium tank.

This is actually number four in JC's popular *Police Story* series. While the Chinese title suggests some continuity with the former *Police Story* movies, only a basic premise survives: JC as a Hong Kong cop. Everywhere else there's the look and feel of generic Hollywood action movies.

JC's charisma and attitude turn what might have been ridiculously silly into humorous action-packed entertainment. For example, after a spectacular downhill ski chase in his shirtsleeves, his teeth chatter!

Police Story 4: Piece of Cake. See **Police Story 4: First Strike**.

Police Story 4: Project S. See **Project S**.

Police Story 4: Simple Mission. See *Police Story 4: First Strike*.

Police Story 4: Story of the CIA. See *Police Story 4: First Strike*.

Police Woman
Alternate Titles: *Rumble in Hong Kong, Young Tiger*
Year of Release: 1972
Cast: JC (a.k.a. Yuen-Lung Chen), Cheung-Lam Chun
Location: Hong Kong

This zero-budget copycat of **Bruce Lee**'s films is interesting only for an early performance by JC, who plays the sidekick of the female lead. But for some unknown reason, he appears on-screen with an ugly clump of hair on one side of his face! JC befriended actor Chun, who taught JC acting lessons in return for kung-fu lessons.

Of the numerous Hong Kong movies that feature JC on screen for but a few minutes and attempt to use his star power to lure viewers, *Police Woman* is perhaps the worst of them. It is, in fact, almost universally considered one of the worst movies JC ever made.

Beware: some versions of this video falsely advertise that a JC interview or documentary is included.

Pom Pom
Genre: Action-Comedy
Hong Kong Release Date: February 22, 1984
Cast: John Sham, Sammo Hung, Richard Ng, Dick Wei, Mars, JC. Biao Yuen
Director: Joe Cheung
Location: Hong Kong
Box-Office Gross: $20.1 million (Hong Kong)

Both JC and Biao Yuen have only cameo appearances, reprising their roles from the *Lucky Stars* hit series to help their colleague, producer-star **Sammo Hung**, launch another film franchise.

Postage Stamps, JC. JC was commemorated on a set of postage stamps in 1997, issued by the government of Gambia, Africa.

Prisoner, The. See *Island of Fire*.

Project A

Alternate Titles: *Jackie Chan's Project A, Pirate Patrol, Schedule A, Superfly 2*
Genre: Period Action-Comedy
Hong Kong Release Date: December 22, 1983
Cast: JC, Sammo Hung, Biao Yuen, Mars, Dick Wei
Director: JC
Other JC Credits: Coscreenwriter, stunt coordinator
Location: Hong Kong
Box-Office Gross: $19.3 million (Hong Kong)
Injuries: JC sustained a neck bone injury when he fell from a clock tower. He also broke his nose (for the second time) and a finger.

A tenth anniversary promotional flyer for *Project A*

Courtesy of Scott Rhodes

JC plays Dragon Ma, an early twentieth-century Chinese Coast Guard sergeant. Due to budgetary problems and the fact that they have failed to nab some mean pirates, the Coast Guard is closed down and all its members are forced to join the police force. JC quits the force and teams up with an old friend (Hung) who's now a professional thief. After JC uncovers a corrupt police official, he gets the Coast Guard reinstated and puts "Project A" into operation to catch the pirates.

Project A is a JC classic with lots of slapstick, Charlie Chaplin–style gags, great fights, and plenty of the big stunts that have now made JC and his stunt team world famous. In the first bar fight between navy and police, JC plays the tough guy with his trademark sense of humor. He gives his adversary the bad eye after taking a chair on the back, only to wince in pain as soon as his opponent's out of sight. A bicycle chase gives Chan a mobile prop to use and he incorporates every object he passes by.

Project A Courtesy of the Everett Collection

Project A also features a brilliant clock-tower fight using the clockwork machinery itself and ending in JC's recreation of silent comedian Harold Lloyd's clock-hanging gag.

The picture also puts the "**Three Brothers**" together again: former Peking Opera schoolmates JC, Sammo Hung, and Biao Yuen.

A sequel, ***Project A II*** (1987), followed.

Project A, Part II. See *Project A II*.

Project A II
Alternate Titles: *Project A, Part II*; *Project B*
Genre: Period Action-Comedy

Project A II (DVD). Mega Star Video: 102 minutes/unrated. In Cantonese and Mandarin with English subtitles.

Courtesy of Scott Rhodes

Hong Kong Release Date: August 19, 1987
Cast: JC, Maggie Cheung, Rosamund Kwan,
    David Lam, Carina Lau, Bill Tung, Regina
    Kent
Director: JC
Other JC Credits: Coscreenwriter, stunt
    coordinator

Location: Hong Kong
Box-Office Gross: $31.4 million (Hong Kong)

JC recreates his role as Sgt. Dragon Ma of the Hong Kong Coast Guard in this sequel that picks up where the original left off. Chan is assigned to help out an overworked corrupt police officer who's running a corrupt department. When his superiors discover his actions, the officer is fired and JC assumes his position, only to learn that criminal groups have been bribing the police force to stay out of their affairs.

In addition to a corrupt police force, JC also has to deal with various revolutionaries, pirates, and an inept and cowardly group of individuals that refuse to uphold law and order because of imminent danger. JC eventually swings into action to right all the wrongs.

Perhaps due to its convoluted plot, this sequel is definitely slower than its predecessor is, but Chan's action scenes make up for any awkward pacing. On the other hand, some film critics feel this movie is *the* peak JC experience.

Project A II's fights, except for the finale, are mainly small-scale encounters compared to the typical, more flamboyant JC offerings. The fight in which he's handcuffed to another man is brief but inspired.

A hilarious highlight is the comic bit of hide-and-seek with five different groups of people in his girlfriend's apartment.

Project B. See *Project A II*.

Project Eagle. See *Armour of God II: Operation Condor*.

Project S

Alternate Titles: *Once a Cop, Police Story 4, Police Story 4: Project S, Police Story 3: Part 2, Supercop 2*
Genre: Action
Year of Release: 1993
Cast: Michelle Yeoh, Emil Chow, Dick Wei, Rong-Guang Yu, JC
Director: Stanley Tong
Location: Hong Kong

JC produces and makes only a cameo appearance in this semi-sequel to *Police Story 3: Supercop*. In it **Michelle Yeoh** reprises her Hana Yang role as the mainland China cop. She's dispatched to Hong Kong to help probe a robbery ring only to learn that her boyfriend (Yu) is behind the crimes.

Protector, The

Genre: Action

Hong Kong Release Date: July 11, 1985

Cast: JC, Danny Aiello, Roy Chiao, Bill
    "Superfoot" Wallace, Victor Arnold, Sally Yeh

Directors: James Glickenhaus; JC directed all the
    reshoots in Hong Kong

Locations: U.S. (New York City) and Hong Kong

Box-Office Gross: $13.9 million (Hong Kong)

Injuries: JC injured bones in his hands and
    fingers.

A New York City undercover cop (JC) and his new partner (Aiello) go to Hong Kong to crack a major heroin ring that's smuggling drug shipments to New York.

The Protector marks JC's second unsuccessful stab at mainstream American audiences, and it was disastrous. Insiders wondered when American filmmakers would realize JC's humor and unrestricted action is universal and package him appropriately for the global market. That question was answered eleven years later, in 1996, when New Line Cinema released an upgraded version of **Rumble in the Bronx**.

The Protector features relatively big-budget action set pieces including chases by car, helicopter, motorboat, and motorized junks. It concludes with JC crushing a helicopter with a crane, but the most enter-

The Protector (DVD). Universe Laser and Video Co.: 91 minutes/unrated. In Cantonese and Mandarin with English subtitles. Courtesy of Scott Rhodes

taining scenes are the one or two short, tightly choreographed martial arts pieces, especially the climactic fight with American kickboxing champion Bill "Superfoot" Wallace.

JC and director Glickenhaus suffered a contentious relationship throughout the shoot. Profanity and gratuitous nudity punctuated Glickenhaus's original version

龍

JC performs a rooftop-high, midair kick in *The Protector*.

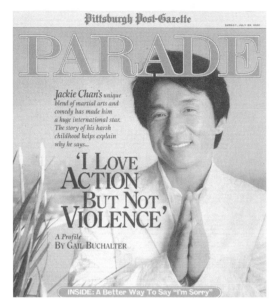

The weekly *Parade* Sunday newspaper supplement has a reported circulation of 32 million copies.

of *The Protector*. Greatly dissatisfied, JC waited for him to leave Hong Kong and then ordered extensive reshoots and delivered a different cut of the film for the home market. Thus, the Hong Kong version of the film, which captures JC's signature fighting style, differs from the predictable elements of the U.S. release.

On the positive side, this picture inspired JC's ***Police Story*** (1985), which set a new action standard for Hong Kong films.

Publications (Mainstream). Since 1980, when JC made his American movie debut in ***The Big Brawl***, he has been featured in countless mainstream media throughout the Western world. These include appearances

in some of the world's most prestigious and highest-circulation publications, including film reviews in the *New York Times* and *Time* magazine, as well as cover stories in *GQ* magazine and the *Parade* Sunday newspaper supplement.

See Appendix 3: Jackie Chan Bibliography.

Ratner, Brett. The director of two JC films: ***Rush Hour*** (1998) and its sequel ***Rush Hour 2*** (2001). Early in his career, he

Director Brett Ratner.

directed music videos for many rap stars, and attended New York University film school.

Moving into feature films, he's directed *Whatever Happened to Mason Reese* (1990), *Money Talks* (1997), and *The Family Man* (2000) starring Nicholas Cage. Ratner is a former martial arts practitioner.

Red Bronx. See *Rumble in the Bronx*.

Red Dragon. See *New Fist of Fury*.

Rhythm. A unique concept personally created by JC as applied to combat choreography. According to him, each and every fight

scene has its own special rhythm based on the moves used by the participants.

In a 1996 interview with Rob Blackwelter for the Spliced Online Internet website, JC explained how he invented his concept of rhythm as applied to cinematic martial arts fights.

"Comedy I learned from Buster Keaton. Then [I looked at actor/dancer] Gene Kelley. Before that, we [were] fighting in Chinese style." He jumps up and makes mechanical kung-fu movements with sounds to match.

"After the editing, we looked at it. [It was] very boring.

"[So] when I looked at Gene Kelley, it give me [a] new idea. Why? Because before they're dancing, you just hear this sound."

He shuffles his feet and makes tap-dancing noises with his tongue.

"If [you dance] ten minutes like this, [it's] very boring. But suddenly, [when] the music come up [he starts singing], then suddenly the music stops [he repeats the tap-dancing noise].

"Then I said, 'Yes! *That's* the rhythm.'"

JC then adapted that kind of fluctuating rhythm to his screen fights.

JC's actual application of rhythm to screen fighting is best described in this personal anecdote by American karate champion and actor **Keith Vitali**, who costarred with JC in *Wheels on Meals* (1984). It's quoted from Vitali's interview with *Screen Power* magazine's editor, Richard Cooper.

"Jackie and I were ready to do our first fight scene. The cameras were almost ready to roll and not one word had been said to me about what the fight was going to look like. Normally, the way we shoot fight scenes in America is that we rehearse over and over until we're ready to shoot.

"Jackie could tell that I was getting anxious about not knowing what we were going to do. Suddenly, to my relief, Jackie said he was ready to begin putting our fight scene together.

"He said, 'Keith, throw a few kicks for me.' So I demonstrated a couple of moves, then I stopped and looked at him and asked, 'What's next?'

"Jackie didn't answer me. Instead he began drumming out a beat on his thigh with his hands. It was as if he was playing the drum on his thigh.

"I asked him what he was doing and he replied, 'First I create a beat, a rhythm in my head and then apply our movements to the beat I create. If you have the two best fighters in the world in a fight scene in a movie and there is no rhythm or beat to the movements, you will not like the fight. You won't even know why you don't like the fight, but it's because your subconscious mind has detected no rhythm. So, first, I create the beat and then when we fight, your subconscious will like it.'

"This was the most incredible information that I've ever received about fight scenes in movies, and I still follow his philosophy in my films today. It has had an impact on every film I've worked on since then."

Roadshow Magazine. A slick, high-quality Japanese fan magazine, which published many special editions about JC and also issued film awards to him for his work. The publication enjoyed its widest circulation in the 1980s.

See Appendix 4: Jackie Chan's Awards, Honors, and Offices Held.

Rothrock, Cynthia. The American actress and martial arts champion who starred in *Inspector Wears Skirts* (1988), produced by JC. A five-time national forms champion and a black belt in five different styles, she has starred in some forty-five martial arts and action films.

ROADSHOW

SPECIAL EDITION

世界初公開!新作『龍少爺』台湾ロケ・スナップ

台北熱写フレッシュ独占カラーぎっしり

JACKIE CHAN

実物大手型足型キスマークもあるぞ!

Roadshow magazine   Courtesy of Neva Friedenn

In her hometown of Scranton, Pennsylvania, Rothrock started taking lessons at her parents' best friend's private gym at thirteen. Little did she know that her casual interest would lead to a full-time professional career. By 1982, she was one of the premier forms and weapon competitors in the United States. Competing in divisions that were not segregated by male-female categories, she literally captured every title in both open and closed karate competition.

From 1981 to 1985, Rothrock was the undefeated National Karate Champion in both forms and weapon competition, a record that still stands today.

Rothrock's status as a champion led to a Kentucky Fried Chicken commercial in the early 1980s, after which she was invited to Hong Kong to star in a string of action pictures, the first American female to do so.

She made her starring debut in *Yes Madam* (1984), paired with **Michelle Yeoh**. Over the next five years, she went on to star in numerous films, among them *Millionaire's Express* (1985) with **Sammo Hung**, *Righting Wrongs* (1986) with **Biao Yuen**, *Magic Crystal* (1987), and JC's *Inspector Wears Skirts*. She left Hong Kong as one of the most celebrated action stars in that colony's cinematic history. **Golden Harvest Studios**, the company that had helped launch the careers of both **Bruce Lee** and JC, tried to launch Rothrock in the United States with a pair of martial arts movies called *China O'Brien* (1988 and 1989). Though they performed poorly at the domestic box office, they became popular on cable television and in video rentals.

Cynthia Rothrock in *Sworn to Justice*

Photo by Jeff Barco; courtesy of Paul Maslak

Her most recent release is *Sworn to Justice* (2001), the largest-budgeted picture in her long career. [Paul Maslak]

Rouge
Genre: Fantasy
Hong Kong Release Date: July 7, 1988

Cast: Anita Mui, Leslie Cheung, Emily Chu, Alex Man, Irene Wan
Director: Stanley Kwan
JC Credit: Producer
Location: Hong Kong
Box-Office Gross: $17.4 million (Hong Kong)

In 1930s Hong Kong, the opium-smoking son (Cheung) of a rich family falls in love with a high-class prostitute (Mui). Refusing to accept her, his rich parents cut off his allowance, forcing him to try working unsuccessfully at several jobs, and forcing her to continue entertaining men. Eventually they make a suicide pact. She dies but he loses his nerve at the last moment. They had planned to reunite in the spirit world, so when he doesn't come, she returns to the mortal world to find him. But one day in the spirit world is fifty years in the human one, and she is lost and helpless in a Hong Kong of the late 1980s. Her distress earns the sympathy of young newspaperman Alex, who helps her in the quest to be reunited with her lover.

Produced by JC and winner of four Hong Kong Film Awards, including Best Picture, Best Director, and Best Actress, *Rouge* belongs to a popular Hong Kong genre, the ghost story, and also to a more select category, the Cantonese art film.

Rumble in the Bronx

Alternate Title: *Red Bronx*

Genre: Action-Comedy

Hong Kong Release Date: January 21, 1995

U.S. Release Date: February 23, 1996 (upgraded
   version)

Cast: JC, Mark Akerstream, Garvin Cros, Anita
   Mui, Bill Tung, Francoise Yip, Chun Wai Sit,
   Morgan Lam, Emil Chow, Raymond To

Director: Stanley Tong

Other JC Credit: Co–stunt coordinator

Locations: Canada (Vancouver, B.C.), United
   States (Washington)

Box-Office Gross: $56.9 million (Hong Kong);
   $32.2 million (U.S.)

Injuries: JC broke his left ankle while jumping
   onto a hovercraft.

Rumble in the Bronx (DVD). New Line Video: 91
minutes/rated R. In English.

Courtesy of Scott Rhodes

In a thin plot, JC plays Ah Keung, a Hong Kong cop who comes to New York to help his uncle sell his grocery store, then befriends the woman who has bought it. While protecting her from thieves and street gangs from the notorious "Fort Apache" neighborhood of the Bronx, JC ultimately gets embroiled in a mobster's diamond-smuggling scheme.

JC's trademark use of nearby props to defeat whole gangs of thugs is once again evident. In *Rumble*, there's a sequence where he uses refrigerators, another one where he improvises with furniture, one involving perfect timing with a knife, and another fight in a grocery store where he does something uncanny with a grocery cart.

When JC broke his ankle jumping onto a hovercraft, his crew placed a sock on his broken foot and painted it to look like a

(Both photos) *Rumble in the Bronx*   Courtesy of the Kobal Collection

sneaker! This is just one of many examples of how he earned his status as the hardest-working man in all of show business.

Actually shot in Vancouver, B.C., Canada, originally for a Chinese audience, *Rumble in the Bronx* was later optioned by New Line Cinema and given a cinematic facelift via a new soundtrack using JC's voice in English. Upon its release in the U.S.

market in January 1996, it shot to number one in box-office receipts, marking JC's breakthrough to the American market after three failed past attempts. (Back in his home territory, *Rumble* was 1995's most profitable Hong Kong movie.)

The New Line connection influenced JC's career in two important ways. First, it finally made him a recognized global movie star in the eyes of Hollywood producers, who began offering him salaries in the $12 million range to star in American productions. Second, New Line (and later, Miramax) upgraded numerous other already completed JC pictures and released them in American theaters, where they all made a tidy profit. These modified versions

(Both photos) *Rumble in the Bronx*   Courtesy of the Kobal Collection

are identifiable by the marketing gimmick of preceding each title with JC's full name and actually using JC's name as the fictional character he portrays.

Rumble is a fun movie with plenty of action and martial arts content, more than enough to amaze viewers with JC's signature acrobatic talents. But what makes it special is JC's spirited enthusiasm for his work and his infectious personality.

Rumble in Hong Kong. See **Police Woman**.

Rush Hour
Genre: Action-Comedy
Year of Release: 1998

Cast: JC, Chris Tucker, Elizabeth Pena, Tom Wilkinson, Ken Leung, Julia Hsu, Tzi Ma, Robert Littman, Chris Penn, Michael Chow, Kai Lennox, Larry Sullivan Jr., Yang Lin, Roger Fan, George Cheung, Lucy Lin
Director: Brett Ratner
Other JC Credits: Stunt coordinator
Locations: U.S. (Los Angeles), Hong Kong
Box-Office Gross: $141.1 million (U.S.); $245.3 million (worldwide)
Injuries: Sliding down a canvas ornamental banner from several stories' height, he brush-burned his buttocks and nearly friction-burned his pants completely off his backside.

JC plays Detective Inspector Lee, the only man capable of capturing Juntao, one of Hong Kong's most powerful and treacher-

Rush Hour. Courtesy of the Kobal Collection

Rush Hour. Courtesy of the Everett Collection

THE UNAUTHORIZED JACKIE CHAN ENCYCLOPEDIA

ous crime lords. With the unwavering support of Han (Ma), the Chinese Consular in Hong Kong, Lee's diligence and cunning have led to the confiscation of more than $500 million in weapons, drugs, and a collection of Chinese art unsurpassed in the world.

However, the elusive Juntao remains at large, and now seeks revenge against those who believe they can bring him to justice.

The action moves to Los Angeles when Consul Han is sent on a diplomatic mission to the United States, where his daughter, Soo Young (Julia Hsu), is abducted in broad daylight. Though the FBI assures Han that they will find the kidnappers and return his daughter safely, Han fears for her life and turns to the only man he believes he can trust: his longtime friend and ally, Inspector Lee.

Unwilling to have their investigation hampered by a meddling outsider, the FBI assigns rogue LAPD detective James Carter (Tucker) to the case. Seizing the opportunity as a chance to impress the FBI and ultimately join the Bureau, Carter enthusiastically accepts—until he discovers that his mission is to "baby-sit" Lee and keep him away from the case at any cost. Carter,

Rush Hour. Courtesy of the Everett Collection

who is as arrogant and fast-talking as he is street smart, covertly embarks on a one-man crusade to solve the case. Of course, he must first distract Inspector Lee.

Within hours, Carter realizes he has greatly underestimated his Hong Kong counterpart, who has quickly seen through the ruse, given Carter the slip, and landed in the middle of the FBI's investigation.

As the impatient FBI agents try to cast off these unwanted misfits, it becomes clear to the two cops from two very different worlds that it is in their best interests to join forces. Together, with the help of LAPD bomb expert Tania Johnson (Peña), they wreak havoc on Los Angeles, the FBI investigation, and each other as they become tangled in a deadly web of revenge, deceit, and betrayal.

Rush Hour is a formulaic but frenetic "fish out of water" saga that effectively teams JC and motormouth comedian Tucker. Directed by **Brett Ratner**, it marked JC's first American-produced

During a 1998 promo campaign in New York for *Rush Hour*, JC (center) appeared on ABC-TV's "The View" with its four hostesses (left to right): Star Jones, Lisa Ling, Joy Behar, and Meredith Vieira. Courtesy of the Everett Collection

JC with taekwondo master Sang Koo Kang of Miami on the set of *Rush Hour 2*

Courtesy of Sang Koo Kang

blockbuster, grossing some $142 million in its domestic (U.S. and Canada) release alone and cementing his status as one of the world's biggest movie stars. He was reportedly paid a $12 million salary for his role. Besides the terrific stunts and fight scenes, JC and Tucker have great chemistry together, leading to some gut-busting comic bits.

Rush Hour was the highest grossing picture in the history of New Line Cinema, its production company, which also claims that it's "the number-one grossing independent film of all time."

A sequel, ***Rush Hour 2***, followed.

Rush Hour 2

Genre: Action-Comedy
Year of Release: 2001
Cast: JC, Chris Tucker, Wong Fei, Alan King, John Lone, Chris Penn, Roselyn Sanchez, Stephen Sable, Ziyi Zhang, Don Cheadle

(Both photos) *Rush Hour 2*   Courtesy of the Kobal Collection

Director: Brett Ratner
Locations: Hong Kong, U.S. (Los Angeles and
   Las Vegas)
Box-Office Gross: $226.02 million (U.S.)

This reported $68 million–budgeted sequel to the blockbuster 1998 original continues the saga of two high-energy cops from different backgrounds. As seen at the end of the first movie, Detective James Carter (Tucker) travels back to Hong Kong with his new friend, Detective Lee (Chan). There they fight Chinese crooks, and end up back in America (Los Angeles and Las Vegas).

Reportedly, JC's *Rush Hour 2* salary was $15 million while Tucker got $20 million. The high budget paid off: *RH2* earned a sensational $226.02 million in domestic (U.S. and Canada) ticket sales. That staggering figure made *RH2* the biggest martial arts–themed film hit in motion picture history. Further, the sequel's amazing profit firmly established Chan as the undisputed king of action films worldwide.

Rush Hour 2
Courtesy of the Everett Collection

Rush Hour 2
Courtesy of the Kobal Collection

A bizarre incident occurred during production of this film in Hong Kong. Hong Kong police arrested a man after protection money was allegedly demanded from Spyglass Entertainment, the film company shooting *Rush Hour 2*.

A police spokeswoman reported that a thirty-year-old with ties to the **Triads**, Hong Kong's version of the Mafia, was arrested in a police ambush as he collected the money in a restaurant. "Tens of thousands" of dollars had been demanded and was fully recovered, according to police. Newspapers put the figure at HK $500,000 ($64,500 U.S.). Police said the extortionist threatened to disrupt *Rush Hour 2*'s shooting schedule if demands for the money were not met.

The man and two accomplices were suspected to be part of a valet-parking syndicate that wanted compensation for parking spaces used by the production crew in the Wan Chi area, which is known for its nightclubs.

Saeba, Ryu. JC's character name in *City Hunter*.

Rush Hour 2
Courtesy of the Kobal Collection

Sammy. JC's character name in *Fantasy Mission Force*.

"Saturday Night Live." The trendy, irreverent American comedy TV show on which JC appeared as the guest host on May 20, 2000. *SNL*, as it is known, has produced dozens of superbly talented cast members who've graduated to films and become major stars, from the late John Belushi to Adam Sandler. Each weekly show also features a prominent guest host and a popular musician or band.

JC as Elvis in a skit from "Saturday Night Live"
Courtesy of the Everett Collection

JC appeared as the guest host for the final show of the 1999–2000 season. In his opening monologue, JC rejoiced at being the "first" martial artist ever to host "SNL," and he assured the audience that there would be no violence on that evening's show. His "guarantee" was immediately challenged by a cast member impersonat-

JC in a guest appearance on "Saturday Night Live"

Courtesy of the Everett Collection

secret ingredient to clean clothes—Calgon detergent!

The JC-hosted show garnered impressive ratings. Some thirty million viewers watched the program, a 13 percent gain over the previous year's finale, which had featured Sarah Michelle Gellar and the Backstreet Boys.

Schedule A. See **Project A**.

Screen Power: The Jackie Chan Magazine. The only magazine in the West completely devoted to JC and his work. Published in England, it is officially endorsed and recognized by The Jackie Chan Group in Hong Kong. Founded by publisher/editor Richard Cooper in 1997, *Screen Power* is published six times a year (bimonthly). Each issue is approximately forty-six pages in length, and is printed on high-quality glossy paper with some color pages.

ing Steven Seagal, who reminded JC that he had already hosted "SNL" nine years earlier!

"I'll bet you were really funny," JC retorted, "because everything you've done is a joke."

As "Seagal" exited, JC was then confronted by a cast member impersonating Jean-Claude Van Damme, whose recent box-office failures sent him scurrying from the stage in embarrassment.

Throughout the rest of the show, he interacted with cast members in numerous comedy skits. He had a fight with a female, impersonated Elvis, and played a Chinese laundryman who uses an ancient Chinese

Each issue of *Screen Power* features exclusive interviews with JC, his directors, costars, bodyguards, and stunt team. It also carries on-set reports from current movie locations, retrospective and current film reviews, and contests offering JC merchan-

Screen Power: The Jackie Chan Magazine is the world's only fanzine officially endorsed by JC.

dise. The magazine's website address is www.screen-power.com.

Seasonal Films Corporation. See **See-Yuen Ng**.

Serious Crimes Squad. See *Crime Story*.

Seven Little Fortunes. The **Peking Opera** performing troupe of the **China Drama Academy**, whose members included JC, Sammo Hung, and Biao Yuen. This troupe's public performances represented the academy's only source of revenue. Troupe members were given five dollars (HK)—and later thirty-five dollars—of every seventy-five dollars they earned for the school. The

big return, however, was learning the art of public performance and stagecraft, which gave them a basic foundation for their later work in films.

Sex and Zen & A Bullet in the Head. See Appendix 3: Jackie Chan Bibliography.

Shanghai. See **Hong Kong Martial Arts Films**.

Shanghai Knights

Genre: Period Action-Comedy
U.S. Release Date: 2002
Cast: JC, Owen Wilson, Fann Wong
Director: David Dobkin
Location: London, England
Concept: The ancient East meets Victorian England.

Set in early twentieth-century London, this sequel to **Shanghai Noon** went into production in February 2002. In it the mismatched buddies, Chon Wang (JC) and Roy O'Bannon (Wilson) uncover a worldwide conspiracy to overthrow the Chinese and British empires.

Shanghai Noon

Genre: Period Action-Comedy
U.S. Release Date: May 26, 2000
Cast: JC, Owen Wilson, Lucy Liu, Brandon Merrill, Roger Yuan, Xander Berkeley, Rongguang Yu, Ya-Hi Cui, Eric Chen, Jason Connery, Walt Goggins, Adrien Dorval, Rafael Báez, Stacy Grant, Kate Luyben
Director: Tom Dey
Other JC Credits: Executive producer
Locations: Canada (Calgary)
Box-Office Grosses: $56.9 million (U.S.); $95.5 (worldwide)

Shanghai Noon (DVD). Touchstone Home Video: 110 minutes/rated PG-13. In English. Courtesy of Scott Rhodes

Shanghai Noon   Courtesy of the Everett Collection

Concept: The ancient East meets the Old West. JC plays Chon Wang, a palace guard in China's Forbidden City who comes to America in the late 1800s to rescue a kidnapped princess (Liu). Chon hooks up with a New-Age, image-conscious train robber, Roy O'Bannon (Wilson), who's more adept at shooting off his mouth than his pearl-handled pistols. Roy also is more interested in the chest of gold coins sent as ransom than in helping to free the princess.

The mix makes for a very amusing interracial buddy flick. Plunking JC into the Old West allows him to unleash another outbreak of his exuberant, inventive acrobatics. Roy mistakes his new partner's name as "John Wayne" and pronounces it a terrible moniker for a cowboy. He laments that when the two become wanted men, his "sidekick," Chon, gets a thousand-dollar reward posted, while Roy gets just five hundred dollars. Roy also envies the cool nickname Chon picks up, "The Shanghai Kid."

Shanghai Noon relies on JC's usual ballet of wild martial arts and stunts as he mixes it up with cops and robbers and cow-

Shanghai Noon

Courtesy of the Kobal Collection

Shanghai Noon

Courtesy of the Everett Collection

boys and Indians. The high-octane action is nicely choreographed by JC and his Hong Kong stunt team. Some of the JC highlights include a runaway train sequence inspired by Buster Keaton's silent film *The General* (1926), a fight in the forest against a gang of Crow Indians involving several things we didn't know could be done with evergreen trees, another fight scene where he uses a horseshoe tied to a rope à la the classical Chinese rope-dart weapon, a new twist on the standard Western barroom brawl, and a tense climactic battle inside a mission using spears. JC was stunt-doubled in some of his action and fight scenes by Andy Cheng.

JC is a very likable Western hero, and there are good turns from Liu as the socially liberal princess, Yuan and Berkeley as scowling villains, and rodeo star Brandon Merrill as Chon's smirkingly stoic Sioux bride.

Wilson rounds up a good share of the laughs, too. Best known as one of the oil-men-astronauts in *Armageddon* (1998) and a ghost-hunter in *The Haunting* (1999), Wilson breaks out in *Shanghai Noon* with a comic take on a goodhearted bandit who's less concerned with booty than how he looks and acts while he's stealing it.

Shanghai Noon was JC's second big-budget Hollywood film after ***Rush Hour***

Shanghai Noon. Courtesy of the Everett Collection

(1998). A sequel, **Shanghai Knights**, has been announced by the production company, Spyglass Entertainment Group.

Shanghai Noon: From East to West. See **Shanghai Noon**.

Shaolin Chamber of Death. See **Shaolin Wooden Men**.

Shaolin Men. See **Hand of Death**.

Shaolin Snake and Crane Arts. See **Snake and Crane Arts of Shaolin**.

Shaolin Wooden Men

Alternate Titles: *Shaolin Chamber of Death*, *36 Wooden Men*, *Young Tiger's Revenge*
Genre: Period Martial Arts
Hong Kong Release Date: November 10, 1976
Cast: JC, Kan Kam, Simon Yuen, Chung-Erh Lung
Director: Wei Lo
Other JC Credit: Co–stunt coordinator
Director: Chi-Hwa Chen
Location: Hong Kong

JC's promotional appearance for *Shanghai Noon* on "Tonight" with Jay Leno.

Courtesy of the Everett Collection

In this straight kung-fu, revenge-oriented piece, JC, in an early role, is a mute who witnesses the death of his father when he is a young child. He then seeks guidance under the monks of the Shaolin Temple. However, he finds the training too slow so he trains under the guidance of a prisoner of the temple. Before JC can leave the tem-ple, he has to take on the awesome wooden fighters, 108 huge, activated warrior dummies controlled with chains and pulleys. In doing so, JC exhibits his mastery of the five animal styles of kung-fu and his skill with the long staff.

As co–stunt coordinator, JC had a degree of creative freedom to express his

(Both photos) *Shaolin Wooden Men*

real martial arts talent for the first time, which drew a few compliments but had no effect on box-office profits.

Shaw Brothers Studios. The post–World War II pioneering Hong Kong film studio that introduced the kung-fu film genre. The studio is named after the two brothers who founded it, Run Run and Runme, each of whom subsequently became a billionaire. The studio's main kung-fu output was period pieces/costume epics, a style of film-making that became the most popular of its time and paved the way for Hong Kong's contemporary action cinema.

The brothers began working as theater owners and expanded to the business of movie production, where they made films to exhibit in their own theaters, much like the Hollywood studios did in the 1930s. They were the first filmmakers to produce a Hong Kong movie with sound.

During the 1960s, Shaw Brothers Studios produced historical dramas, comedies, romances, documentaries, and an occasional kung-fu film. Due to its enormous film production output, the studio was dubbed "Movie Town." But with the growing popularity of martial arts pictures, the studio decided to focus all its considerable energies on the kung-fu genre in 1970 and quickly became its biggest producer. One of its biggest franchise hits was the *One Armed Swordsman* series starring **Jimmy Wang Yu.**

The studio was renowned for its frugality. It signed stars to exclusive contracts for very little pay and cranked out feature films on as little as one-week shooting schedules. On the other hand, it developed talent, giving many filmmakers their first breaks and providing a training ground in which to learn their craft.

This was the studio for which JC worked as a freelance stuntman after leaving the China Drama Academy in 1971. His first job was as an extra, and eventually he moved up to a position as a stuntman. Two years later, his training and determination paid off with a promotion to stunt coordinator, which ultimately led to his discovery. Watching JC direct stuntmen in the finer points of fighting and dying, a producer spotted his talent and gave him his first role as an adult performer in *Little Tiger from Canton* in 1971.

Historians point to the Shaw Brothers as one of the main culprits reportedly responsible for permitting the **Triads**, Hong Kong's powerful organized crime syndicate, to infiltrate the film industry. Because they were paid such low salaries, many Shaw Brothers contract players reputedly also worked for the Triads on the side. **Jimmy Wang Yu** is one of the most striking examples. Since then, the Triads have gained a sinister hold on Hong Kong filmmaking and filmmakers to this day, a hold against which prominent industry figures like JC started publicly protesting in the 1990s.

The Shaw Brothers Studios' decline began in the early 1970s, coinciding with the rise of **Golden Harvest Studios**, whose first superstar, **Bruce Lee**, made enormously profitable pictures for them. By the mid-1980s, the Shaw Brothers Studios became a full-fledged television production facility. Today the Shaw Brothers are inactive.

See also: **Hong Kong Martial Arts Films**.

Shaw, Runme. See **Hong Kong Martial Arts Films**; **Shaw Brothers Studios**.

Shaw, Run Run. See **Hong Kong Martial Arts Films**; **Shaw Brothers Studios**.

Shek, Dean. The veteran Hong Kong actor (a.k.a. Dean Shek Tien) who's worked in eight of JC's films: *Little Tiger from Canton* (1971), *Drunken Master* (1978), *Snake in the Eagle's Shadow* (1978), *Spiritual Kung Fu* (1978), *The Fearless*

(Both photos) *Snake and Crane Arts of Shaolin*

Hyena (1979), ***Dance of Death*** (1976), ***Half a Loaf of Kung Fu*** (1980), and ***Fearless Hyena II*** (1980).

Sheng, Alexander Fu. See **Hong Kong Martial Arts Films**.

Shing, Lung. JC's character name in *The Fearless Hyena*.

Simple Mission. See *Police Story 4: First Strike*.

Snake and Crane Arts of Shaolin
Alternate Titles: *Shaolin Snake and Crane Arts*

Genre: Martial Arts
Hong Kong Release Date: March 8, 1978
Cast: JC, Nora Miao, Kan Kam
Director: Chi-Hwa Chen
Other JC Credit: Co–stunt coordinator
Location: Hong Kong

In southern China, eight kung-fu masters create a powerful style called "The eight steps of snake and crane" and place these secrets into a book. Then they and the book mysteriously disappear. Yin-Fung Hsu (JC) turns up with the book and fights off a multitude of opposing clans who try to take it away from him.

Although this is another serious kung-fu picture, JC considers it his first "dream" project since the director, Chi-Hwa Chen, was a friend and gave him more creative freedom than he had ever had before. It consequently became the first picture that drew serious attention to JC from Hong Kong filmmakers.

As the co–stunt coordinator, JC shot for the sky. He took two days to film the main title credits, a series of fifty-eight actions performed in one continuous take, the moves of which are timed and positioned to point up the opening credits as they appear.

In the film itself, JC invented one of the techniques that would become his lifelong trademark: using everyday objects as combat props. He also offers some swashbuckling single-sword work against multiple opponents.

Snake Fist Fighter. See *Little Tiger from Canton*.

Snake in the Eagle's Shadow

Alternate Titles: *Bruce vs. Snake in Eagle's Shadow, The Eagle's Shadow, Snaky Monkey*
Genre: Comedy Kung-Fu
Hong Kong Release Date: March 1, 1978
Cast: JC, Jang-Lee Hwang, Simon Yuen, Roy Horan

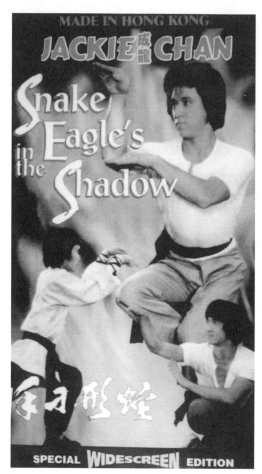

Snake in the Eagle's Shadow (VHS). Arena Home Video: 94 minutes/unrated. In English. Courtesy of Scott Rhodes

Director: Woo-Ping Yuen
Other JC Credit: Original story
Location: Hong Kong

(Both photos) JC in training with the wily master played by veteran actor Simon Yuen in *Snake in the Eagle's Shadow*

Courtesy of Seasonal Films Corporation

Box-Office Gross: $2.7 million (Hong Kong)
Injuries: JC's front tooth was kicked out by Jang-
   Lee Hwang during the climactic fight scene,
   and his arm was slashed during a sword
   fight, causing profuse bleeding.

JC plays a brawny menial at a kung-fu school where sadistic, pompous masters and students treat him like a human punching bag. He befriends a wily old vagabond (Yuen) who, in reality, is the last living master of the Snake-Fist style. JC saves the old man's life when he's bullied by a bunch of mean students from the rival Eagle Claw school.

In gratitude, the master teaches JC rudimentary martial arts techniques, like how to escape from attacks, but avoids showing him the secret Snake-Fist style until an encounter with two Eagle-Claw stylists almost costs JC his life. JC ultimately learns Snake-Fist and dukes it out with the evil Eagle-Claw master (Hwang) to save his and his master's lives. To win he employs a mixture of Snake-Fist techniques and tricks learned from his pet cat!

JC is brilliant during his comically difficult solo and duo training sequences. This film is also a terrific platform for introducing his impish humor and theatrical flair.

The fights are meticulously choreographed, dramatic, and frequently punctuated by outrageous humor, demonstrating just how good this genre can be when it's at its best.

Snake in the Eagle's Shadow marked JC's ninth starring role and was a breakthrough film—his first box-office hit. This genre trendsetter is considered the first of the **comedy kung-fu** films, despite the earlier *Half of Loaf of Kung-Fu* (1978), which remained unreleased until 1980. An equal share of the credit must go to producer **See-Yuen Ng**, who leased JC's services from **Wei Lo**'s company and gave the young star almost total creative control, and director **Woo-Ping Yuen**, who adeptly captured JC's humor and acrobatic flair.

Originally, *Snake* was intended as a vehicle for Alexander Fu Sheng, but a limited budget led to JC's casting in the lead role. The film's enormous success—it grossed over $2 million Hong Kong on its first run—propelled JC to stardom as a growing Asian box-office force.

Snaky Monkey. See **Snake in the Eagle's Shadow**.

Son, JC's. See **Jason Chan**.

Son of Master with Cracked Fingers. See **Little Tiger from Canton**.

Soup, JC's Favorite. Green bean.

Spartan X. See **Wheels on Meals**.

Spiritual Kung Fu

Alternate Titles: *Karate Bomber, Karate Ghostbuster*
Genre: Martial Arts Fantasy
Hong Kong Release Date: November 23, 1978
Cast: JC, James Tien, Shih Tien (a.k.a. Shek Kin)
Director: Wei Lo
Other JC Credit: Stunt coordinator
Location: Korea

JC meets *Poltergeist*! Five spirits rise from a meteor that crashes on earth. In a burned-out scripture hall, rumored to be haunted by these spirits, JC, a happy-go-lucky bumpkin, falls asleep, and tiny ghosts of the Dragon, Snake, Tiger, Crane, and Leopard styles emerge from hiding to make fun of him. He turns the tables and blackmails the ghosts into attaining human size and teaching him their lost fighting arts, collec-

Spiritual Kung-Fu

Spiritual Kung-Fu

tively known as "Spiritual Kung-Fu." He uses these supernatural techniques to retrieve a secret kung-fu manual, which had been stolen thirty years earlier.

Spiritual Kung Fu is a mostly straight role for JC, but it features the innovation of a superimposing camera, which produces special effects wherein Chan, who also choreographed the fights, can engage in combat with the ghosts.

This was director **Wei Lo**'s misguided attempt at humor, which turned out more vulgar than funny. The real laughs come from the cheesy special effects, which actually give this JC vehicle a special charm all its own.

Sport, Favorite Outdoor. Soccer.

Sports, Favorite Indoor. Badminton, bowling.

Stage Door Johnny
Genre: Drama
Hong Kong Release Date: March 24, 1990
Cast: Anita Mui, Kara Hui, Yin-San Lai, Yuk-Lin Chan, Ma Wu
Director: Ma Wu
JC Credit: Producer
Location: Hong Kong

JC produced and does not appear in this period piece about a group of Shanghai performers who overthrow a crime syndicate boss.

Star Power Ratings. Each year The Hollywood Reporter compiles its Star Power Survey, which looks at the global bankability of selected actors in the theatrical marketplace. Having a bankable actor, or actors, is probably the most important factor in the process of filmmaking today. Every year, the importance of the star becomes greater and greater in the presales business.

In its 2002 poll of more than 100 industry executives worldwide, 1,000-plus actors were rated on criteria such as potential opening-weekend box-office power and ability to secure financing and theatrical distribution based on their attachment to a project.

Actors with a perfect 100 percent rating are in the number-one position. JC was the top-scoring Asian actor globally (86.84 rating), with Malaysia-born Michelle Yeoh the top-scoring Asian actress (35.84). Fourteen actors finished in the top category (Maximum Star Power), with JC placing seventeenth overall and high in the next category (Strong Star Power). JC tied with veteran actor and multiple Oscar winner Jack Nicholson.

The two stars nearest to JC who also perform martial arts in their action films were Wesley Snipes (64.91) and Jet Li (57.68).

With box-office figures outside North America estimated at $13 billion—or more than 60 percent of the $21 billion-plus worldwide theatrical pot in 2001, according to investment banking firm Houlihan Lokey Howard & Zukin—the importance of global star appeal continues to be a critical component. Many say its importance is growing in an increasingly crowded marketplace. Whether you're a major studio looking to minimize risk or an independent trying to presell rights, star power is a crucial component of the package.

Here's how JC placed against Hollywood's megastars: Tom Cruise (100), Tom Hanks (100), Julia Roberts (100), Mel Gibson (98.68), Jim Carrey (98.46), George Clooney (95.18), Russell Crowe and Harrison Ford (94.74), Bruce Willis (94.30), Brad Pitt (92.98), Nicholas Cage (91.23), Leonardo DeCaprio (91.01), Will Smith (91.91), Denzel Washington (89.04), Sandra

Bullock (87.28), Robert De Niro (87.17), JC and Jack Nicholson (86.84).

Star Profile: Jackie Chan Monthly. See Appendix 3: Jackie Chan Bibliography.

Story of Drunken Master, The. See *Drunken Master*.

Story of Qui Xiang Lin, The. JC's third child role, a drama released in 1964.

Story of the CIA. See *Police Story 4: First Strike*.

Stranger in Hong Kong. See *Little Tiger from Canton*.

Strike of Death. See *Hand of Death*.

Style, Favorite Kung-Fu. Drunken boxing.

Subject, Favorite School. Physical education.

Superchef. See *Mr. Nice Guy*.

Supercop. See *Police Story 3: Supercop*.

Supercop 2. See *Project S*.

Superfly 2. See *Project A*.

Tang, Edward. JC's longtime screenwriter, he wrote or cowrote *The Young Master* (1980), *Dragon Lord* (1982), *Wheels on Meals* (1984), *Armour of God* (1986), *Project A II* (1987), *Police Story 2* (1988), *Police Story 3: Supercop* (1992), *Rumble in the Bronx* (1995), *Mr. Nice Guy* (1997), and *Who Am I?* (1998).

Tang (a.k.a. Edward Tang King-Sang) was studying Chinese literature when he became interested in theatrical plays, and while changing from one job to another, he wrote scripts. His writing talent first surfaced in television dramas. In the late 1970s, he became a scenario writer for **Golden Harvest Studios**. After his first collaboration with JC in *The Young Master*, he became JC's favorite screenwriter.

Tang, How-Yuen. JC's character name in *Dragon Fist*.

Tan, Little. JC's character name in *Hand of Death*.

Target, The. See *Twinkle, Twinkle, Lucky Stars*.

Television. JC appeared as himself in a two-part episode of the American TV show "Martin." The first, entitled "Scrooge," aired on December 16, 1996; the second, entitled "I Saw Gina Kissing Santa Clause," aired on December 17, 1996.

He also hosted "Saturday Night Live" on May 20, 2000.

Ten Fingers of Death. See *Little Tiger from Canton*.

36 Crazy Fists, The
Alternate Titles: *Blood Pact*, *Jackie Chan's Bloodpact* (U.S.), *Master and the Boxer*
Genre: Martial Arts Comedy and partial Documentary (The Making of 36 Crazy Fists)

Year of Release: 1979
Cast: Cha-Yung Liu, Feng Ku, Pei Chin
Director: Chi-Hwa Chen
JC Credit: Stunt coordinator
Location: Hong Kong

JC only choreographed the action for this forgettable movie about an orphaned youth who learns kung-fu from monks to avenge his father's death. Without JC's permission, the unscrupulous producers compiled a behind-the-scenes documentary about the making of this movie and released it as a "Jackie Chan" film.

36 Wooden Men. See *Shaolin Wooden Men*.

Thomas. JC's character name in *Wheels on Meals*.

3 Brothers; Three Brothers. A reference to former **China Drama Academy** classmates JC, **Sammo Hung**, and **Biao Yuen**. The trio worked together on numerous pictures, which ultimately came to be referred to as the "Three Brothers" films. The first such film was **John Woo**'s *Hand of Death*

(1976), in which they had small roles. The three went on to make some of the most entertaining martial arts films ever made: **Dragon Lord** (1982), **Wheels on Meals** (1984), **Project A** (1983), **Winners and Sinners** (1983), **My Lucky Stars** (1985), and **Twinkle, Twinkle, Lucky Stars** (1985).

Thunderarm. See **Armour of God**.

Thunderbolt

Alternate Title: *Dead Heat*
Genre: Action-Comedy
Hong Kong Release Date: August 5, 1995
Cast: JC, Anita Yuen, Michael Wong, Ken Lo, Chor Yuen, Thorsten Nickel
Director: Gordon Chan
Other JC Credit: Co—stunt coordinator
Locations: Hong Kong, Japan, Malaysia
Box-Office Gross: $45.6 million (Hong Kong)

In perhaps the corniest plot of all the JC films to date, JC is a car-racing mechanic forced into competing in a race against a murderous speedster named Cougar. Former Miss Hong Kong Anita Yuen is thrown in as a romantic interest, but makes absolutely no difference to the movie since the relationship dead-ends.

While the plot is an obvious excuse for JC, a car enthusiast in real life, to make a car-racing movie, *Thunderbolt* does have several non-vehicle action sequences to recommend it. They are, however, more violent and less comical than in the majority of films JC has made in the last two decades.

In one phenomenal scene, JC's house, a train car, gets completely demolished when it's lifted upside down by a crane and dropped to the ground. If you enjoy multiple-opponent fight sequences, *Thunderbolt* is definitely your kind of movie. Each of the two major fights has flashes of brilliance from JC's past work. The fight in the Pachinko parlor is amazing, and reminiscent of **Dragons Forever** (1987).

Due to the ankle injury sustained in his previous picture, **Rumble in the Bronx** (1995), JC used a double in a lot of the fight action for *Thunderbolt*. **Sammo Hung**'s protégé, Kar-Lok Chin, a gifted stuntman and martial artist, is a worthy double who's come to be called "Jackie Junior."

Thunderbolt is also noteworthy as the most expensive Hong Kong film ever made up to that time, $2 billion ($25 million U.S.).

Tien, Shih. See **Dean Shek**.

Ting, Lord Chung. JC's character name in *Magnificent Bodyguards*.

To Kill with Intrigue

Alternate Title: *Jackie Chan Connection*
Genre: Period Martial Arts
Hong Kong Release Date: July 22, 1977
Cast: JC, George Wang, Feng Chu (a.k.a. Feng Hsu)
Director: Wei Lo
Location: Korea

In this Shaw Brothers imitation costumer notable only for some dazzling sword scenes, JC plays a man seriously injured by a gang that kills his family who then embarks on the conventional vengeance-seeking mission. Director **Wei Lo** once again fails to effectively employ JC's considerable talents.

To Kill with Intrigue was filmed on location in Korea in freezing weather conditions, where the filmmaking equipment froze and chilled the cast and crew's enthusiasm.

Tokyo Powerman. See *Winners and Sinners*.

Tong, Stanley. The director of three of four of JC's greatest works—*Police Story 3: Supercop* (1992), *Project S* (1993), *Rumble in the Bronx* (1995), and *Police Story 4: First Strike* (1996)—and one of JC's favorite collaborators.

Born in 1953, Stanley Tong (a.k.a. Kwai-Lai Tong) got his start in the film industry as a stuntman, and he learned his trade as a filmmaker only after surviving years of death-defying stunts. Determined to make films of his own, he started his own production company.

He made his directorial debut with *A Chinese Ghost Story* (1987), whose success necessitated a sequel in 1990. He followed up with the swashbuckling *Swordsman II* (1991).

As a film director with an intimate knowledge of stunt work, it soon became apparent that a collaboration between Tong and Hong Kong superstar JC would be an ideal match.

Tong was among those filmmakers and performers who relocated to America in anticipation of the reunification of Hong

Kong and mainland China in 1997. His first Hollywood outing as a director was a live-action version of *Mr. Magoo* (1997), a moderately successful slapstick comedy starring Leslie Nielsen. He also coproduced with fellow Hong Kong filmmaker **Sammo Hung** the short-lived American TV series "Martial Law."

Top Squad. See *Inspector Wears Skirts.*

Top Squad II. See *Inspector Wears Skirts II.*

Touch of Zen, A
Genre: Period Martial Arts
Year of Release: 1968

Directed by King Hu, *A Touch of Zen* is notable as the first major role for **Sammo Hung**, who was just sixteen at the time. He plays a Japanese swordsman. In it, Xu Feng stars as Hui-Zhen Yang, a female swash-buckler who teams up with allies to defend a provincial town from imperial enforcers. JC has a small cameo role.

Training, Martial Arts. At four or five years old, JC began learning the fundamentals of a rare form of Shaolin kung-fu called Kung Kar from his father, Charles Chan. These daily sessions commenced at sunrise and lasted several hours. He then learned a number of acrobatic styles during his ten-year apprenticeship at the **China Drama Academy** from 1961 to 1971. Since then, he's studied and employed in his films karate, judo, hapkido, and Western boxing.

These styles were reflected in the fight scenes of his early straight kung-fu and **comedy kung-fu** pictures. In *Project A* (1983) and after, JC abandoned conventional kung-fu fighting for a more realistic, eclectic application of combat.

Triads. Hong Kong's secret organized crime societies that have entrenched themselves in the local moviemaking business. The gangs, which are also involved in prostitution, illegal gambling, copyright piracy, and smuggling, regularly demand protection money from producers, and are even known to coerce popular entertainers into working for low-grade, X-rated films, which they finance.

The organization's move into the entertainment industry is often blamed for the deteriorating quality of Hong Kong movies in the 1990s and the exodus of talent overseas. JC and other Hong Kong stars have led public protests against the Triads and their involvement in Hong Kong filmmaking.

Director Hark Tsui (right)   Photo by Alan Markfield; courtesy of Columbia Pictures

Tsui, Hark. The codirector of JC's *Twin Dragons* (1991). Recognized as a one-man film industry and revolutionary in the changing face of Hong Kong cinema, Tsui has become one of the world's foremost action directors.

Born in Vietnam in 1951, he moved to Hong Kong with his parents as a child, becoming fascinated with film from an early age. His stint at the University of Texas in the United States studying film, while his father in Hong Kong thought he was studying medicine, is just part of the Hark Tsui legend.

After graduation, Tsui remained in the States, producing documentary work. Returning to Hong Kong, he worked in television on the acclaimed miniseries "The Gold Dagger Romance" (1978). The following year he directed his first feature, *The Butterfly Murders* (1979), which drew critical notice through screenings in film festi-

vals across Europe. His brutal satire *Dangerous Encounters* (1980) raised the ire of Hong Kong censors with its presentation of urban youth violence and street crime.

Tsui drew international fame with his *Zu, Warriors of the Magic Mountains* (1983), which awakened the overseas film community to the revitalized face of Eastern cinema. In 1986, Tsui set up the production organ Film Workshop, whose first project was to succeed beyond everyone's wildest dreams. The Tsui-produced *A Better Tomorrow* (1986) not only launched the film career of Hong Kong superstar Yun-Fat Chow, it relaunched former Shaw Brothers player Lung Ti back into the limelight, brought Leslie Cheung to world notice, and established one of the world's finest action directors, **John Woo**. The success of *A Better Tomorrow* necessitated two sequels.

In the 1990s, Tsui's stellar producing-directing career was divided between the fantasy/horror genre, with *A Chinese Ghost Story 2* and *3* (1990 and 1991), and martial arts epics like *Swordsman* (1990) and its sequels (1991 and 1993); *Once Upon a Time in China* (1990) and its sequels (1991 and 1992), all starring the dynamic Jet Li; and *Iron Monkey* (1993). The original *Once Upon a Time in China* made Li a star and won Tsui the best action director award at the Hong Kong Film Awards.

He codirected with colleague **Ringo Lam** *Twin Dragons*, starring JC, in a unique collaboration of Hong Kong filmmakers.

Tsui made his American directorial debut in *Double Team* (1997), starring Jean-Claude Van Damme, with fellow Hong Kong filmmaker **Sammo Hung** serving as fight choreographer, and followed up with Van Damme's *Knock Off* (1998).

Tuxedo, The
Genre: Action-Comedy
U.S. Release Date: June 7, 2002

Cast: JC, Jennifer Love Hewitt, Richie Coster, Jason Isaacs, Debi Mazar, Romany Malco, Mia Cottet, Peter Stormare
Director: Kevin Donovan
Location: Toronto, Canada

The working title for one of JC's planned films that went into production in September 2001. In it bumbling cabdriver Jimmy Tong (JC) is hired to chauffeur rich, debonair businessman Clark Devlin (Isaacs), who is actually the head of a secret government spy unit. When Devlin gets sidelined with an injury, Tong steps in for his boss and, working with his sexy young sidekick (Hewitt), goes about saving the world himself—with the help of an extremely well-crafted Armani tuxedo that enables him to fight villains and perform feats of derring-do skillfully.

The storyline gives JC a chance to showcase the full spectrum of his own remarkable skills—from dancing to shimmying up a twenty-story cement silo.

The action-comedy is intended to be a film series, much like **Rush Hour**.

DreamWorks, the studio behind the film, is co-owned by legendary director Steven Spielberg, with whom JC has dreamed of working for many years. Spielberg is not directing the film, however.

Twin Dragons

Alternate Titles: *Brother vs. Brother, Double Dragon, Duel of Dragons, The Twin Dragons, When Dragons Collide, When Dragons Meet*

Hong Kong Release Date: January 25, 1992

U.S. Release Date: April 9, 1999 (upgraded version)

Cast: JC, Maggie Cheung, Nina Li, Teddy Robin Kwan, Nina Li Chi, Philip Chan, Kar-Leung Lau, Hark Tsui, Ringo Lam, See-Yuen Ng

Directors: Hark Tsui, Ringo Lam

Other JC Credits: Stunt coordinator

Location: Hong Kong

Box-Office Grosses: $33.2 million (Hong Kong); $8.3 million (U.S.)

Injuries: JC had glass shards embedded in his buttocks.

Twin Dragons

Courtesy of the Kobal Collection

In a dual role, JC plays twin brothers who are reunited after being separated at birth. One grew up in the United States and became a famous conductor; the other was raised in Hong Kong and became a petty thief. All manner of mayhem ensues when the siblings meet and the good brother gets caught up in his twin's life of crime.

The highlight of *Twin Dragons* is JC's stunt-laden fights in an auto production factory.

Twin Dragons was a unique collaboration of Hong Kong filmmakers, which explains the participation of **Hark Tsui** and **Ringo Lam**, two of Hong Kong's most renowned directors. All profits from this film were donated to erect a new Director's Guild headquarters.

The film's audio and soundtrack was upgraded for American audiences and released in 1999 after JC had become a box-office star in the United States.

Twin Dragons, The. See *Twin Dragons*.

Twinkle, Twinkle, Little Stars. See *My Lucky Stars*.

Twinkle, Twinkle, Lucky Stars

Alternate Titles: *My Lucky Stars II: The Target*, *The Target*

Genre: Action-Comedy

Hong Kong Release Date: August 15, 1985

Cast: JC, Andy Lau, Sammo Hung, Biao Yuen, Richard Ng, Shui-Fan Fung, Charlie Chin, Ying Ching, Dick Wei, Rosamund Kwan, Michelle Yeoh

Director: Sammo Hung

Location: Hong Kong

Box-Office Gross: $28.9 million (Hong Kong)

Twinkle, Twinkle, Lucky Stars (VHS). American Imperial: 90 minutes/unrated. In English. Courtesy of Scott Rhodes

The cockeyed crime-busters from *My Lucky Stars* take a break in Thailand to celebrate their undeserved success from their previous case. Their vacation is cut short when they learn that Thai assassins are on the way to Hong Kong to kill a local drug lord. Detective JC finds his assignment switched from giving the drug lord a hard time to protecting him from the assassins.

Twinkle, Twinkle boasts a wonderful cast in a wacky film featuring two humungous fights that allow viewers to compare JC's and Yuen's combat styles side-to-side. Costar-director Hung steals the show in a hilarious sequence where he wages history's first clash of the sai-versus-tennis racket!

Due to its vast array of alternate titles, the *Lucky Stars* trilogy is the second most confusing related film series in all of JC's body of work (***Police Story***, 1985–96, is by far the *most* confusing.) To avoid confusion, *Twinkle, Twinkle, Lucky Stars* is the third and final entry—in other words, the second sequel—in the *Lucky Stars* trilogy.

The first and second entries, in order of release, are **Winners and Sinners** (1983) and **My Lucky Stars** (1985). In this trilogy, JC is part of an ensemble cast and has only a supporting role.

Two in a Black Belt. JC only appears in a small cameo role in this 1984 martial arts movie. Very little is known about this picture and it has faded into oblivion.

Urquidez, Benny "The Jet." The American World Kickboxing Champion who costars as a villain in two JC films, **Wheels on Meals** (1984) and **Dragons Forever** (1987), and has a cameo as a villain in a third, **My Lucky Stars** (1985). His exciting screen fights with JC are considered some of the best ever filmed.

Known as Benny "The Jet" for his flamboyant fighting style during his long and distinguished ring career, Urquidez scored fifty-seven knockouts in sixty-three fights and established himself as a legend in kickboxing circles. Starting in 1977, he was the first American to defeat Asian kickboxing champions at their own sport and thus establish American kickboxers as respected world-class fighters. His ring victories led to his portrayal as a hero in a series of Japanese comic books entitled *Benny "The Jet."*

Altogether, Urquidez has appeared as an actor in a dozen motion pictures, but he's been far more prolific as a stunt coordinator, stunt fighter, and martial arts trainer. In those capacities, he has worked with major stars like Patrick Swayze (*Road House*, 1989), Michael Keaton (*Batman Returns*, 1992), Chuck Norris (*Hellbound*, 1993), Jean-Claude Van Damme (*Street Fighter, The Movie* 1994), John Cusack (*Grosse Point*, 1997), Nicholas Cage (*Con Air*, 1997), and Cuba Gooding Jr. (*Pearl Harbor*, 2001).

Los Angeles Magazine recently named him "Los Angeles' Best Personal Trainer."

Vitali, Keith. JC's costar in **Wheels on Meals** (1984). The former number-one-ranked American karate champion for three consecutive years (1978–80), Vitali made a successful transition from tournament fighting to a movie career. He was discovered by Priscilla McDonald, a Hollywood producer's assistant at Cannon Films, in 1982, through a cover-story appearance in a national martial arts magazine. To date he has starred in seven films and has produced three others.

See also: **Rhythm**.

Wallace, Bill "Superfoot." The retired American world middleweight kickboxing champion (1974–80) who played JC's main nemesis in the finale of *The Protector* (1985). One of the most rugged warriors in martial arts ring history, he and **Benny "The Jet" Urquidez** were the first "television" fighters during professional kickboxing's embryonic era.

Wallace was dubbed "Superfoot" because he kicked only with his left foot and, at the height of his career, his kicks were measured at a spectacular impact velocity of 60 mph. He costarred in a number of other martial arts films beginning with Chuck Norris's *A Force of One* (1979).

Actor/producer Keith Vitali. Courtesy of Keith Vitali

Wang, Chon. JC's character in *Shanghai Noon*.

Wa, Wu-Bin. JC's character name in *Killer Meteor*.

Weapon, Favorite. The spear.

Weapon X. See *Wheels on Meals*.

Website, Official. www.jackie-chan.com.

Wei, Dick. A veteran Chinese actor who's appeared in more than fifty Hong Kong films, he appeared in seven JC pictures. They are *Winners and Sinners* (1983),

Project A (1983), *Twinkle, Twinkle, Lucky Stars* (1985), *Heart of Dragon* (1985), *Dragons Forever* (1987), *Miracles: Mr. Canton and Lady Rose* (1989), and *Project S* (1993).

Weintraub, Fred. The American producer who produced JC's first American production, *The Big Brawl*, in 1980. This low-budget B film was JC's first stab at Hollywood filmmaking and his first failure to generate the mass interest of the American audience.

Based on the wild success of Bruce Lee's 1973 classic *Enter the Dragon*, which Weintraub produced, he went on to also produce a host of B-grade martial arts films starring some of the world's most skilled martial artists. In addition to JC, they include Jim Kelly (*Black Belt Jones* and *Golden Needles*, 1974), Joe Lewis (*Force: Five*, 1980), and Cynthia Rothrock and Keith Hirabayashi Cook (*China O'Brien* and its sequel, 1988 and 1989).

None of them became stars as Lee did. This sheds strong suspicion on Weintraub's longtime claim that he made Bruce Lee a star.

All of these films were directed by American Robert Clouse, Weintraub's longtime collaborator, who cranked out consistently mediocre movie fare. Clouse brought films in on budget, but in doing so constantly sacrificed the quality of the fight scenes. Under Clouse's helm, any suggested fancy or flamboyant stage combat was quickly forsaken for basic ho-hum kicks and punches. His restrictions on fight-scene choreography were unmistakably self-defeating. Audiences watch martial arts films chiefly for the fight action, not for the acting.

Whang, Inn-Shik. See **Inn-Sik Whang**.

Whang, Inn-Sik. The Korean hapkido master who played the main villain in JC's *The Young Master* (1980) and also appeared with him in *Dragon Lord* (1982).

Whang (a.k.a. Inn-Shik Whang), whose body of work includes about a dozen pictures, also appeared in the classic *Hapkido* (1972), which marked **Sammo Hung**'s first lead role, and played the Japanese fighter in **Bruce Lee**'s *Way of the Dragon* (1972).

Wheels on Meals

Alternate Titles: *Meals on Wheels, Million Dollar Heiress, Spartan X, Weapon X*

Genre: Martial Arts Action-Comedy

Hong Kong Release Date: August 17, 1984

Cast: JC, Sammo Hung, Biao Yuen, Lola Forner, Benny "The Jet" Urquidez, Keith Vitali, Herb Edelman

Director: Sammo Hung

Location: Spain

Box-Office Gross: 21.4 million (Hong Kong)

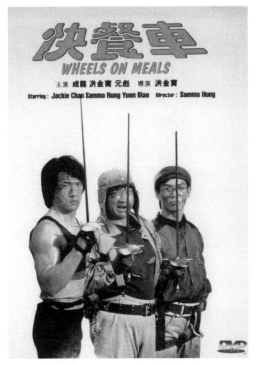

Wheels on Meals (DVD). Universe Laser and Video Co.: 99 minutes/unrated. In Cantonese and Mandarin with English subtitles.

Courtesy of Scott Rhodes

Wheels on Meals follows the fortunes of two Chinese youths living in Barcelona, Spain, Thomas (JC) and David (Biao), who make a living selling fast food from their high-tech Mitsubishi van. Hung, who also directed, plays a dimwitted apprentice private detective, and the three principals become separately involved with the lovely Sylvia (Forner, a former Miss Spain) who, unknown to all, is really an heiress whose uncle, a count, plots to keep her from her rightful inheritance. When henchmen disguised as monks kidnap the heiress, the heroic trio storms a medieval fortress where she's being held and save her.

Wheels on Meals is a masterpiece of action-comedy. In fact, it's the textbook example of how to add humor to combat as demonstrated by the masters of the genre. The film marks the second time the so-called **"Three Brothers"**—JC, **Sammo Hung**, and **Biao Yuen**—teamed up in one

Benny "The Jet" Urquidez (right) versus JC in *Wheels on Meals* Courtesy of Benny and Sara Urquidez

Wheels on Meals cast members (left to right): Keith Vitali, Biao Yuen, JC, and Benny "The Jet" Urquidez Courtesy of Keith Vitali

picture. In fact, the team works so well together in this one that you'll want to watch it again and again.

JC's superb climactic fight against American kickboxing champion **Benny "The Jet" Urquidez**, whose ring savvy has made him a folk hero in both the United States and Japan, is considered by many the greatest ever captured on celluloid. JC himself rates it as the all-time best screen fight of his entire career. Urquidez's kickboxing combinations and techniques work very well against JC's kung-fu style. Despite its serious nature, the battle also contains elements of comedy relief. One kick where Urquidez blows out some candles behind a ducking Jackie with the breeze from the sheer force of the kick is terrific. Toward the end you can visibly see just how tired both men are getting and the exchanges just get better as each puts forth even more effort.

Rumors still abound today regarding the reported rivalry between JC and Urquidez on the set of *Wheels on Meals*. Some sources say there was a clash of egos and the two ended up brutalizing each other during the filming of their tooth-and-nails fight scene. Costar **Keith Vitali**, who was an eyewitness to it, explains it this way.

"I consider Jackie's sheer athletic ability the best worldwide. One phenomenal kick he pulled off in the film was in his fight scene with Benny. It's almost a cartwheel type of kick that was thrown with his back leg upside down. Overall, if Jackie had chosen the path of fighting in the ring instead of in movies, he would have been one of the best.

"On the other hand, he chose to do movies, and Jackie as a martial arts ring *fighter* is another thing altogether. Jackie never had the fight training in his career to ever consider jumping in the ring with someone as great as Benny Urquidez, for example. It has been written about before that Benny and Jackie exchanged some tense words during one scene, and Jackie jokingly talked about putting on boxing gloves and going a few rounds with Benny.

"I was in the middle of that encounter, and I remember telling Jackie that the ring was a different world than the movies, and that he wanted nothing to do with fighting Benny for real. In one fight scene, for example, I remember Jackie was continuously hitting Benny with full force to his head. Each time Benny would smile and would reply to Sammo's concerns about the contact by saying, 'No problem.' All of the Chinese stuntmen couldn't believe how Benny could take those blows over and over and not be hurt."

The humor in *Wheels on Meals* also works very well, and is made extra enjoyable by the playful interaction between the three opera school "brothers."

The nonsensical title, *Wheels on Meals*, was originally correctly entitled *Meals on Wheels*, like the mobile vehicle that delivers food. But Golden Harvest, the production company, changed the name when it decided that "M" was an unlucky letter with which to begin a film title. Nonetheless, it sort of captures the movie's wacky nature.

When Dragons Collide; When Dragons Meet.
See *Twin Dragons*.

Who Am I?
Alternate Titles: *Jackie Chan's Who Am I?* (U.S.)
Genre: Action
Hong Kong Release Date: January 17, 1998
Cast: JC, Michelle Ferre, Mira Yamamoto, Ron Smerczak, Ed Nelson, Tom Pompert, Glory Simon, Johan van Ditmarsch, Fritz Krommenhoek, Dick Rienstra
Director: Benny Chan, JC
Other JC Credits: Coscreenwriter, stunt coordinator

Locations: South Africa, Rotterdam, Holland
Box-Office Gross: $38.8 million (Hong Kong)

Three scientists studying strange meteorites are abducted by a crew of commandos in a top-secret military operation, but the commando squad is sabotaged by someone higher up and only JC survives, but he can't even remember who he is after a tumble from an airplane. He is adopted by an African tribe, and becomes one of them, but flashbacks to his past haunt him and he is determined to discover his identity. Along the way, he gets caught up in a web of international intrigue with his life threatened at every step.

Although the first hour of *Who Am I?* is relatively slow for a JC picture, the last hour certainly makes up for it. His spectacular slide down the sloped exterior of a twenty-one-story office building in Rotterdam, Holland, could very well be the most dangerous in motion picture history and the capper to his own daredevil career.

The relentless creativity with which JC uses his environment to his benefit is also of particular note, and he employs some extraordinary escapist antics in one sequence while handcuffed.

Who Am I? outgrossed even the megahit *Titanic* (1997) in some Asian territories.

Who Am I? Courtesy of the Kobal Collection

For JC's fans, it's quite a treat, but moreover, it's the perfect choice to introduce newcomers to his work.

Wife, JC's. See **Feng-Chiao Lin.**

Wilson, Owen. See *Shanghai Noon.*

Winners and Sinners
Alternate Titles: *Five Lucky Stars*, *5 Lucky Stars*, *Tokyo Powerman* (Europe)
Genre: Action-Comedy
Year of Release: 1983
Cast: Sammo Hung, Richard Ng, Charlie Chin, John Sham, JC, Biao Yuen

Director: Sammo Hung
Location: Hong Kong
Box-Office Gross: $21.9 million (Hong Kong)

A group of former prisoners set up a cleaning company to try to earn an honest living. It isn't their fault that one of the buildings they are hired to clean is the headquarters of a ruthless gang of counterfeiters. It isn't their fault that the set of fake printing plates turns up in their van. And it isn't their fault that they get mixed up in a war over the plates between two rival gangs and just about every law enforcement organization in Hong Kong.

JC's character, named Muscles in the U.S. version, is a cop who, in one scene in a café, is out to catch a group of robbers led by a midget! In a daring roller-skating sequence, JC chases fleeing robbers down a busy highway, skating under a fast-moving truck and, while apprehending the criminals, ultimately causing a fifty-car collision.

Outside of JC's scenes, *Winners and Sinners* is more noted for its comedy than for its action, thanks to a wonderful supporting cast of comedians.

Due to its vast array of alternate titles, the Lucky Stars trilogy is the second most confusing in all of JC's body of work (**Police Story**, 1985–96, is by far the *most*

confusing). To avoid confusion, *Winners and Sinners* is the first entry in the Lucky Stars trilogy. The sequels, in order of release, are **My Lucky Stars** (1985) and **Twinkle, Twinkle, Lucky Stars** (1985).

In this trilogy, JC is part of an ensemble cast and has only a supporting role. *Winners and Sinners* also marks the second time JC and his Peking Opera school "brothers" **Sammo Hung** and **Biao Yuen** worked together in one picture in leading roles. (The first was 1983's **Project A**.)

Wire-Fu. See *Wirework*.

Wirework. The science of attaching wires and/or cables to actors and stuntpeople and jerking or pulling them in order to enhance their movements or reactions during action sequences. When performed expertly, this technique gives the impression of fantastic, gravity-defying, exaggerated maneuvers—men and women literally flying, twisting, and somersaulting in midair while engaged in combat. When performed badly, it has been called "wire-fu," a cynical spin-off on the word *kung-fu*.

Although wirework has recently impacted both Eastern and Western action

Hong Kong–style wirework was reinvented in 1999's *The Matrix*: Neo (Keanu Reeves, left) versus Agent Smith in their midair subway battle.

films, JC and his famed stunt team have seldom employed the device. He still prefers to perform his own stunts without wires—or even safety nets or ropes of any kind. One movie in which JC does employ wirework is ***Drunken Master II*** (1994).

Wirework was a cinematic staple of the Hong Kong kung-fu movies produced by the **Shaw Brothers Studios** in the 1960s and 1970s, as well as in Japan's samurai films that featured villainous ninjas leaping from and over trees during swordplay. In this era, wirework defied the credulity of Western audiences and became the brunt of jokes about its cheesy action applications. This type of fantasy action was especially transparent to viewers when it was compared with Bruce Lee's intensely realistic fight portrayals.

Wirework returned to prominence for martial arts sequences and, in fact, rose to unprecedented popularity because of its use by, quite surprisingly, Western filmmakers in the Hollywood blockbuster *The Matrix* (1999). This film's cutting-edge special effects and wireworked Hong Kong

Charlie's Angels stars Cameron Diaz (center), Drew Barrymore (left), and Lucy Liu in their wire-assisted fighting poses

fight scenes blended to create amazing new heights of stylized on-screen action.

Using filmmaking technology that brings to life Japanese anime comics, *The Matrix* introduced numerous novel fight scenes including a mind-blowing climactic encounter, all masterfully choreographed by Hong Kong legend **Woo-Ping Yuen**. The main cast members, Keanu Reeves, Laurence Fishburne, and Carrie-Anne Moss, trained hard for months with Yuen and his assistants not only to learn martial arts fundamentals, but the nuances of complex wirework as well—and it showed in the film's spectacular results.

The huge success of *The Matrix* also launched a whole new martial arts subgenre called "kung-fu chic," where the women look like heaven and fight like hell. Yuen's work was once again evident in the

Michelle Yeoh in action from *Crouching Tiger, Hidden Dragon*

critically acclaimed, Oscar-winning action-romance *Crouching Tiger, Hidden Dragon* (2000) and will also be seen in the upcoming *The Matrix II* (2002).

The subgenre really took flight with the stylized fight action and wirework of pictures such as *Charlie's Angels* (2000), expertly choreographed by Woo-Ping's brother, Cheung-Yan Yuen, and *Lara Croft: Tomb Raider* (2001).

See also: **Hong Kong Martial Arts Films**.

Wong, Billy. JC's character name in *The Protector*.

Wong, Curtis. Chinese-American publisher and a close friend of JC's. Wong is one of the world's foremost publishers of martial arts magazines, starting with *Inside Kung-Fu* (1973), his flagship publication, followed by a score of others through the years including *Martial Arts Movies*

(1980). He was the first U.S. publisher to publish stories about JC and his films.

In 1998, Wong cowrote the book *Jackie Chan* (Contemporary Books).

Wong, Fei-Hung. The legendary martial artist portrayed by JC in his ***Drunken Master*** films (1978 and 1994). By far the most famous screen character in Hong Kong cinema, Fei-Hung Wong is China's most adored folk hero. Born in 1847 in Lingnan, Canton, China, he mastered the hung kuen martial art system and subsequently devised the style's most powerful fighting forms.

Wong became famous not only for his superior kung-fu skills, but for his commitment to social issues and helping the downtrodden. Legend has it that he once single-handedly defeated thirty axe-wielding opponents using a wooden staff.

Not much else is actually known about the legendary martial artist, but more than one hundred full-length feature films—most of them highly fictionalized—have been done about him. Tak-Hing Kwan (1905–1996), Hong Kong's first true martial arts action star, played the true-life Chinese folk hero in nearly one hundred of these pictures. After JC, Jet Li portrayed

Jet Li portrayed Fei-Hung Wong in four of the groundbreaking *Once Upon a Time in China* films, starting in 1991. Shown here is a current DVD version of *Once Upon a Time in China*. Mega Star Video: 128 minutes/unrated. In Cantonese and Mandarin with English subtitles. Courtesy of Scott Rhodes

Wong in four of the groundbreaking *Once Upon a Time* in China films, starting in 1991.

Woo, John. Director of JC's ***Hand of Death*** (1976), he is today recognized as one of the

Li also played the same character, Fei-Hung Wong, in *The Legend*.

Director John Woo

Courtesy of Twentieth Century Fox

world's foremost action directors who has turned cinematic action into an art form.

Born in southern China, he grew up in Hong Kong, where he began his film career as an assistant director in 1969, working for **Shaw Brothers Studios**. He made his directorial debut in 1973 and worked prolifically in that capacity in a series of Shaw Brothers' kung-fu films. These include *Belles of Taekwondo* (1974), *The Young Dragons* (1975), and *Shaolin Men* (1975).

Woo then worked in a wide variety of genres before *A Better Tomorrow* (1986) established his reputation as a master stylist specializing in ultraviolent gangster films and thrillers, with hugely elaborate action scenes shot with breathtaking panache. His slow-motion gun battle sequences and *noir* camera angles and lighting gave his films an atmosphere akin to a ballet of death. As such, he rose to the top of Hong Kong's New Wave filmmakers.

After gaining a cult reputation in the United States with *The Killer* (1989), Woo was offered a Hollywood contract to work on *Hard Target* (1993), starring Jean-Claude Van Damme. Since then, he has rocketed to A-list status as the director of such mega-budget, action-oriented blockbusters as *Broken Arrow* (1996), *Face/Off* (1997), and *Mission: Impossible II* (2000).

Woo's unique vision of stylized action has been imitated by other Hollywood directors like Quentin Tarantino in *Pulp Fiction* (1994) and Robert Rodriguez in *Desperado* (1995).

World of Jackie Chan, The
Genre: Documentary
Year of Release: 1989

British comedian Jonathan Ross hosts this incisive one-hour study of Hong Kong's biggest box-office star and king of kung-fu comedy. Made in Hong Kong, the documentary is in the English language. In it, JC discusses every aspect of his spectacular career, from his rugged training as a youth in the Peking Opera school, to his methods of setting up stunts, to his near-fatal accident performing a stunt on *Armour of God* (1987). He also candidly addresses his minor successes and major failures in American films up to that time.

The interviews are interwoven with plenty of film clips from JC's pictures, including outtakes of behind-the-scenes accidents and injuries he sustained during filming. *The World of Jackie Chan* is one of the most informative and entertaining studies of the action master on the market.

World Stunt Awards. See Appendix 4: Jackie Chan's Awards, Honors, and Offices Held.

Yang, Eddie. JC's character name in ***Highbinders***.

Yang, Jeff. The coauthor of JC's autobiography, ***I Am Jackie Chan: My Life in Action***. Yang is the publisher and founder of *A. Magazine: Inside Asian America*, which he launched upon graduating from Harvard University in 1989. Since then, *A. Magazine* has grown into the nation's largest publication for English-speaking Asian Americans.

Yang is also the author of *Eastern Standard Time: A Guide to Asian Influence in American Culture, from Astro Boy to Zen Buddhism* (Houghton Mifflin, 1997). A New York City resident, he has also been a columnist for *The Village Voice* and a featured contributor for Vibe.

Yeoh, Michelle. The actress who starred opposite JC in two of his films, *Police Story*

III: Supercop (1992), one of his best pictures ever, and *Project S* (1993). Her career parallels the ascendance of modern Hong Kong films.

Malaysian-born and London-trained as a ballerina, Yeoh (a.k.a. Michelle Khan) was cast in a lead role in *Yes! Madam* (1984), a film that paired her with **Cynthia Rothrock**, an American martial arts champion nicknamed "The Blonde Fury." The movie was a hit, and Yeoh went on to make *Royal Warriors* (1986) and then *Magnificent Warriors* (1987) before retiring.

Yeoh's triumphant comeback came in 1992 in JC's *Police Story III: Supercop.* Yeoh's Hong Kong career was resparked, and her early 1990s' roles in movies like *The Heroic Trio* (1993)—with **Maggie Cheung** and **Anita Mui**, both of whom have also worked in numerous JC films— became popular with Western audiences.

After the semiautobiographical *Ah Kam* (1996), that featured a stunt that hospitalized Yeoh, she relocated to Hollywood and emerged as the "Bond Girl" in *Tomorrow Never Dies* (1997). But rather than a googly eyed helpless type, Yeoh's character in *TND* is a competent warrior woman, actively helping Bond (Pierce Brosnan) subdue the forces of evil. Reviewers raved

Michelle Yeoh (right) with Pierce Brosnan in the James Bond adventure *Tomorrow Never Dies*   Courtesy of the Kobal Collection

and movie fans in her native Malaysia so loved *TND* that the Malaysian grosses actually exceeded those of James Cameron's blockbuster *Titanic*.

Yeoh perhaps eclipsed all her former work in the stunning action-romance *Crouching Tiger, Hidden Dragon* (2000), which won four Academy Awards, including Best Foreign Film, and was the first Asian picture to earn over $100 million.

In it, her combination of a ballerina's grace, an athlete's power, and intense charisma has never been more evident. [Stefan Hammond]

Ying, Angela Mao. The star of *Hapkido* (1972), in which JC had a cameo role early in his career. A veteran star of some thirty-five films, she was a pioneering actress in Hong Kong cinema and a genuine black belt in the Korean martial art of hapkido.

Born in 1950, Angela Mao Ying (a.k.a. Angela Mao) was enrolled in Taiwan's Fu Shing Academy at the tender age of five, where the harsh training rivaled that of JC in the Peking Opera school. She gained international attention for her role as **Bruce Lee**'s sister in the martial arts masterpiece *Enter the Dragon* (1973).

Ying retired in 1980.

See also: **Hong Kong Martial Arts Films**.

Yong Yao Film Company. See *Hong Kong Martial Arts Films*.

Young Dragons, The. A 1973 relatively routine kung-fu film noted only for JC serv-ing as stunt coordinator. It's a story about Chinese **Triads** selling guns and ammunition to Japanese troops during the Sino-Japanese War.

Golden Harvest Studios later bought this independently produced film and reedited it for rerelease.

Young Master in Love. See *Dragon Lord*.

Young Master, The
Genre: Comedy Kung-Fu
Year of Release: 1980
Cast: JC, Shih Tien (a.k.a. Shek Kin), Biao Yuen, Kam Chiang, Lily Lee, Inn-Sik Whang
Director: JC
Other JC Credits: Stunt coordinator
Location: Hong Kong
Injuries: JC sustained a broken nose and also was almost suffocated when he injured his throat.

JC plays a young martial arts student called Dragon. Orphaned from an early age, he and his Big Brother are raised by Master Tien (Tien). After Dragon's brother supposedly hurts his leg too severely to compete in the Lion Dance competition celebrating the prosperity of the city, Dragon has to take his place. During the competition, Dragon discovers that Big Brother has secretly allied with the rival school and is facing off directly against him. The brother wins the competition underhandedly.

When Master Tien learns of the brother's deception and traitorous actions, he sends him away from the school. The school is disgraced by the loss in the competition, and the students blame JC and Big Brother for their situation. Dragon tells Master Tien that he is grateful for all that he has done for him and his brother, but he must depart, and is told that if he leaves, he must come back with his brother.

After a brief visit to the rival school, Dragon learns that Big Brother is not there anymore. Shortly after leaving the school, Big Brother assists several fighters in ambushing an armed group of marshals transporting Master Kim to court. A short but spectacular battle takes place between the unarmed bandits and the sword-wielding marshals. Although outnumbered, Big Brother and his comrades make quick work of their opposition and free Master Kim. A reward is then set for the capture of Big Brother, and Dragon must come to his brother's aid.

The Young Master (VHS). Tai Seng Video Marketing: 105 minutes/unrated. In Chinese with English subtitles.
Courtesy of Scott Rhodes

When Dragon continues his search, marshals mistake him for Big Brother. In another fantastic fight, Dragon holds off five marshals, all armed with swords, before the lead marshal flees to the constable's house. The constable is at the station, but his son (Yuen) sets out to help the cross-eyed marshal find Big Brother and ends up finding Dragon.

Yuen carries a small wooden bench that he uses in two brief fight sequences with Dragon. After these first encounters the constable takes Dragon captive, mistaking him for Big Brother. After repeated unsuccessful attempts at escape, Dragon finally leaves when the constable realizes he has the wrong man. The constable learns that Big Brother and his new partners are trying to rob the bank. During the robbery, his cohorts trap Big Brother so that they can avoid paying him his share of the stolen loot. Dragon, now disguised as an old man, fights the robbers and frees Big Brother.

After some bargaining and threats back and forth, the constable agrees to drop the charges against Big Brother if Dragon tracks down Master Kim and returns him to custody. In the finale, Dragon is finally able to overcome Master Kim and clear the charges against his brother.

This was JC's first film for **Golden Harvest Studios**. With complete creative control as star, director, and stunt coordinator, he incorporates all of his raucous trademark ingredients in *The Young Master*: good-natured humor, rapid fight scenes, and the inventive uses of props.

JC's main-title sequence, a Lion Dance fight over, under, and around obstacles, is jaw-dropping. So are his brilliant uses of props in a fan-fight (for which one of the actions reportedly required 329 takes), a sawhorse fight, and the frenetic "skirt-foot" fight with a female opponent. Then, posing as a female impersonator while sporting a rugged-looking beard, he engages in some hilarious skirt-foot fighting himself. JC's masterful use of unconventional props in these various fight scenarios is riveting.

The picture wraps with perhaps the longest climactic fight ever staged, and thus becomes tedious for Western viewers. The best fight scenes in *The Young Master* are the brief ones spread throughout the movie. The martial artists make excellent use of weapons and other, more obscure props. It is fantastic to see JC hold off five marshals by stealing their swords and making good use of his surroundings.

The Young Master broke all previous box-office records in Hong Kong at the time of its release. Fans maintain that this is JC's last thoroughbred classical kung-fu film. After this, he created a more realistic style of fighting for use in his films.

Young Tiger, The
Year of Release: 1980
Genre: Martial Arts and partial Documentary

A ninety-minute forgettable Chinese movie followed by a twelve-minute documentary on the inimitable JC. A novelty.

Young Tiger. See **Police Woman.**

Young Tiger of Canton. See **Little Tiger from Canton.**

Young Tiger's Revenge. See **Shaolin Wooden Men.**

Yu, Jimmy Wang. The former star with whom JC made three inferior films: **Killer Meteor** (1977), **Fantasy Mission Force** (1982), and **Island of Fire** (1991). JC's brief appearances in the latter two pictures were done only as a favor to Yu, who had helped him get out of a difficult contract situation with director **Wei Lo.**

The veteran Yu, a one-time swimming champion, is one of the few Hong Kong actors who worked for both **Shaw Brothers Studios** and **Golden Harvest Studios**. His acting career hit its peak with his striking swashbuckler role in the *One-Armed Swordsman* series, launched in 1967. Overall, he's acted in some fifty motion pictures and directed about a dozen.

Wu has reputed ties to the **Triads**, Hong Kong's version of the Mafia, and he was reportedly charged with murder in 1981 in Taiwan. His career probably suffered because of it. He was never fully embraced by audiences and his career eventually fizzled. Residing in Taiwan, he still occasionally dabbles in filmmaking.

Yu, Jim-Yuen. The sole proprietor and strict master of the **China Drama Academy**, with whom JC held a love/hate relationship over a ten-year period during his youth. Yu's authoritarian discipline and harsh training was responsible for developing JC's phenomenal physical skills.

Yuan, He-Ping. See **Woo-Ping Yuen.**

Yuen, Biao. The Hong Kong actor and childhood friend of JC who gained fame as a featured player in the films of JC and Sammo Hung. Known as the "**Three Brothers**," the trio worked together on some of the most entertaining martial arts films ever made: *Dragon Lord* (1982), *Wheels on Meals* (1984), *Project A* (1983), *Winners and Sinners* (1983), *My Lucky Stars* (1985), and *Twinkle, Twinkle, Lucky Stars* (1985).

Born Ling-Jun Hsia in 1957, Yuen attended the **China Drama Academy** as a child, where he met JC and Hung and was a member of the Seven Little Fortunes Peking Opera troupe. After leaving the academy, he got a number of small roles through Hung. His first major break was in JC's *Young Master* (1980), and his real talent was finally showcased in the Hung-directed kung-fu farce *Knockabout* (1980). Since then, aside from his "Three Brothers" work, he's appeared in about a dozen Hong Kong films.

Yuen, Cheung-Yan. See **Wirework**; **Woo-Ping Yuen**.

Yuen, Hsiao-Tien. See **Simon Yuen**.

Yuen, Lung. See **Sammo Hung**.

Yuen, Simon. The Hong Kong actor who played JC's inebriated and demanding kung-fu master/mentor in three hit films: *Shaolin Wooden Men* (1976), *Snake in the Eagle's Shadow* (1978), and *Drunken Master* (1978). The roles rejuvenated his career and he reprised his character in a whole string of subsequent drunken-style pictures.

A veteran actor from the **Shaw Brothers Studios**, Yuen (a.k.a. Simon Yuen Siu-Tin and Hsiao Tien Yuen) is the father of prominent director/fight choreographers **Woo-Ping Yuen** and Cheung-Yan Yuen (*Charlie's Angels*, 2000).

Yuen, Siu-Tin. See **Simon Yuen**.

Yuen, Wah. One of JC's classmates at the **China Drama Academy** who also launched a career in motion pictures.

Upon graduating from the academy, Yuen found work as **Bruce Lee**'s stunt double, performing all the acrobatics required in Lee's roles. Although he ultimately built his career playing villains in countless kung-fu and action films, Yuen also played a member of JC's SWAT team in *Heart of Dragon* (1985) and has had more recent straight comedy roles.

Yuen, Woo-Ping. The director of two influential 1978 JC movies, *Snake in the Eagle's Shadow* and *Drunken Master*.

The eldest son of illustrious actor **Simon Yuen** (a.k.a. Siu-Tin Yuen), Woo-Ping Yuen (a.k.a. He-Ping Yuan) was born in Guangzhan in 1945, one of twelve children. He began his career with bit-part roles and stunt work in numerous martial arts movies.

In 1977, Seasonal Film's owner and producer **See-Yuen Ng** approached Yuen to choreograph the surprise hit *Secret Rivals II*. In 1978, Yuen made his directorial debut for Ng in the hugely successful *Snake in the Eagle's Shadow*, followed by *Drunken Master*, both starring JC. It was, in fact, Yuen who brought JC to Ng's attention, and Ng who gave JC his big break—a starring role with freedom to do a film his own way.

By 1979, Yuen had formed his own production and choreography company. The timing proved fortuitous, as kung-fu was fast securing a following outside of China. Through the years, Yuen has worked with or directed many of China's top film talent including **Sammo Hung** and **Jet Li**. One of Yuen's most highly regarded films is the modern classic *Iron Monkey* (1993), starring the popular Donnie Yen.

Yuen's work caught the attention of the Wachowski brothers, Larry and Andy, two Hollywood directors who hired him to choreograph the fantastic fights in their science-fiction blockbuster *The Matrix* (1999) and also train the principal actors, Keanu Reeves, Laurence Fishburne, and Carrie-Anne Moss, in martial arts techniques.

The success of these intricate fight scenes launched the ongoing Hollywood trend called "kung-fu chic."

American action film tycoon Joel Silver, who produced *The Matrix*, so admired Yuen's fanciful martial arts choreography that he put him to work in the same capacity on his sequel, *The Matrix II* (2002). Yuen followed up with the striking choreography for director Ang Lee's critical and commercial hit *Crouching Tiger, Hidden Dragon* (2000).

Woo-Ping's brother, Cheung-Yan Yuen, choreographed the fights for the block-buster *Charlie's Angels* (2000) and provided martial arts training for its three stars, Drew Barrymore, Cameron Diaz, and Lucy Liu.

See also: **Hong Kong Martial Arts Films; Wirework**.

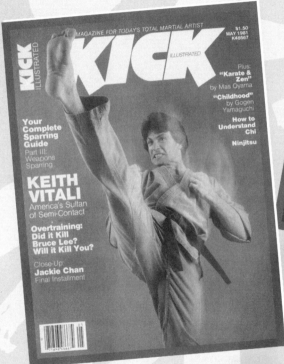

The March–May 1981 issues of *Kick Illustrated*, in which JC's
"Lost Interview" originally appeared

Courtesy of Neva Friedenn

Appendix 1

JACKIE CHAN'S LOST INTERVIEW
(His First in the English Language)

Author's Introduction

I became an instant fan of Jackie Chan's in 1979, early in his career, after seeing *Drunken Master* at the Pagoda, a Los Angeles Chinatown theater. His humorous antics and physical genius were equally extraordinary and captivating. They represented a stunning new approach to martial arts films, "Comedy Kung-Fu."

Until Chan's arrival the heroes of the genre were almost invariably portrayed with intense seriousness by Herculean figures who never made a mistake and never lost a fight. Chan broke all the established genre rules by playing the comic underdog who more often than not got beat up by villains on the way to winning his fights by accident. In doing so, he became the reigning superstar of Asian cinema with a rapidly growing cult following throughout the Western world. This was years before he began personally performing the death-defying stunts that have now become his cinematic trademark.

As the founding editor of two new national martial arts magazines in early 1980, *Martial Arts Movies* and *Kick Illustrated*, I began assigning freelance journalist and filmmaker Neva Friedenn to write about Chan and his films. Friedenn was the ideal choice for these assignments. Her writing credits extended from genre publications to major magazines like *Playboy*.

And her company, Condor Films, was at that time distributing about a hundred Far East–produced kung-fu pictures to U.S. theaters throughout the thirteen Western states. She was intimately familiar with Chan's body of film work and, as you'll see, she was able to accurately articulate key scenes that greatly enhanced her question-and-answer session with Chan.

Friedenn's three-part interview with Chan, reprinted here with her permission, first appeared in the March through May 1981 issues of *Kick Illustrated*, and it was a landmark. Conducted over approximately four hours at the Westwood Marquis Hotel in Los Angeles, it was Chan's first in-depth interview ever in his then new language of American English.

In it Chan's enthusiasm for his work, his personal charm and charisma, and his high-energy humor have perhaps never been more forcefully abundant. When Jackie struggles for the right words or when he can't finish a statement in English, he simply leaps up and physically enacts his meaning complete with sound effects. The interview unexpectedly took on the semblance of a game of charades, all of which Friedenn interprets exquisitely in bracketed descriptions. Chan's physical vocabulary and Friedenn's interpretations of it are often hilarious.

These days, Friedenn is an established film producer, and she says that conducting this interview was like having a lengthy private audition from the comic genius. For Jackie, it clearly demonstrates that he's the King of Cool.

This three-part series could genuinely be considered Jackie Chan's "Lost Interview," since the magazine in which it originally appeared has long been defunct, and the interview has never been resurrected in print until now—over twenty years later.

UP CLOSE & PERSONAL WITH . . .

Jackie Chan
An Outrageous Interview with the New Martial Arts Marvel
Part 1

© 1981 by Neva Friedenn

They said it couldn't be done. Bruce Lee's fans obstinately and faithfully maintained that absolutely no one could ever surpass the late great kung-fu king in any way, shape, or form. This consciousness pervaded martial arts circles; for some six years it was held as a virtually unanimous opinion. After all, Bruce left a phenomenal legacy of achievement that established unprecedented standards of excellence almost impossible for any subsequent artist to match, a legacy that will certainly live on for generations.

Then, enter Hong Kong movie sensation Jackie Chan. At first glance, Chan seems an unlikely candidate for superstardom. He does not immediately project the potent unleashed fury so common to all of Lee's film performances. He is not, like Bruce, strikingly even-featured. Unlike Bruce, he shows vulnerability; on-screen, he frequently lets himself get hit. And *Kick* learned that

off-camera, he also let himself get stabbed—and frozen!

Yet Jackie Chan is, like Bruce Lee, a phenomenon. He is the undisputed new king of kung-fu cinema. He is an accomplished actor, an extraordinary natural comic, a superb kung-fu artist, a director, a producer, and a magician of motion whose astonishing physical repertoire represents an encyclopedia of martial arts movement never before seen on film. On top of all of that, he is warm, charming, and approachable. As [then] prominent Los Angeles newscaster Connie Chung described him, he's "the type of guy you would want to take home to meet your mother."

Indeed, Jackie Chan is not Bruce Lee's successor—he's the first Jackie Chan.

Chan rose to prominence when three of his films broke all existing box-office records, including those set by Bruce Lee, in the Orient. He was

continued

龍

promptly discovered by Hollywood and cast in his first starring role in an American-made film, *The Big Brawl*, which boasted the collaboration of the same team that made *Enter the Dragon*, producers Raymond Chow and Fred Weintraub and director Robert Clouse. In large metropolitan areas, *The Big Brawl* opened to turn-away first night crowds, and it has still to play various cities throughout the country.

Any sketch of his background indicates that Jackie Chan distinguished himself by making possible a new type of martial arts movie: the "Comedy Kung-Fu." On the way to this development, he starred in a number of Chinese films of two other genres, straight kung-fu pictures and ancient Chinese costume martial arts epics.

Here, in Part 1 of this three-part interview, Chan explains—and at times enacts—the play-by-play on his progress from glorified stuntman in 1976 to bona fide film star in 1978. As he demonstrates muscle-rending forms and bone-wracking kicks and punches, as he recounts the physical rigors of location shooting, and the emotional drain of archaic costume drama filming with its resultant box-office disillusionments, he often reveals not only the philosophical detachment of a man three times his age but also his own unique brand of zany humor.

Jackie's birthday animal is the Horse. In person, he is a presence of incredible and steady vitality, up and moving "mustang-style." When he demonstrates actions, he vocalizes his kicks, punches, and armed movements in a very low but very rapid voice, keeping the emphasis on a slightly pulled-back representation of the compelling physical stamina one can see in the movies he describes.

Chan's Chinese-language movies have not been seen by mainstream audiences in the U.S. In talking to *Kick*, Jackie has his work cut out for him as, in relation to these unfamiliar films, he sheds light on such specialized filmmaking fields as martial arts choreography (action design) and martial arts directing (realization of action for camera). He discusses—sometimes outrageously and always with sound effects—working with everything from the latest in cameras to the bulkiest in stunt equipment and most antique in story lines. Whether on personality conflicts or career disappointments, Jackie Chan delivers candidly, according to his experience, the fortunes and misfortunes of a "fighting actor."

And now for his next trick, Chan performs all of the above—without a net—meaning that he speaks for himself, no longer needing a translator. What follows is Part 1 of the first extensive interview with Chan in his new language, American English. Now presenting, the *real* Jackie Chan.

Kick Illustrated: In 1976, you starred in *New Fist of Fury*, the sequel to *Fist of Fury* that starred Bruce Lee. If there are similarities between your martial arts style and Bruce Lee's in those two pictures, can the similarities be accounted for by any factor other than imitation?

Jackie Chan: The martial arts director on *New Fist of Fury* was the same as for *Fist of Fury*. He was my "brother"—big, big brother.

Kick: From what you've said, this means he comes from the same school of kung-fu training but is very much your senior.

Chan: Yes, he's much older. So I have some ideas, but see, he's my "big brother"; it's his [place to make a final] decision. So when he wants me to do a piece of action like Bruce, I just can't do it. Yet I'm not the martial arts director, I'm only the actor, you understand. [So] I try what he wants [to do]. And he wants things Bruce Lee is not known for doing, but some of these things are things even Bruce did for my "brother."

In *New Fist of Fury*, I do a lot of things because my "big brother" wants them.

Kick: Give us some background on *Shaolin Wooden Men*, the other picture you starred in that year.

Chan: It was the second picture for Wei Lo. The director was Chan Chi Hua, a friend of mine. Because in Hong Kong a martial arts director might have as many as three movie companies he has signed contracts to work for during the same period of time, he might go up to the location and need the action to move along fast, bam-bam-bam! If one of his pictures has a lot of fighting scenes, like *Shaolin Wooden Men*, he has to let the fighting actor do some of the martial arts planning and directing. I was able to do this in Shaolin Wooden Men; so it's my first "dream" movie.

Kick: In this picture you fight not only the "heavy," who's a Shaolin monk, but you also pit yourself against activated warrior dummies in the Shaolin monastery. Can you tell us about these Shaolin wooden men?

Chan: Yes, they really have this! The Shaolins, in China, they really have this! A student, after ten years or maybe twenty years, wants to get out of the Shaolin temple, wants to see the world. The final trial is like in kung-fu movies—SSSST!—dragon [burned onto one inner forearm], tiger [burned onto the other].

But before this, the student fights a hundred-oh-eight [one hundred eight] wooden men. The Shaolins have a long alley lined with the wooden

continued

men going *whish, whish, whish* [striking out into the alley]! A student fights past a hundred wooden men. He gets tired enough to faint, but the wooden men just keep on: *whish, whish, whish*—really! It's a real fight! Throughout Shaolin history, all the students try to go out of the temple, but some of them die inside. The alley of the wooden men is the next to last trial. There are still wooden men, even in China today!

Kick: Incredible!

Chan: Maybe the wood is broken, but they're still there.

Kick: We hear that the main titles segment of this movie looks visually terrific. This opening has you center-screen doing a kata [form] of the five traditional animal styles, right?

Chan: Yes. This is called in Chinese, just "five" [Chinese word]. In American, you translate [it as] "five-style punch," but that doesn't mean very much. Really, it's a five-in-one: dragon—dragon is big in China—snake, tiger, crane, leopard.

Kick: Monkey is only a style of ground-fighting movement, so it's not included in this five-style series?

Chan: Monkey is a style, also. But many years ago, when one of the younger kung-fu masters made up these five styles into one set, he didn't choose the monkey style. Maybe tiger was his style; the basic one for him, and everything was tiger, tiger, tiger. Then maybe he began to make changes: tiger, crane, whatever. He finally just changed all five styles into one. That's the way a five-style-in-one combination happened. Put together, the five gained more power and popularity and new students every day.

Kick: A nice introduction, to establish the time of the story of *Shaolin Wooden Men* with your version of a set of movements so popular that they were handed down to the traditional kung-fu movie period of about eighty years ago.

But we've been curious how you, as a versatile actor and as a young man of today, could relate to the requirements of making pictures set hundreds of years in the past. The ancient Chinese costume period movies.

Chan: Oh! The worst movies of my whole life! You know, the director wanted me to be a big hero, like this [striking an antique macho pose]. He wanted me to do a love story. Oh! I *hate* that! I'm only twenty-one then. But he wants me to do a love story. And the girl is bigger, older than me . . . thirty-two, something like that. So [miming a smooching scene] how can I do it?!? The director says, "You *must* do it!" [and I do] because he is the director.

The acting goes like this [putting on a heart-sick expression and faking some dialogue]. "What are you talking about? Sniff-sniff [arch, controlled weeping sounds], sniff-sniff." You know, even when you cry, you cry like this. "Sniff! Sniff!" No "Yaaaahhh" [wailing], no [gesturing to convey letting it out]. In a story with truth, like *Fearless Hyena*—"Aaaaahh!" I also cry, but it's different, the way people really cry. "Waaaahh!"

Kick: But not here in one of these stylized ancient period pieces.

Chan: Why not here? Here, they—the makeup man and assistants—they come up, they stop, they're waiting for me. *Sheeees*!

Kick: You mean they wait at the precise blocking for the next scene, ready to check for perfect makeup?

Chan: Yeah, and if you've been doing this [rubbing eyes], then you're like a [Chinese word] because you have makeup here. I mean, if you go [sniffling, fists in eye sockets] like this, then you look like a big bear, you know, like China gives Americans!

Kick: Panda bear!

Chan: Yeah. So whenever I cry they come up [and] stop; they're waiting for me. But in my films, *Young Master* and everything after—no makeup.

Kick: Just how corny do those ancient Chinese costume dramas get?

Chan: Films where people cry like this, "Sniff-sniff?" Ugh! I said, "I can't."

But I did love stories anyway. In one, when I'm sleeping, I dream the girl comes to me . . . [twirling and humming, "La-la-lah . . ."]. Yeah, really! Oh! It hurt my feelings! But [laughing], I'm with the girl out in the country, you know, the pr-r-retty landscape [humming, "Tra-la"], it's in [singing] slow mo-o-tion, [spinning and miming, hugging and kissing all at the same time]—Aw-Gak!

Yeah, when the movie comes out, the audience goes "BOOOO!" The girl—the girl on the mountain's like this [using hand movements to show the girl rolling down the mountainside]—she stops: [lengthy kissing scene . . .]. Yoi-oh-ee-yooh! My God!

[Much laughter all around from Chan's publicist, manager, and assistants who've dropped in on the interview.]

And in one of these movies, two girls fall in love with me.

Oh! These are the *best* movies. But I don't want to say these pictures are no good.

Kick: They're fine, for the type of pictures they're intended to be?

continued

龍

JACKIE CHAN'S LOST INTERVIEW

Chan: Yes, and one director even put a lot of work into one of the screenplays. Every day he wrote and wrote because he had his ideas. He thought the script was good.

But now it's the 1970s, 1980; people don't need those stories. Audiences today like new ideas—because we're young! I know what you want; I know what you want to see! This one director, he's still like [impersonating a conservative grandee] *No comedy.* Eee-yech! You know? It's not that he's a fool; he's just out of date.

Kick: These ancient Chinese costume pictures sound as if they carefully follow a trend created by some of the successful Shaw Brothers films of a few years back. The action scenes make heavy use of trampolines, and the weapons are swords?

Chan: Tam-tam-tam [conveying swashbuckling swordplay]! Oh, too easy. Yeah, it's too easy for me, tam-tam-tam-tam, then *sheeeew* [flying through the air]! Tam-tam, tam-tam—*Sheew*! Yeah, the fighting scenes, they're all chum-chum-chum [more outlandish swordplay moves]! And you know, if one day you want to try something, change something, the director gets upset. So most of the time on those movies, I'd just go to the set: Pam-pam, tam-tam, nothing much to do.

Kick: In the theater, it must have been quite an experience to watch yourself up on the screen in one of those artificial period pieces when a sophisticated Hong Kong movie audience was sitting all around the real you.

Chan: Everybody's going, "BOOOO!" Like this [through cupped hands] "BOOOOOH!" I'm sitting in the theater, I'm crying, really. How can I do this? Oh! I'm upset. I get up and run away!

Kick: So with the ancient Chinese costume pictures, filming then was never the hardest part.

Chan: No. One of them was a very tough movie. We went on location to Korea. It was cold! Below zero—*thirty* [degrees] below! Yeah, every day, when I put the makeup on my face [patting shivering cheeks], really, I'm like this [teeth chattering].

They want to get a good take in one shot, the way they can in Taiwan—because in Taiwan, it's hot.

Then I go to Korea, and they're still saying, "Only one shot." But [shivering] oh! You don't believe how cold [it is]! When I talk dialogue, you know, smoke comes out my mouth because the air is ice—ice cold. I have to drink cold water first. If I don't, it'll look to audiences in south Asia like I'm talking and smoking a cigarette they can't see. So if I want no smoke, I have to drink cold water before saying each line in Korea.

Every day, it's very tough to [apply] makeup. Not like in America, where big stars have big dressing-room trailers. I'm standing [out] on the street! Brrrrr! Then the makeup people try, but it's just like this: my face is [cheeks shaking uncontrollably].

The *jum-ling* [trampoline]—the *jum-ling* springs and everything are frozen. My first leap goes *Poh* [smacking a hand down; absolutely flat, no give]! Nothing! Then, you know, they warm up the trampoline over a fire, and I try to take off again. "Okay, one, two, three," new camera: *Poh*! I can't jump; I have nothing to help get me up over the house, maybe this high [gesturing seven or eight feet up], nothing.

But it's a cold day. And the director wants it in one shot. I say, "Okay, I'll do it." I jump over the house, go into the fall. I'm like this: [demonstrating a rigor-mortis-legged landing] PUM!

The director says, "Run! Quick! *Run*!"

I say, "M-m-m-my foot [indicating that his foot is frozen stiff]!" My god! Yeah, really, I swear!

The director said, "Quick! My film! You're *spending* my film!" He keeps on saying, "You spend my film! You run!"

I say, "No-o-o-o, my f-f-foot."

Okay. We do it again. Yeah, the second time: PUM-*PAH*! [thighs-and-butt pancake landing]. My whole body is like, Pah! Broken!

I stand . . . up . . . again. It's cold, the wind is very cold. I have no shirt, nothing like that. Uh! The *worst*!

[Smiling wryly] The box office? The worst.

Kick: *Snake and Crane Arts of Shaolin*, in which you learn traditional kung-fu to help a monk retrieve a stolen book of martial arts secrets, must have been more rewarding.

Chan: *Snake and Crane Arts* is, I can say, my second "dream" [project]. Now for this one, I really—like the *Wooden Men* picture—make an effort. It had a serious movie script, but I was my own martial arts director. The fighting scenes were good, so my name grew.

Kick: This is the first picture with you as star that other martial arts directors and movie-industry people in Hong Kong thought would gross more than one million Hong Kong dollars there. What happened?

Chan: Publicity's no good. You know, in the daily newspaper? [Mimes squinting at fine print.] You need a magnifying glass to find the ad. So it doesn't do a million [dollars]. But then, I really

continued

don't care. I put a lot of energy into this movie, so I don't get upset because I know I really *did* it in that picture.

Kick: In *Snake and Crane Arts of Shaolin*, for the first time you had complete control, from design through execution, of the martial arts action for a picture. How did you test yourself?

Chan: Oh! The main title for this one! Okay. Main title: Two spears. The first spear . . . here [picking up one imaginary spear, then another]. I do it in one shot while all the subtitles come up. First the picture title comes up. By then I'm holding the spear [striking] Cha-cha-cha-*whish*! I stop. The next title comes up, director's credit [in motion with the spear again]. Chum-chum-chum, chum-chum-chum, *cha*! We did the whole main title segment in just one take.

For two days I did fifty-two, no, fifty-eight actions [demonstrating a sample kata section]. Da-da-da-da, da-da-da, *paht*—that's one action.

The director is standing over the camera counting off the seconds it will take for a credit to come and go at one side of the frame while I just watch him, you know? Then I do another part of [a] two-spear kata. Pah, pa-da-da-da-da, *dah*! Fifty-eight actions like that! I have to do them *all* in just one shot.

Then at the end—ow, my legs—chi-chi-chi-chi-chi, chi-chi, pah! Then I jump over, shum-shum [leaping and turning in mid-air], shum-shum-shum! *Sha*! Then I'm like this [half-sprawling, half-kneeling, huffing and puffing]. My legs are really sore, I can't walk. Because it took two days for filming the titles.

Then, in the movie, I have a sword and fight two people at once. Oh [claps hands]! That was great.

Kick: Still later, you also have a scene where you fight against three attackers, each with a spear?

Chan: Oh, this one's a bastard. Really. Three guys come at me at the same time. Then I move. But three people, they have three different ways to move, you know [demonstrating], one guy is here, one guy over there. I go down on my stomach, fight the one and then the other and then the big guy.

Oh! Great scene! It took one month because I knew some martial arts directing by that time, and I wanted all of that job partly to make more money. Before, on acting pay, I was very poor, very poor. Anyway, I didn't have a right hand [assistant] and a left hand; I just did the action direction by myself.

Kick: Tell us about *Half a Loaf of Kung Fu*. What type of picture is it?

Chan: Big comedy. Slapstick, with not much of a story.

Kick: You did the choreography?

Chan: Yes. I did *Half a Loaf* because, after my two dream movies, I had lost confidence. You know, in *Shaolin Wooden Men* and also *Snake and Crane Arts of Shaolin*, I do a lotta work.

Kick: Sounds as if you made every effort . . .

Chan: Yeah, but still the box office is not good.

Kick: The pictures you liked didn't catch on with the general public.

Chan: So along the way came those other ones.

Kick: The ancient period pictures?

Chan: Yeah. I was just fooling around [in *Half a Loaf*]. Because, how can I give it everything again? "No more." I think, "No more." I told the company director. I said, "No more, I want to go back to Australia [his residence]. The audiences don't like me!" But he just keeps starting up new movies, while I'm still just fooling around!

This one, this *Half a Loaf* movie, in it I put [singing] "Dah-dah-dah, Superstar." I include comedy, yeah? I'm running from some people, you know how it is in Chinese movies [acting out a mob hurling throwing stars from various direc-

tions]? Ping, pi-ew! Lotsa people, about twenty people yelling, "Don't go!" Ping, zing! Piew-pah! Then I go up against the wall [demonstrating being pinned, arms outstretched to the sides, singing *Jesus Christ, Superstar*] "Dah-dah-dah, Superstar." Big comedy.

I'm no fighter in this movie. The bad guys beat me, every time. So I dream one day that they are chasing the girl. I'm helping the girl, but four guys come up and beat me and beat me. Then I see some spinach [gobbling imaginary spinach while humming the *Popeye, the Sailor Man* theme, then singing the Jesus Christ, Superstar theme alternately!] [Much general laughter.]

Kick: That film would have appeared as the first comedy if its release hadn't been delayed until mid-1980. Let's hear more about the circumstances at the time.

Chan: Back then, I was thinking, "How can I use my martial arts? Even if the picture's good, people just pass it by." So for this movie, I figure maybe if, with just one punch, ka-pow! The bad guy's all broken, people will be thinking, "Oh! *Funny movie!*" You know? So I just do the singing and everything.

I have my hand like this [up in the air], and I can fly, you know? Zoom! If bad guys want to

continued

chase me again, I—Zoom!—go out [flying on a wire over their heads], and people go, "Oh my gaahd! How can he do that?!?" Ah! *Ah*! [Slapping himself, because to this day he wonders at the absurdity, too.] I'm upset; I'm upset.

Throughout the picture, I play no good as a fighter. I just do everything wrong. Maybe at the end of the film with people trying to kill me, I just [throws a quick elbow]. *Pum*! The people are dead! [Looking down in complete surprise] I don't know why! I'm like this [trying to kick, but stumbling], then maybe I hit their leg, then they fall down, and they just lie there! I just go, "Oh! What? What? What's happening?!?" You know? I have nothing to use, not even martial arts like this [making a traditional fist]. I don't know fighting, so everything I do looks ugly.

Here's one: The biggest guy is standing in back of me with his knife here while I'm [gawking around]. I don't know what I'm doing when I strike everywhere. I just pow-pow-pow, slash-slash, slam. I fight on and on, then [suddenly looking down] "Oh, he's dead. Dead? *OH*!"

Yeah, this comedy made over a million [dollars] in Hong Kong. Yeah. My best stuff, you know, when I first got into the Lo Wei Company, my best stuff I'd say is *Snake and Crane Arts of Shaolin*,

pictures like that. *Snake-Crane* box office was only half a million [dollars].

But this movie [*Half a Loaf of Kung Fu*] in Hong Kong? One million [dollars], by just fooling around. One million!

Kick: That proved to be a crafty decision on the part of the company director, holding back *Half a Loaf of Kung Fu* until your stardom was well established. Do you remember his first reaction to the picture?

Chan: He says, "What the hell you guys *doing*?!? You spend my money! And you're not *fighting*! You're not doing anything!"

Kick: After that, Lo Wei made some clever movies starring not only you, but also some of the more unusual technical possibilities of filmmaking. There was *The Magnificent Bodyguards* in 3-D, with feet, snakes, your fists, and a rousing final fracas of the bodyguards against a mountain bandit tribe all leaping out at the audience. A bit later there was *Spiritual Kung Fu*, a picture that used special effects, or a kind of split-screen or superimposing technique.

Chan: That was something very difficult for me, when they were shooting those parts of *Spiritual Kung Fu* using the new camera.

Kick: It's been explained to us as a camera with one lens in front and another on the side, designed to shoot two actions taking place separately, but to blend the actions during the filming process, rather than later in the lab. The "spirits" of *Spiritual Kung Fu* are played as tiny ghost-masters of the traditional kung-fu animal styles. So one lens is shooting their shadowboxing small, while the other lens is picking up your fight movements in full human size.

Chan: For those scenes, I'm always ducking the special effects. Maybe I want a kick. "Oh, no-no-no, you cannot kick, because the ghost's here [indicating where]; your punch should be like this [demonstrating]. You know, the ghost's here, right here . . ."

Kick: Never exactly where you'd think, right?

Chan: Yeah. So it's difficult for me to react. I should kick here [at a certain angle], because the ghost will appear over here [in another direction]. Then I say lines to where the ghost will be. When the fighting gets faster—shew, shew!—I still cannot be kicking where I want and I have to pull my punches.

Kick: So your kicks and punches don't go right through the special-effect ghosts.

Chan: Yeah, you know. Everything is moving; then my hand just stops. It's very difficult to do.

Kick: But you like the results, the look of the choreography you planned?

Chan: Yes, it *looks* fun.

Kick: The story has more magic and fantasy than it does comedy?

Chan: Yes. And the fighting really is good. But I do not like the story, you know?

Kick: You mean, the basic device of having to find one particular book with the lost secrets of the dragon, snake, tiger, crane, and leopard styles?

Chan: Yes, only if I become master of these five styles can I kill the villain. I [could] use another book, so why only this book? I can fight monkey style; I can kill a monkey-style fighter, I should be able to win. But no, I'm only scared of the five-style.

The teacher says, "Oh, you are nothing. After you learn the five animals, then you can kill the powerful guy" [the villain].

SSSSsss-jaa-aah! You know, that's why I don't like the story.

Kick: But take a simple story, one without that kind of phony plot device, and save the exaggerations for some outrageous kung-fu parody moves in the fight scenes, and we get closer to Jackie Chan's "Comedy Kung-Fu?"

Chan: As in *Snake in the Eagle's Shadow*, where I gave a lot of ideas. The story is not mine, but what I want to do, they just say, "Okay!"

continued

Kick: Seasonal Films producer Ng See Yuen and director Yuen Woo Ping gave you this first opportunity to extend your creativity beyond acting and choreography. They said, "Okay," every time?

Chan: Yeah, just, "Okay." You know? I'd say, "Oh, I want to do this one" [showing a training exercise]. "Okay." Or I'd say, "I want to be . . ." "Okay!" You know?

Not like before, when I'd say, "I want to do this one," and I'd hear: "No! [It costs] Too much money!" [Laughter from all present.]

How Jackie Turned Pain into Profit
by Neva Friedenn

If Jackie Chan's persistence and endurance can be read between the lines of his filmography [see Appendix 2], these qualities—plus the flair for comedy that made them work—are also evident in an account of a mishap which occurred on location during shooting of the breakthrough "Comedy Kung-Fu" picture, *Snake in the Eagle's Shadow*.

Fighting barehanded against a sword that should have been fitted with a guard, Chan took an accidental but bloody slash on the arm. Significantly, Chan reacted not with raging anger but with convincing body language. Spewing red stuff, he immediately executed a spectacular series of rolls and writhings. He uttered half-butchered koala-bear noises. He illustrated to those present every reason why he deserved to keep his original number of nerves and arteries.

Through all of this, Chan's energy level was tremendous, even terrifying. There were no further slip-ups. Seasonal Films' brilliant and jovial producer, See Yuen Ng, got himself a hit movie, and Jackie Chan got himself a giant step closer to superstardom.

Jackie Chan

An Outrageous Interview with the New Martial Arts Marvel

Part 2

© 1981 by Neva Friedenn

With the 1980 Warner Bros. release of *The Big Brawl*, the latest team effort of producers Raymond Chow and Fred Weintraub and director Robert Clouse of *Enter the Dragon* fame, general American audiences were introduced to the irrepressible new king of kung-fu, Jackie Chan.

Prior to this introduction, Jackie had already socked, kicked, winked, tumbled, and charmed his way to the top of many parts of the world in a handful of amazing, trendsetting Chinese-language martial arts movies.

In Part 2 of his interview, the never-say-die kid charts the course onward to his present preeminence as certified superstar. He now has to his credit the invention of a new film genre— "Comedy Kung-Fu"—and four solid cinema hits, the latter three of which have broken Bruce Lee's

Far East box-office records. Of these pictures, Chan starred in *Snake in the Eagle's Shadow* and *Drunken Monkey in a Tiger's Eye* in 1978.

In 1979–80, moving into positions of creative control of his projects at the ripe old age of twenty-four, he starred in, choreographed, wrote, and directed *Fearless Hyena*, the second highest grossing of all pictures to play Hong Kong in 1979, and *Young Master*, the all-time top grossing movie in Hong Kong history. Here Jackie Chan gives a high-spirited guided tour of the terrain behind the camera on the first two of these four considerable filmic and commercial achievements.

Continuing his first extensive interview in his new language, American English, Chan is always careful to provide animated physical and vocal demonstrations of martial arts actions as he dis-

continued

cusses various technical and artistic aspects of his kung-fu filmmaking methods and intentions.

And looking in on the interview proceedings, a few of Chan's associates add their reactions, which we've preserved here within brackets, as they realize that even without Cantonese their friend is more fun than a barrel of drunken monkeys. So much fun, in fact, that we decided to expand his outrageous interview into three parts.

Kick Illustrated: *Snake in the Eagle's Shadow* is certainly a showcase for your martial arts abilities. It has your Snake-style kata in the main title sequence, your practice and training scenes, the Mantis versus Snake-Fist battle, and your final fight against the Eagle-Claw master. Can you pick out an additional one or two of your creative contributions that helped Seasonal Films make a box-office success of this picture as the first "Comedy Kung-Fu"?

Jackie Chan: I designed two more parts. You know the one where I have to scrub the floor?

Kick: Where you follow faster and faster on the heels of the assistant boxing instructor who's purposely messing up the floor? That and the later scene where you've become so quick you can slide the scrub rags under his feet before he takes a step?

Chan: Right. And also the scene where I fight with the old teacher behind me, and I don't know what the old man is doing.

Kick: In this scene, at first you're very clumsy using the long stake, and then all at once you're very adept and powerfully accurate with it. And it looks as though the stake is striking by itself.

Chan: Yes, yes, yeah. Yeah, I want to help the old man. But! [to those present who might not be able to follow] . . . you saw the movie?

[Several respond that they haven't seen *Snake in the Eagle's Shadow*. So for this scene in which he meets the rambunctious old gent who is to transform his general klutziness into Snake-Fist expertise, Chan launches into a slightly scaled-down depiction of all the characters and actions involved.]

A lot of people, they hate the old man; they think the old man's bad luck. What they don't know, because he doesn't want everybody to know, is he's the Snake Master. So everybody hits him. Then suddenly I come.

"Don't hit him!" *Hah*! I have no kung-fu, but I say it anyway. "Stop hitting him!"

[Impersonating a cocky gang member] "Who are you?" Then the gang is coming up, you know, to kick me or knock me down. But when a fighter hits me, then the master puts my arm up [showing a lightning-fast arm extension]. *Pah*! I designed this fight.

I designed more. When a fighter shoves a stick so it comes to here [reacting to a swipe a quarter-inch from his nose]—Oooh! I close my eyes! That's when the master goes [taking the part of the old man, who's really the one skillfully manipulating the long stake from behind Chan's back and aiming the blows] one here, one here! The stake goes [really fast] weh, weh, weh-weh-weh, weh-weh, and I react, "Oh, my god!"

And the gang goes, "Oh, what good kung-fu!"

Then I stop. [Turning and reassuring the old master.] "Don't be scared, don't be scared!" Then I win! I get 'em, pah-pah-pah-pah!

See, I have a fighter come here [gesturing a few feet away], and the master takes my leg [executing a magnificent kick while looking amazed]. Pah-pah-puh—"Good!"—*Boom*! It goes something like that.

Kick: Clever.

Chan: And the gang comes here, right here [indicating inches away]. The master takes my pants [reacting to having his imaginary pants yanked down].

"Uh-oh, my pants!" [Ducking down to pull up his pants while the master's strike goes over his back, then pulling up pants and looking around.] And people are falling over.

[While everybody in the room breaks up at these renditions, Chan finishes a series of alternately proud and mystified double-takes and comes out of movie character.]

Kick: Who was the director of *Snake in the Eagle's Shadow*?

Chan: My friend, Yuen Woo Ping.

Kick: And did you create the choreography throughout?

Chan: Same as with the story; I just gave a lot of ideas.

Kick: After that you starred in two more pictures, *Spiritual Kung Fu* and *Dragon Fist*, basically straight kung-fu pictures made simultaneously or during the same period of time in Korea. *Spiritual Kung Fu* used special effects to convey a kind of fantasy feeling. What distinguishes *Dragon Fist*?

Chan: The punch fight and weapons fight at the end. My enemy in the movie is an older karate master who ruined my master and then got ashamed of his actions and cut off his own leg. I want to kill this master, but I cannot challenge a man that has only one leg. When I find out that the gangsters who are this master's enemies are my enemies too, I just join up with the master, and

continued

together we have three legs [demonstrating balancing a partner while kicking]—pah-pah!—instead of only his one leg.

Kick: Did you do the choreography for that fight?

Chan: Oh! [Laughing] Yes!

Kick: Why are you laughing?

Chan: Because in the weapons fight at the end, one of the gangsters has a knife, and I have nothing. The karate master has the—[hobbling a few steps]. You know?

Kick: A crutch?

Chan: The crutch, yes, that he gives me. So I use that on the bad guy [showing how], whuh, whuh, whuh, whuh! [Laughter all around the room.]

Kick: If *Dragon Fist* is an example of a kung-fu film without comedy, maybe you should tell us about *Drunken Master* or *Drunken Monkey in a Tiger's Eye*, the picture journalists in the Far East have called the breakthrough "Comedy Kung-Fu."

Chan: Really, *Snake in the Eagle's Shadow* is the first comedy film. The second one is *Drunken Monkey*.

Kick: *Drunken Monkey* captured public attention even more widely than *Snake in the Eagle's Shadow*?

Chan: Yes, so after *Snake in the Eagle's Shadow* and after *Drunken Monkey* came out, oh!

I have big power. In a picture, I can do whatever I want to do, everything I want to do.

Kick: The way *Drunken Monkey* begins, you play the reckless son of a kung-fu master who decides that only a crafty old "kung-fu brother" of his can tame you. Since you've heard of your "uncle's" sadistic training methods, you run away; but you accidentally meet up with this very same master. He captures you, takes you to his place, and starts the strenuous training. First he teaches you how to fall, right?

Chan: Yeah, he teaches me, [but] I still don't want to learn. Then I run away from him. And this other fellow, a professional assassin, beats me [up]. So I know my kung-fu is really no good. Then I go back to my mean master and I say, "Teach me, teach me." Okay? "Really teach me." Then at the end, I fight the professional killer again.

Kick: By that time, the old guy has taught you drunken-style fighting. The movie makes it seem as if, for the best technique, your master has to get drunk to teach you as well as he does. And your character has to get drunk in order to fight well.

Chan: Yes, yes. Oh, the part where the teacher has no wine left to drink. He asks me to go buy it. Because I've hated the teacher all this time, I only want one thing—to get away. When he asks me to go buy this drink, I love it because I cannot be training when I go into town to buy wine. He gives me ten dollars. I eat up nine dollars worth [of food]; I eat chicken legs and everything. And meanwhile the teacher back at home, his hand is like this [doing the "shakes"], because, you know?

Kick: He's an alcoholic—

Chan:—Without a drink. Suddenly, some bad guys come and want to fight my master. But I'm in town, still eating. Then I buy one dollar's worth of his drink and fill the rest of the jug with water. Then I come back home: "Oh, somebody's beating my master!" [Imitates the master taking a swig of his drink and disgustedly spitting it out:] "It's water!"

So the fight is lost. Then I'm upset a whole lot, all night. After I calm down, he really teaches me.

The more we drink, the more comedy. Audiences, you know, go, "Ha-ha-ha!"

Before the end, I've been drinking maybe like, uh, 7-Up with gin, you know? At the end, the master gives me *whiskey*! [Feigning as if his throat's on fire and the top of his head blown off.] "Whoa! How strong! *Whis*-key! Oh!" At this part, Chinese people really laugh a lot. Why? Because when he gives me the drink, he says it's san-ping wine.

Kick: Let us in on the joke.

Chan: San-ping wine is a very strong drink. In China, they have tigers. They use the tiger's penis—the tiger's and the waterdog's [to make the wine].

Kick: What's a waterdog? A retriever?

Chan: [Chan enacts a four-second imitation of a google-eyed, back-floating, bubble-blowing critter whose identity is then immediately obvious.]

Kick: Oh, an otter.

Chan: Like a water seal, yeah, yeah. And lo, lo . . .? [There's a brief assist via a sidelines translation.]

Deer? Deer. So from three kinds of animals, they take the penis and make this drink. It's very *good*! In Chinese, everyone knows how good. And it's expensive. So at the end, the master gives me this san-ping wine.

I say, "Ooh! Too strong! What's this?!?"

My master says, "Three [Chinese word] wine!"

All the people in the audience go, "Yaa, yaa, yaa!" And I go [lurching and jogging into battle] dum-dum-dum . . . [Everybody present howls with laughter.]

Oh, this is the best part. And then . . . Americans, they have the little people they believe in?

Kick: Elves and leprechauns and fairies? Yes, but we probably don't get as much good out of them as you do your Eight Drunken Immortals in this story. Seven of the Immortals are men, and

continued

the master has taught you each of their fighting techniques. But since the eighth is a girl, Lady Ho, you've only pretended to learn her technique. Yet you need all of the Eight Drunken Forms to beat the assassin and win the last fight.

Chan: So I say, "What's the last one [fighting technique]?"

The master yells, "I [already] taught you!"

"But I didn't learn!"

The teacher says, "How could you *do* that?!? You can just figure it out for yourself!"

I say, "Okay." [Mincing through some limp-wristed pseudo technique.] Tee-tee-tee. "The Girl Puts on Makeup . . ." The bad guy's like this [doing an astonished take]. I do it some more [flirting and sashaying, powdering his nose, then flicking a fist at the opponent].

The girl puts on makeup. This part was very easy for me, but this is the part that makes all the money.

Through all of the other seven Immortals, oh! [Punching] Pah, pah, pah, I have really been fighting. Then at the end, with the girl, I just go [singing] "Lai-lai-lai." But people like it, "Ha, Ha, Ha!" Even though it's easy to do, just [singing and mincing around].

Kick: Audiences love the impersonation you do in *Fearless Hyena*, too. Throughout *Drunken Monkey*, both in fighting and acting, you were able to show a variety of abilities as never before.

Chan: Oh, it's a good part, it's a *good* part.

Kick: The Drunken Forms have that off-center, off-balance, unpredictable-looking style of movement. What do you add to that through the Monkey Style?

Chan: It's like this: [In a flash, with a few low-slung, fluid and yet bouncing cross-legged steps, Chan illustrates the Monkey-Style movement. Nobody says a word, hoping for more.]

It's just the name; really, I didn't fight in the Monkey Style in that movie. But in Japan, all my movies have [the word] "monkey" in the title. *Snake Monkey, Drunken Monkey, Fearless Monkey*.

Kick: Monkey has to do with your screen image, then?

Chan: Yes, everything's monkey . . . that means me. But the Monkey's like this [two-stepping into a crouch with one arm curled up]. Then like this [loping along monkey-like]. So far I have never used Monkey [maneuvers] throughout a fight scene.

Kick: Never? Well, that's because your birthday animal is the horse.

Chan: Oh, yes. Next movie [that I do], I am Crazy Horse! [Chan throws his head back and lets forth a little whinny. This is such a culturally rich moment that everybody has to crack up.]

Kick: Tell us about your influence on the martial arts choreography for *Drunken Monkey*.

Chan: For one thing, I changed the training scenes. First, the director asks me what kind of training I can do. I say, "Okay, this kind," and, "Okay, this kind." Then maybe because I can't do what he's thinking of, I use my kind. Whatever kinds I can do, those are the kinds we choose from. That's how we really worked together well.

Kick: *Drunken Monkey* was the first of your three pictures, including *Fearless Hyena* and *Young Master*, that bested Bruce Lee's box-office record in Hong Kong. How did *Drunken Monkey* do outside Hong Kong, in Tokyo, for instance?

Chan: Twenty or twenty-two million.

Kick: The producer must love you.

Chan: Oh, Mr. Ng is a *good* person. Every question, he asks me. Planning the fight at the end of *Drunken Monkey* with Mr. Ng and the director and me sitting there, it comes up, "How does the villain die?" I show a move. That will work, and then we change things around in the *Drunken* set to lead up to that.

I say, "This one?" "Yes." "Oh, then this one?" "Yeah, yeah," they say.

Where we are could be number seven of the Drunken Immortals. "The last one?" I ask. "The girl. Maybe the girl can make the last one."

They say, "Comedy."

I say, "Yes! Then I can do it—oh, yeah!"

The ideas keep coming. Before, I'd have lots of ideas. "Oh, yeah, I can do it like this, Pah-pah-papa!" [Impersonating a dignified producer-type] "No," they'd say. Before, I think, during a whole month, I'd get only one answer. "No!" *Sheeez*! [General laughter]

Kick: But for *Drunken Monkey*, this second film for the Seasonal Films company, it sounds as if you were communicating with the producer and the director so actively that—

Chan: —Oh, everyday! *Ev-er-y* every night! In the Sheraton Hotel with the director. "What do we shoot tomorrow?" Then I'd think, "Okay, tomorrow: This, this, and this." "Okay," he'd say.

The director is quite good. I don't know why, you know, but he'd want me in on everything. Everything is "Jackie!"

You get a lot of martial arts directors that just go along like this [taking cautious formal steps], and then they always say, "No good."

But this martial arts director says [cheering-section voice], "Jackie come on, come on!" I can

continued

just go to the set [demonstrating seemingly freestyle moves] "One, two, three, four, five—how's it?"

"Good!" he just says about everything I'm doing. "Jackie's doing that? *Good!*" he says.

Every night, they say, "Jackie, Jackie," [indicating himself, the producer, and the director leaning into a huddle] at the Sheraton, and we talk-talk-talk-talk. And the minute it's all set for the next day, "Okay, go to sleep!" they tell me. The director just wanted to hear from me, though.

Kick: He sounds somewhat unconventional for a director.

Chan: Oh, he's . . . he's a crazy director. Yeah, when I'm fighting very hard, really fighting, and he starts a shot—"Camera!"—he's concentrating on the action, going, "Oooh!" and doesn't realize when the camera's out of film. He's just [rooted to the spot]. And when he notices, he says [embarrassed], "Oh! Sorry!"

And then sometimes he'll pick up something off the ground right before he says, "Camera!" [Mocking the director, staring fixedly ahead while chewing on a twig.] "Oooh!" he'll say, and he doesn't think when to cut. "Good!" he'll say, [but] he doesn't want to cut. I'll be through with the fight, but he'll still be so lost in it, he'll eat the last piece of the twig!

You know, he's crazy. Even when he's wearing a new shirt [playing this director who just can't help it, breathing so hard with involvement that he swells up], the shirt goes *Shssssshhh* [rips up the side seam], and he goes, "*Gahh!*"

Kick: All frustrated, huh? Who is this funny guy?

Chan: Same as for *Snake in the Eagle's Shadow*, Yuen Woo Ping. He is still my "kung-fu brother." But all directors are different. All of them are funny.

UP CLOSE & PERSONAL WITH . . .

Jackie Chan
An Outrageous Interview with the New Martial Arts Marvel
Part 3

© 1981 by Neva Friedenn

In the 1970s, U.S. film fans made a movie star of Chuck Norris and gladly renewed the superstar status of Bruce Lee with each rerelease of *Enter the Dragon*. But it took moviegoers throughout the Far East, their ballots cast in the form of box-office dollars, to elect as their top drawing star of all time a young man who is, like Norris and Lee, a superb martial artist.

The recipient of this phenomenal acclaim is the ebullient Jackie Chan.

Chan's fame spread outward from Hong Kong when, beginning in 1978, three of his pictures surpassed the grosses of Bruce Lee's films in Asia: *Drunken Monkey in a Tiger's Eye* was followed by *Fearless Hyena*, which was runner-up to a James Bond picture in Hong Kong in 1979. These two hits were capped in 1980 by *The Young Master*. This picture currently stacks up second to none, having sold more tickets, according to Golden Harvest Film Group, than any picture of any genre ever to play in Hong Kong.

For both *Fearless Hyena* and *The Young Master*, Chan served as writer, martial arts director, and director, as well as its star. By the time he attained this level of creative control, at age twenty-four, Chan already had seventeen years of intensive kung-fu and acting training under his sash. So, understandably, his taste in martial arts action for film runs from the unusual to the downright esoteric. And his approaches to the technical aspects of filmmaking run from professional to perfectionist.

In Part 3 of this interview, *Kick* presents a "monkey's" eye view of the inventor of Comedy Kung-Fu at work, as Jackie continues his hilarious—not to mention, educational—demonstra-

continued

tions and descriptions from his own unique blend of martial arts and movie arts. Notably, he reveals the little known "wire technique" from *Fearless Hyena*. The "wire technique" shows the range of four emotions—happiness, melancholy, joy, and anger—and represents one of the most brilliant acting devices ever enacted in a martial arts film, Chinese or otherwise. Chan integrates these four emotions into the hyperkinetic final fight, and it's unlike anything ever seen on film. Imagine fighting a man who starts crying, or laughing hysterically, in the middle of combat!

In discussing *Fearless Hyena* and *The Young Master*, he also reveals qualities not indicated by his playful on-screen image as presented in T*he Big Brawl*. As a director, Chan is one cool cucumber but, during the process of editing his movies, he says he turns into a white hot whirling dervish!

Here, in the final installment of the new kung-fu king's first extensive interview in English, *Kick* gets Jackie Chan to tell it his own way. The segments appearing in brackets represent the reactions of those present during the interview, as well as Chan's own physical and vocal demonstrations that he uses to punctuate his narration.

Kick Illustrated: You've said all film directors are different, but all of them are funny. We imagine you're a little peculiar as a director yourself.

Jackie Chan: Yes, I'm a director like this [assuming a line referee's eagle-eyed, hands-on-knees stance, extremely self-contained]. I never move. Even when the fighting goes all over. I just say [with a very low, calm voice], "Cut." From that, all the people know we have to do it again.

Kick: How did you come to direct your favorite picture for the Lo Wei Company, *Fearless Hyena*?

Chan: For *Hyena* . . . oh. I really did it for that one. With that picture I almost knew beforehand how it would turn out if I had the power.

Kick: Creative control of the project? Your successes in *Snake in the Eagle's Shadow* and *Drunken Monkey in a Tiger's Eye* were certainly making your innovations seem like a good gamble . . .

Chan: Yeah, I was growing from the little power I had before as a fighting actor under other directors. So with *Hyena*, I did this [standing full height but with head respectfully bowed], and I said, "No. I want to direct it myself." [Waiting out any counterarguments, then looking up and saying urgently] "Yes! I want to direct!"

I'm upset, you know? [Taking on the pose of the company director considering the angles, then coolly and offhandedly saying] "Okay."

Then I change the script, change everything. And I direct. And the picture goes [gesturing a grand explosion] POOM! Ha-ha!

Kick: You were right.

Chan: Pow! *Fearless Hyena* comes out, and the money [gesturing a torrential rainfall] comes down.

Kick: It has the second highest box-office record of all films to play in Hong Kong in 1979; and it plays to full houses at the Kim Sing Theater here in Los Angeles, too. Audiences have a great time with that movie. They react to every shift in the mood of your story and character, there's such a continuity established by your use of remarkable comedy bits and unusual martial arts action. Tell us how you came up with the chopsticks fight over the food. Is that in any way related to kung-fu technique, or does it derive from your Chinese Opera training?

Chan: No. I just designed it. It came about because I wanted to show my character after my grandfather dies. Also, I had another couple of scenes in there to show how, every day, I'm just like this [moping] and not training. If I want to kill the bad guy, I should be training, but I'm not, I'm just [looking dejected].

I cut down these scenes so I start to change faster, when the eating scene comes up.

[Taking on the character of his crippled old clan "uncle," Eight-Legged Unicorn.] "Now come on, eat." And it's true, even if your grandfather has died, you'd still want to eat. I say, "Okay." Then he makes me laugh. I pick up the chopsticks. When I go to pick up a piece of food, then he [doing an almost invisibly fast intercept] Shew! He takes it away [with his chopsticks]! Then I look for it. Then I pick up another one—Shew! He takes that away! Then I forget my grandfather's dead, I just [acting out his part of the chopsticks food-fight contest]—Shew! Pah-pah-pah!—get quicker and quicker. Oh! [It is a] good scene?

Kick: A wonderful scene.

Chan: When I want to eat [leaping up open-mouthed after an imaginary flying morsel of food], there it goes again! Then, he puts a little bit on the sawhorse. And when I start after it, he—Pop!—tips the sawhorse. Zhoo! The food slides down out of reach. At the end, I'm [grabbing for another morsel] ch-ch-CHA! I get one! [Popping it in his mouth, laughing] Ha-hah! Then—Oomp!—I find out, it's a stone [and not a piece of food]!

All of this, I just designed the same way I devise different fights. But, oh, for this part I did a lot of takes. This scene with the chopsticks is very

continued

hard for me, you know. Usually, I use a knife and fork! [The room explodes in a giant guffaw.]

Kick: Tell us about the grueling upside-down sit-ups training scene?

Chan: Oh, that's a rough one to do. You only see fourteen of those sit-ups on the screen, but I really did twenty-six of them in a row.

Kick: Unbelievable! But we believe you, anyway. Can you explain a basis in kung-fu for the four emotions—happiness, melancholy, joy, and anger—that you use for the final fight in *Fearless Hyena*?

Chan: Those are part of what is called the "wire technique." The whole exercise [indicating a circle of about three feet in diameter], the whole action is only this big.

[Chan takes a symmetrically balanced position at the center of the imaginary ring. He draws himself up with a breath, then expels it forcefully, "Aah!" He demonstrates several series of the wire-technique exercises, for each of which he positions and flexes his arms differently, breathes in and out to a variety of depths, and uses the framework device of assuming one of the four emotions through facial expression and vocal quality. He continues, exercising and explaining simultaneously.]

Aah! It [the wire technique] is not really for fighting, but for training the blood and breathing.

If you finish the whole sequence, you—Ahhw!—get tired like this [going limp]. But [quickly pumping up with the "happiness" series] gah, ha-ha-ha-ee-*AH*! The power! [Repeating the series with variations] It's for power and everything like that. But I put it in the movie [Chinese word].

[After another brief translation assist from the sidelines:]

Yeah, exaggerated for the audience. [Doing the series again at a hyperactive tempo.] Exaggerated because these things are used just for training [breathing out at length, smoothly]—Phhrnm—never for fighting. It would be really funny if you could see a hundred people doing it all at the same time.

Kick: So the wire technique is a set of breathing exercises for circulation, and for oxygenating the blood.

Chan: Yeah. And some like this [doing a high-energy version]. But then, relaxed, some like this [doing the same series slowly with shoulders lowered, then expelling the last breath completely.] Hahhh! And then some like this [doing a series with emphasis on the last four breath expulsions]. It's all for the body; for control. And it's really tough.

In Hong Kong, not many people understand the wire technique because the last people to know it don't want to teach it. [Taking on the persona of a master from the previous generation.] "Now I know these things, but I don't want to teach everybody. I'll only teach my son."

Kick: Keeping the secrets in the family?

Chan: Yeah. That's why not many people know the wire technique.

But everybody in the whole of Asia knows what this is [making a traditional fist], even if many people don't actually do it. If everybody can recognize a technique, I never use it the way they'd expect; if I used it the traditional way, they'd say [disappointed], "Aw, what's this?"

But out of a total of a hundred million people in Asia, only about one hundred know the wire technique. It's not common.

Kick: Even at that, you've made the technique still less common by translating it from exercise to combat.

Chan: To fighting, yes. But it wouldn't really make a fighting technique itself—ha! Ha! Ha-ha-ha-ha—*Eep*! [In a tiny child's voice] Jack-ie-Chan!

Kick: Right, it's entertainment. That "Eep!" you make when you're learning to take a punch in *Fearless Hyena*, that sound is the reason the villains spare you when you attack them before you're completely trained. They think you're crazy and a

mute, when it's only that you've been getting hit so often—

Chan: —Yeah, every time I've been going "Eep!" [In the film] I've been hit, and said "Eep!" so much I've lost my voice.

Kick: How do you come up with comical, odd, but credible coincidences like that one?

Chan: When I designed the earlier part of the story, I wanted it to show real life. For instance, if a person's sitting on a bench in a bad mood and someone comes up and asks where a certain place is located, the moody person won't give complete directions; instead, he'll just point.

Just after the beginning of the story, I'm always fighting, fighting. Then [clasps hands], my grandfather finds out! See? He knows I've been showing how I fight [meaning, showing the secret fighting techniques of their family clan, which has been forced into hiding from the ruler and his general]. I run and run through the mountains; Ah, god! I *cannot* go home. I'll go home, [and] my grandfather will kill me.

At this time, the general and his three swordsmen come: Zum, zum, zum—their weapons ring when they walk. For this part, after I see the footage of the film, I'm really unhappy because the camera setup I have doesn't make it clear enough that I

continued

never really see who they are. The camera should show only my point of view and pan up no higher than their feet and legs.

But, anyway, they ask for my grandfather by his proper name. But since I'm depressed and since I never think of my grandfather by his name, I just point the way. Zum, zum, zum—I hear them more than see them as they go away. I keep on thinking how I cannot go home because if I do, my grandfather will kill me. Then suddenly I realize, the man they asked for? He's my grandfather!

That's how I get that kind of thing into a movie.

Kick: It's another perfect example of the way you come up with distinctive twists in a story because you're always looking for ways to represent natural behavior.

Chan: Yes. And with this script, every day we'd shoot and every day I'd still be making changes.

Kick: It's an excellent film. You're a good director.

[Chan smiles, nods a modest thanks; and then he almost giggles. We get the feeling there's more to learn about how he makes movie magic.]

Fearless Hyena might be our favorite of your movies, because of the camera style, Jackie. You know, where often the camera is simply set up for a master shot and you perform in front of it so that the viewer can see an entire movement, rather than short angles and a lot of quick cuts of fists and feet. That kind of coverage wouldn't adequately capture what you do—

Chan: Right. Look [standing up] . . .

Kick: But the camera for *Fearless Hyena* does get it.

Chan: Because the cameraman is my own.

Kick: He's your own?

Chan: Yeah. And he knows what I want, what I don't want. Every time when I practice, he never goes away, he just sits, sits, sits behind the camera—and looks. When he can see I've designed a series of punches [punching rapid-fire five times]—puh, puh-puh-puh-puh—he just zooms in, shooting only to here [indicating a shot down to a little below waist level].

When he knows I'm going to use my foot, okay? It'll be ten punches, then one kick. [Counting and shadow-boxing] On the eighth punch, he zooms out . . . When he's zoomed out [indicating a full shot], my kick goes *POOU*! You see? [demonstrating exactly this punch and kick sequence] Pa-pa-pa-pa, pah, pah, pah, pah, zoop-CHA!

He knows *everything*. If he says the shot's no good, okay, I know I'm not [well covered].

Kick: What a pro. Give us his name and how you got together with him?

Chan: Chen Chin Chu. He's the same camera-man as for *Shaolin Wooden Men* and *Snake and Crane Arts of Shaolin*. I really got to know him on Snake and Crane Arts, because on that picture I was martial arts director. Since, in Asia, martial arts directors have much power, I worked with him close enough to find out: Oh, he's *good*. When I became a big star, I signed him as my own man. Then I got a $600,000 [Hong Kong] camera for him.

Kick: So he also filmed the next picture you directed, *The Young Master*?

Chan: Yes.

Kick: You created the story, is that right?

Chan: Yes, but—if you saw *The Young Master*, you saw nine thousand feet. But you lost more than that.

Kick: Really? How could we have been so careless?

Chan: In Hong Kong, they *cut* my film. So I said, "Send *The Young Master* to be cut [edited] in San Antonio. If you don't, I'll stop working on *The Battle Creek Brawl*." [a.k.a. *The Big Brawl*]

Kick: You were ready to walk off *The Big Brawl*? What happened next?

Chan: I cut *The Young Master* in San Antonio. They assigned the cutting—editing—here in the U.S. First I put all the footage back in. But I knew by then that I couldn't use all three hours' worth.

Kick: What were the limitations?

Chan: I had wanted three hours' running time with only three showings a day. But the studio boss said no, [that's] not good business for the theaters. The exhibitors can't make enough [profit] without seven shows a day.

Besides, Raymond Chow said, "In Asia, people want to see you fight, they don't want to see you talk." It's true that people know I'm the fighting director. But along with becoming a big star, I also want to be [known as an] acting director.

Yet I have to cut *The Young Master* to ninety minutes; if don't cut it, the studio boss in Hong Kong will cut it for me. I'm looking at three sections; I should cut out one of them. But I don't want to cut out any of them.

So it's tough for me. When I cut, I'm really crying. I say to myself, "I want to keep *this* part. Also, I want to keep *this* part. Also, I want to keep *this* part."

Finally, I cut out a whole scene where people pick on me and beat me because I'm an orphan and then I get mad. And I cut a lot of the ceremonies from the opening sequences, from the part with [doing the ceremonial drumbeat] dah, chum, dah-dah-dah, chum—

Kick: You cut some of the lion dancing?

continued

Chan: Yeah, how to open the lion, how to do the kicking: Pah-pah; pah, pah, pah. How to put on the lion.

Kick: But that introduction to lion dancing, which you use in the opening of *The Young Master*, has such pageantry and gives such a spectacular look at the traditions.

Chan: [Now] You see how much you lost.

Kick: The fighting is very good in *The Young Master*.

Chan: Did you like the fan fight? I like that one [slicing the air with an imaginary fan], piew, piew-piew-piew! But when we did that scene, three hundred and twenty-eight takes were no good.

Kick: Three hundred and twenty-eight shots were no good? What were you trying for?

Chan: In the middle of the fight, I was just waving the fan, and it was supposed to flip out and flip back. But it didn't. Again [swishing the fan], it wouldn't flip back. Another one, new one [trying again]. Phew-sh-sh-sh—the fan doesn't come back. People wander away while we try to find a fan that works. On the three-hundred-and-twenty-ninth take, finally it comes back! You know? [Resuming energetic fighting.] People have to get back to work [still heavier fighting] when the fan works.

Kick: That's funny! But you got a nice scene there, and also with the sawhorse fight. Tell us about the fight against the robbers in the town square. You're in a silly guy disguise similar to the one you use in *Fearless Hyena*, and you start defending yourself with bolts of fabric from a merchant's stand, and then you remember what you saw the sheriff's daughter do with her skirts.

Chan: Yes. Yes.

Kick: The way she used her skirts when she was fighting you, is that an authentic style of fighting for women?

Chan: Yes, *really*. It's called "skirt-foot." Like techniques in wing chun [kung-fu], many years ago, skirt-foot was designed to be proper and effective for girls to use.

The kung-fu mother, Wing Chun, designed her style to include some snake and bird movements and this punch [showing close-in power jabs]; wing chun kung-fu became popular, and now everyone knows this punch.

Skirt-foot was designed long ago in China when it was proper only for men to use the foot like this [doing a high straight-front kick]. When it's done the real, traditional way with a big skirt, you never see the leg, never see where the foot is coming from.

Kick: But when you improvise a skirt with the fabric for this fight in *The Young Master*—

Chan: You see a lot of my movements in that scene because [lifting an imaginary skirt to improper heights, showing off strange-looking angled kicks] I'm not supposed to know skirt-foot; I've only seen it once and never tried it before. In the movie, these things are exaggerated for comedy.

Kick: Then you turn your "skirt" into a bull-fighter's cape, and the fight goes from hilarious to outrageous. You seem to have so many great improvisatory ideas for a scene such as this one that we've been wondering whether you ever lose any of these inspired bits along the way. How do you keep from forgetting some of the good things you want to include?

Chan: I have two script men. With *The Young Master*, at first I'm thinking and thinking until I know where I'm going and where to start: "Ah!" I say. Then I call my script men.

Okay, the opening scene [goes fast]—pah, pah, pah-pah—because me, I'm a difficult or funny person. When I talk story, my story keeps coming. Now maybe I have three minutes of story when I talk to the first script man. But now I turn and talk to the second script man: Another three-minute section of story is coming! I don't know where it's coming from; it's just *coming*. Yeah, I just keep talking, keep talking. "Okay, it's finished! Tomorrow, give me the script, the whole story."

The next day, I just sit [concentrating] while they talk to me. They talk-talk-talk. Then I say,

"Okay, stop!" It happens fast again, pah-pah, pa, pa, pah. I say, "This part's no good, I have a new one. Change it."

Working like this, it takes only one week to get *The Young Master* story. I just keep changing it, keep changing it.

Kick: How do you know when the script is good?

Chan: Maybe some scripts are better than mine, but that doesn't matter if the movies don't make money. Doing scripts my way, I make money. I'm good.

Kick: Yes, you are. You revise until you're sure you have it?

Chan: What I'm going to use in the movie, that's just what I want in the script. I design the important fights first, so I already know I want to use, maybe a three-finger punch and one kick style in the first fight. Then I take the script; it has the beginning of the first fight. We shoot the fight; then I follow the script to the next fight. Okay, for this part, we use a three-finger punch, never forgetting how it was used earlier.

Kick: You take a technique like the three-finger punch and use it as a kind of stylistic "theme" for the fighting?

Chan: I never forget the three-finger punch, all the way to the finish. People say, "What's he

continued

doing?" But I keep going, putting in a three-finger punch here, maybe a little finger punch there, a new one next. Then I follow the script, follow it to the next big scene, maybe a table fight or sawhorse fight, an important one that I've designed already. Then it's back to the script, on up to the next important fight.

The script might say I want a girl to use her skirt, a man to use a sawhorse, another man to have a knife, maybe a couple of men to have stakes. Myself, I'll use a fan. Okay?

Kick: Yes.

Chan: Now, this is important: Maybe when I designed the fight, I was thinking "Oh, the skirt-fight is *good*." But when we get into the scene, even though I do my best, it's not possible to use that idea to the fullest. There's not enough time to develop it, so there's no way to include it.

"Okay, okay," I tell everybody, "[we'll use it in the] next movie!" For the next movie, I'll try to design a scene around that idea, among other good ideas. But the next movie may need new kinds of fighting. Every movie is different, so it's hard to know in advance what will work.

Kick: It must be easier to improvise a small bit on the spot than to carry over a complex idea from an earlier picture. Give us some improvised touches from *The Young Master*.

Chan: Singing "London Bridges" in the swamp. And the little part with the goldfish—that's the kind of last, small idea that you don't get until you're on the set.

Kick: In choreographing an important fight, have you ever been influenced by concerns not really related to the story or the characters or the quality of the martial arts action?

Chan: For *The Young Master*, one of my leading fighters didn't know how his first scene would come across. I said, "Okay, don't worry."

"You'll teach me?" [he asked.]

I said, "Don't worry, I have a good idea." Then I designed the fight to get the best out of the fifteen stuntmen who were just sitting around the set getting paid $600 (H.K.) every day for a week, just gambling and, "HA-HA-HA," fooling around. After seven days, I announce: "BIG JOB." Everybody's in it—POUM! OOF! PAHNG! What a fight!

Kick: For that and other supercharged scenes, you determined what would come out as slow motion or speeded-up action?

Chan: Oh yes. Those things and also the editing.

Sometimes I do the easy editing myself. But for more important parts, I stand in the back of my cutting man . . .

[Chan now takes a position as if peering over his editor's shoulder and demonstrates how he revs himself up, reaching a feverish pitch during picture editing, which many other filmmakers would describe as the least personally involving part of the moviemaking process. Chan starts striding back and forth, excited:]

"Cut! Yes! *Cut*! Ah, *Yes*!" Oh, editing's very funny: "Cut—oh, no-no-no, *CUT*!" I just stand there in my office going, "CUT. Yes, ah [whirling around in a 360-degree spin], *God*! Yes!"

Then I'm waiting. The cutting man [makes the sound of running a moviola] again; "Ah, good . . . okay . . . Let's see another one; cut this one, yes, *good*!" This goes on the whole night. The cutter's [drooping and starting to nod] because he's just sitting there. But I move, you know? So in the morning, by six o'clock, he's like this [putting on a glazed-over zombie face].

[Everybody breaks up, watching Jackie try to look like a man who's run out of steam.]

Kick: What are your plans for your next picture in the Far East? Do you think you might use the downtrodden student and the wily old master as elements in your stories?

Chan: In Hong Kong, after *Snake in the Eagle's Shadow* and *Drunken Monkey in a Tiger's Eye* came out, about three hundred comedies came out that tried to copy those characters. Now, no matter which way I take a story, other movie people follow me this way and that way.

So when people ask me, "What's your new working title?" I say [obviously and coolly lying], "I dunno."

When they've stopped copying my last movie, that's when I'll come back to do one of the two new scripts I have ready. But each new movie has a new style, different story ideas. One of them uses a "master" idea, but not as in any movie that's been done before.

Kick: Choose your favorite one of all of these pictures we've been talking about?

Chan: The last three, *Fearless Hyena*, *The Young Master*, and *Drunken Monkey in a Tiger's Eye*.

Appendix 2

JACKIE CHAN FILMOGRAPHY

All of the following JC films are listed by their original titles. All roles are starring roles unless otherwise indicated. Multiple job descriptions are also included.

The Accidental Spy (2001)

Rush Hour 2 (2001)

Shanghai Noon (2000)

Gorgeous (1999)

Rush Hour (1998)

Who Am I? (1998)

An Alan Smithee Film: Burn, Hollywood, Burn (cameo) (1997)

Mr. Nice Guy (1997)

Police Story 4: First Strike (1996)

Thunderbolt (1995)

Rumble in the Bronx (1995)

Drunken Master II (1994; upgraded in 2000)

Crime Story (1993)

Project S (1993)

City Hunter (1993)

Actress (1992)

Once Upon a Time in China (1992) (soundtrack song only)

Police Story 3: Supercop (1992)

Twin Dragons (1992; upgraded in 1999)

A Kid from Tibet (1991) (cameo)

Island of Fire (1991) (small role)

Armour of God II: Operation Condor (1990)

Stagedoor Johnny (1990) (producer)

Miracles: Mr. Canton and Lady Rose (1989)

Outlaw Brothers (1989) (stunt coordinator)

Inspector Wears Skirts II (1989) (producer; stunt coordinator)

Inspector Wears Skirts (1988) (producer)

Rouge (1988) (producer)

Police Story 2 (1988)

Dragons Forever (1987)

I Am Sorry (1987) (coproducer)

Project A II (1987)

Naughty Boys (1986) (producer; stunt coordinator)

Armour of God (1986)

Police Story (1985)

Heart of Dragon (1985)

The Protector (1985)

Pom Pom (1985) (cameo)

Twinkle, Twinkle, Lucky Stars (1985)

My Lucky Stars (1985)

Two in a Black Belt (1984) (cameo)

Wheels on Meals (1984)

Project A (1983)

Cannonball Run II (1983) (cameo)

Winners and Sinners (1983)

Ninja Wars (1982) (cameo)

Fantasy Mission Force (1982) (small role)

Dragon Lord (1982)

Cannonball Run (1981) (cameo)

The Big Brawl (1980)

The Young Master (1980)

Fearless Hyena II (1980)

The Odd Couple (1979) (stunt coordinator)

The 36 Crazy Fists (1979) (stunt coordinator)

The Fearless Hyena (1979)

Drunken Master (1978)

Snake in the Eagle's Shadow (1978)

Dragon Fist (1978)

Spiritual Kung Fu (1978)

Magnificent Bodyguards (1978)

Half a Loaf of Kung Fu (1978)

Snake and Crane Arts of Shaolin (1978)

To Kill with Intrigue (1977)

Killer Meteor (1977)

Iron Fisted Monk (1977) (co–stunt coordinator)

Dance of Death (1976) (stunt coordinator)

Shaolin Wooden Men (1976)

New Fist of Fury (1976)

Hand of Death (1975) (small role)

The Dragon Tamers (1975) (stunt coordinator)

All in the Family (1975) (supporting role)

The Himalayan (1975) (small role and stuntman)

Golden Lotus (1974) (supporting role)

The Young Dragons (1973) (stunt coordinator)

Enter the Dragon (1973) (stuntman)

Not Scared to Die (1973) (supporting role)

Hapkido (1972) (cameo)

Police Woman (1972)

The Heroine (1973) (supporting role; stunt coordinator)

Little Tiger from Canton (1971)

Fist of Fury (1972) (stuntman)

A Touch of Zen (1968) (cameo)

Come Drink with Me (1966) (child role)

The Story of Qui Xiang Lin (1964) (child role)

The Love Eternal (1963) (child role)

Big and Little Wong Tin-Bar (1962) (child role)

JC's official autobiography, *I Am Jackie Chan: My Life in Action*, became a *New York Times* bestseller.

The *Los Angeles Reader*'s cinema editor Andy Klein was an early and earnest JC editorial patron.

Courtesy of Neva Friedenn

This 1996 cover story drove home the point JC had been making for years. *Boxoffice* caught on years later.

Courtesy of Neva Friedenn

Appendix 3

JACKIE CHAN BIBLIOGRAPHY

For those interested in researching JC, his body of film work, and the progress of his high-powered career, here's a thorough guide to most of the published books and magazine stories devoted to him in the English language. This bibliography lists articles about JC that have primarily appeared in U.S. newspapers and periodicals, as well as books written about and by him.

In 1980, *Martial Arts Movies* (*MAM*), under the helm of founding editor John Corcoran, this book's author, was the first American publication to devote feature-length and cover stories to the then new phenomenal talent from Hong Kong. In August 1981, *MAM*'s sister magazine, *Kick*

Illustrated, also edited by Corcoran, featured the very first extensive interview with JC in his new language, English (see Appendix 1).

Others, in and outside of the martial arts field, including domestic filmmaking publications, only truly caught on to JC's unique talents in the late 1980s and, en masse, in the mid-1990s when *Rumble in the Bronx* became a domestic box-office hit and finally cemented JC's stardom in the U.S. market.

The following entries span 1980 to 2001 in reverse chronological order, from the latest publications featuring JC to the very first. Understandably, many of the listings derive from film sources.

The format is very user friendly. Each book entry cites the title, the author(s), the publisher, and the year of publication. Each periodical and newspaper entry lists the article's title, the type of story (brief article, feature, etc., when available), the name of the writer or writers when available, the publication in which it appeared, the publication date and, when available, the page number.

All references to *Variety* in this bibliography indicate *Daily Variety*, the Hollywood trade magazine.

Books

The Best of Jackie Chan's Screen Power
(foreword by Jackie Chan),
Richard Cooper.
Screen Power Publishing Group (U.K.),
2001.

*The Ultimate Martial Arts Q & A Book:
750 Expert Answers to Essential
Questions*
(one chapter devoted to JC),
John Corcoran and John Graden.
McGraw-Hill/Contemporary Books,
2001.

*Hollywood East: Hong Kong Movies and
the People Who Make Them*
(one chapter devoted to JC),
Stefan Hammond.
Contemporary Books, 2000.

I Am Jackie Chan: My Life in Action
(JC's official autobiography; paperback),
Jackie Chan with Jeff Yang.
Ballantine, 1999.

Jackie Chan
(pictorial biography),
Wade Major.
Michael Friedman Publishing Group,
1999.

Jackie Chan,
Curtis F. Wong and John R. Little.
Contemporary Books, 1998.

I Am Jackie Chan: My Life In Action
(JC's official autobiography; hard cover),
Jackie Chan with Jeff Yang.
Random House, 1998.

The Essential Jackie Chan Sourcebook,
Jeff Rovin and Kathy Tracy.
Pocket Books, 1997.

Jackie Chan: Inside the Dragon,
Clyde Gentry III.
Taylor Publishing Company, 1997.

*Jackie Chan: The Most Dangerous Hands
in Hollywood,*
K. S. Rodriguez.
HarperCollins, 1997.

*Dying for Action: The Life and Films of
Jackie Chan,*
Renee Witterstaetter.
Warner Books, 1997.

Asian Cult Cinema,
Thomas Weisser.
Boulevard Books, 1997.

Sex and Zen & A Bullet in the Head,
Stefan Hammond and Mike Wilkins.
Fireside/Simon and Schuster, 1996.

Hong Kong Action Cinema,
Bey Logan.
The Overlook Press, 1996.

Encyclopedia of Martial Arts Movies,
Bill Palmer, Karen Palmer, and Ric
Meyers.
Scarecrow Press, 1995.

The Martial Arts Sourcebook
(extensive reviews and ratings of JC's
films),
John Corcoran.
HarperCollins, 1994.

Star Profile: Jackie Chan Monthly,
Grant Foerster and Rolanda Chu.
Hong Kong Film, 1994.

The Essential Guide to Hong Kong Movies,
Rick Baker and Toby Russell.
Eastern Heroes Press, 1994.

*From Bruce Lee to the Ninjas: Martial Arts
Movies,*
Richard Meyers.
Citadel Press, 1984.

Jackie Chan: His Privacy and Anecdotes,
Danny Lee Hing-Kwok.
Kung Fu Supplies Company.

Exclusive Jackie Chan Magazines

Screen Power: The Jackie Chan Magazine
(officially endorsed by JC).
Bimonthly, England.

Periodicals and Newspapers

Jade Screen: The Hong Kong Movie Magazine (occasional JC articles/interviews). Launched bimonthly in September 2001, England.

"The 'Hour' Strikes 2" (feature; *Rush Hour 2*), Wade Major. *Boxoffice*, July 2001, page 36.

Impact: Action Movie Magazine ("Impact East: China Beat" section features occasional JC articles/interviews). Launched in January 1992, England.

"Chan's Spy Games Sleuth Big Local B.O." (brief article), Don Groves. *Variety*, February 5, 2001, page 20.

"Tooned Out" ("Jackie Chan Adventures" TV program; brief article). *Entertainment Weekly*, January 26, 2001, page 83.

"Harvest Sows U.S. Seeds in Chan's Spy: Jackie Chan Stars in Golden Harvest Entertainment's *The Accidental Spy*" (brief article), Don Groves and Charles Lyons. *Variety*, November 20, 2000, page 45.

"Arts & Sciences/People: Jackie Learns to Take It Slow" (feature). *Asiaweek*, November 7, 2000.

"When He-Men Meet G-Men: Movie Violence? Congress Wants Action; What Do Action Heroes Want?: Film Stars Weigh in on Violence in Movies" (in "Scoop/Focus" column; brief article). *People Weekly*, October 23, 2000, page 20.

"The Legend of Drunken Master" (movie review), Joe Leydon. *Variety*, October 23, 2000, page 41.

"Set 'Em Up, Joe, for Roaring Kung Fu" (movie review), Elvis Mitchell. *New York Times*, October 20, 2000, page B29.

"Martial Arts for Americans" (in "Living Arts" pages; movie review), Rick Lyman. *New York Times*, October 13, 2000, page B3, column 1.

"'Adventures' Series Is Like Chan's Movies, Only for Kids" ("Jackie Chan Adventures" TV program), Dennis

Hunt. *USA Today*, October 13, 2000, page 11E.

"Kids' WB! OKs more 'Jackie'" ("Jackie Chan Adventures" TV program; brief article), Paula Bernstein. *Variety*, October 10, 2000, page 33.

"Shanghai Noon" (movie review). *New York Times*, October 6, 2000, page B29.

"Family Notes" ("Jackie Chan Adventures" TV program; brief article). *Newsweek*, October 2, 2000, page 78.

"Playmates into Action on Chan Toy Figures" ("Jackie Chan Adventures" TV program; brief article), Paula Bernstein. *Variety*, September 14, 2000, page 8.

"Celler's Market" ("Jackie Chan Adventures" TV program; brief article), Judith Rumelt. *Hollywood Reporter*, International Edition, September 9, 2000, page 9.

"Jackie Chan Faces 'His Shanghai Noon'" (feature), Mike Leeder. *Impact: Action Movie Magazine*, August 2000, page 14.

"Chan's Noodle Western: Shanghai Noon" (brief article), S. T. Karnick. *Insight on the News*, June 26, 2000, page 27.

"The Golden Talents of Chan and Woo: Jackie Chan and John Woo" (brief article/interview), Mathew Scott. *Variety*, June 26, 2000, page 45.

"Chatter" (various celebrity news items; brief article), Chuck Arnold. *People Weekly*, June 12, 2000, page 164.

"At Home on the Range: Jackie Chan Kicks up a Rousing Good Time in the Multicultural East Meets Western Shanghai Noon" (in "The Arts/Cinema"; movie review), Richard Schickel. *Time*, June 5, 2000, page 82.

"Chan Tests Warrior Skills in Emperor Pic" (brief article), Kevin Kwong. *Variety*, June 5, 2000, page 11.

"Noon Rides into H'wood: Jackie Chan Motion Picture *Shanghai Noon*" (brief article), Greg Reifsteck. *Variety*, May 29, 2000, page 75.

"Sony (Finally) Gets Its Man; Chan Hype Rises" ("Jackie Chan Adventures" TV program; brief article), T. L. Stanley. *Brandweek*, April 17, 2000, page 11.

"Looking Back: Enter the New Dragon: Hong Kong, July 1979" (feature). *Asiaweek*, April 7, 2000.

"Midway Delivers Jackie Chan to the Playstation" (brief article). United Press International, April 7, 2000.

"Ani Chan on Kids' WB!" ("Jackie Chan Adventures" TV program; brief article), Cynthia Littleton. *Hollywood Reporter*, International Edition, April 4, 2000, page 4.

"Joy Shtick: Jackie Chan Stuntmaster" (game; brief article), David Kushner. *Entertainment Weekly*, March 31, 2000, page 75.

"Chan Helps Media Asia Vie for Action Film Crown" (feature), Davena Mok. *Variety*, December 6, 1999, page 44.

"Too Much Action for Jackie Chan" (brief article), *Newsweek*, November 22, 1999, page 71.

"Rockem Stockem" (feature), *Advertising Age*, November 15, 1999, page 76.

"*Who Am I?/Wo Shi Shui*" (movie review), Jamie Graham. *Sight and Sound*, September 1999, page 60.

"From Asia's Film Factories, 10 Golden Greats: Time 100" (movie reviews), Richard Corliss. *Time International*, August 23, 1999, page 115.

"Horsing Around: Jackie Chan Takes to the Saddle in a New Western: *Shanghai Noon*" (brief article). *Maclean's*, August 16, 1999, page 29.

"Gorgeous" (movie review), Derek Elley. *Variety*, July 26, 1999, page 36.

"Rush Hour" (movie review), Mel Neuhaus. *Stereo Review's Sound & Vision* 64, Issue 6 (July 1999), page 117.

"*Twin Dragons/Shuanglong Hui*" (movie review), Kim Newman. *Sight and Sound*, June 1999, page 54.

"Protest Targets Piracy in H.K." (brief article), Maureen Sullivan. *Variety*, March 22, 1999, page 13.

"King of Hong Kong" (feature), Richard Corliss. *Time South Pacific*, January 25, 1999, page 56.

"*Rush Hour*" (movie review), Philip Kemp. *Sight and Sound*, December 1998, page 60.

"*I Am Jackie Chan: My Life in Action*" (book review), *People Weekly*, October 26, 1998, page 43.

"On Tour with . . . Jackie Chan," Grace Lim. *People Weekly*, October 26, 1998, page 44.

"Chan Do: Actor Jackie Chan" (brief article). *People Weekly*, October 19, 1998, page 182.

"To Our Readers: Jackie Chan Makes It in Mainstream Hollywood" (brief article), Donald Morrison. *Time International*, October 19, 1998, page 2.

"For Hong Kong Action Star Jackie Chan, His New Hit *Rush Hour* Is a Real-Life Hollywood Success Story" (feature), Richard Corliss. *Time International*, October 19, 1998, page 50.

"Interview with Chan" (brief article). *Time International*, October 19, 1998, page 52.

"*Rush Hour*" (movie review), David Denby. *New York*, October 5, 1998, page 53.

"*Rush Hour*" (movie review), Tom Gliatto. *People Weekly*, September 28, 1998, page 39.

"*Rush Hour*" (movie review), Richard Corliss. *Time*, September 21, 1998, page 113.

"*Rush Hour*" (movie review), Joe Leydon. *Variety*, September 21, 1998, page 105.

"*I Am Jackie Chan: My Life in Action*" (book review), Neal Baker. *Library Journal*, September 15, 1998, page 81.

"*Mr. Nice Guy*" (movie review), Gerald Kaufman. *New Statesman*, September 4, 1998, page 39.

"*Mr. Nice Guy*" (movie review), David Tse. *Sight and Sound*, September 1998, page 49.

"*I Am Jackie Chan*" (book review). *Publishers Weekly*, July 13, 1998, page 68.

"*I Am Jackie Chan: My Life in Action*" (book review), Gordon Flagg. *Booklist*, July 1998, page 1826.

"Jackie Chan: From Stuntman to Superstar" (feature). *Martial Arts Illustrated*, July 1998, page 13.

"Chan Throws His Weight Behind Antipiracy Fight" (in "Spotlight: Hong Kong"; feature), Davena Mok. *Variety*, June 22, 1998, page 35.

"Critic's Assessment of H.K. Film's 2nd Wave" (in "Spotlight: Hong Kong"; feature), Andy Klein. *Variety*, June 22, 1998, page 36.

"The Dabbler: Lack of Clear Strategy for Actor Jackie Chan's Business Ventures" (feature), Joanna Slater. *Far Eastern Economic Review*, January 8, 1998, page 76.

"Chan, Jackie. (Actor)." *Current Biography*, November 1997, page 5.

"*An Alan Smithee Film: Burn, Hollywood, Burn*" (movie review), Deborah Young. *Variety*, October 6, 1997, page 54.

"*Mr. Nice Guy*" (movie review), Leonard Klady. *Variety*, August 25, 1997, page 74.

"*Operation Condor*" (movie review). *Variety*, July 21, 1997, page 39.

"*Rumble in the Bronx/Hongfan Qu*" (movie review), Tony Rayns. *Sight and Sound*, July 1997, page 51.

"*First Strike*" (movie review), Stephen Alter. *Far Eastern Economic Review*, February 6, 1997, page 40.

"He Gets a Kick out of Pop: Talking with . . . Jackie Chan" (brief article: interview), Andrea Pawlyna. *People Weekly*, October 28, 1996, page 34.

"Jackie Chan Signs with William Morris Agency" (brief article). *Mediaweek*, October 14, 1996, page 18.

"*Supercop*" (movie review), Fred Lombardi. *Variety*, July 29, 1996, page 59.

"*First Strike*" (movie review), Leonard Klady. *Variety*, May 6, 1996, page 86.

"See Jackie Break His Neck: Actor Jackie Chan Does His Own Stunts" (feature), Andrew Tanzer. *Forbes*, April 22, 1996, page 229.

"Return of the Dragon: Fifteen Years After His First Attempt, Asia's Most Popular Action Hero Finally Kicks His Way to the Top of the U.S. Box-Office Charts" (feature), Lynette Clemetson. *Far Eastern Economic Review*, March 14, 1996, page 46.

"Feat of the Feet: Jackie Chan, Worldwide Star, Would Like to Kick His Way into Your Heart" (feature), Gregory Cerio. *People Weekly*, March 11, 1996, page 57.

"Lethal Laughter: Asia's Top Star Is an Ace at Comedy and Combat" (feature), Brian D. Johnson. *Maclean's*, March 4, 1996, page 74.

"*Rumble in the Bronx*" (movie review), Tom Gliatto. *People Weekly*, February 26, 1996, page 17.

"Go West, Hong Kong: John Woo and Jackie Chan Meet Hollywood" (feature), Richard Corliss. *Time*, February 26, 1996, page 67.

"Movies: Chinese Takeout: U.S. Films with Hong Kong Action Flavor" (feature), David Ansen. *Newsweek*, February 19, 1996, page 66.

"Rumble in the Box Office" (feature), Andy Klein. *Los Angeles Reader*, February 16, 1996, page 8.

"Jackie Chan, Superstar" (feature), Ray Greene. *Boxoffice*, February 1996, page 10.

Jackie Chan (theme issue coinciding with the U.S. release of *Rumble in the Bronx*), edited by John Corcoran. *Martial Arts Movies*, February 1996.

"Jackie Chan, American Action Hero? Movie Star Is Highly Successful in Asia" (feature-length interview), Jaime Wolf. *The New York Times Magazine*, January 21, 1996, page 22.

"Auds Give Thumbs Down to Canton-Language Pix: Hong Kong Films in

Asia" (feature), Fionnuala Halligan. *Variety*, December 11, 1995, page 54.

"Hong Kong Babylon: Its Movies and the Domestic Industry That Produces Them" (feature-length industry overview), Fredric Dannen. *The New Yorker*, August 7, 1995, page 30.

"Jackie Can! Hong Kong Film Star Jackie Chan" (feature), Richard Corliss. *Time*, February 13, 1995, page 82.

"More Than 'The Next Bruce Lee': (Millionaire-Actor Jackie Chan)" (feature), Derek Elley. *Variety*, January 23, 1995, page 56.

"Spectacular Cinema," Charles Oliver. *Reason*, November 1994, page 59.

"Soft-Boiled," Andy Klein, *L.A. Reader*, September 9, 1994.

"Martial Arts Mayhem" (video recording reviews), Richard Kadrey. *Whole Earth Review*, Winter 1992, page 58.

"*Police Story III: Supercop*" (movie review), Fred Lombardi. *Variety*, September 7, 1992, page 49.

"Double Boy," David Chute. *L.A. Weekly*, August 30, 1991

"Fast-Moving Jackie Chan's Slow on the Set" ("Director" feature), Bruce Ingram. *Variety*, March 18, 1991, page 11.

"Frisco Fest Slates Over 80 Features" (San Francisco International Film Festival feature), Jim Harwood. *Variety*, February 15, 1989, page 34.

"Jackie Chan's Big Dilemma: How Long Can He Keep It Up?" (feature). *Variety*, February 1, 1989, page 84.

"A Film Scholar's Infatuation with Hong Kong Action Pics" (feature), Barbara Scharres. *Variety*, February 1, 1989, page 94.

"Chan Can Do" (in special section, "Made in Hong Kong"; feature), Dave Kehr. *Film Comment*, May–June 1988.

"Jackie Chan: Risking His Life for American Approval" (feature), Jane Hallander. *Inside Kung Fu*, February 1987, page 36.

"*The Armour of God*" (movie review). *Variety*, September 17, 1986, page 24.

"*The Protector*" (movie review). *Variety*, May 22, 1985, page 24.

"*Wheels on Meals*" (movie review). *Variety*, September 12, 1984, page 18.

"*Winners and Sinners*" (movie review). *Variety*, August 3, 1983, page 24.

"The One-and-Only Jackie Chan" (feature reprint), Neva Friedenn. *Official Karate*, Summer 1983, page 41.

"Chan Isn't Missing" (feature), Tony Page. *Fighting Stars*, April 1983, page 18.

"The One-and-Only Jackie Chan" (feature), Neva Friedenn. *Official Karate*, January 1983, page 18.

"*The Young Master in Love*" (feature), Sandra Seagal. *Martial Arts Movies*, March 1982, page 14.

"Jackie Chan's 'Old Master': Sifu Yu Chan-Yuan" (feature), Sandra Seagal. *Martial Arts Movies*, November 1981, page 16.

"Jackie Chan: The Struggle for Success" (feature), Sandra Seagal. *Martial Arts Movies*, July 1981.

"Jackie Chan: Welcome to L.A." (feature), Ben Singer. *Fighting Stars*, April 1981, page 16.

"Jackie Chan: Up Close and Personal" (feature-length interview series), Neva Friedenn. *Kick Illustrated*, March–May 1981.

"Inside Jackie Chan" (feature), Paul Maslak and James Lew. *Inside Kung Fu*, October 1980, page 26.

"*The Big Brawl*" (movie review). *Variety*, August 27, 1980, page 20.

"*The Big Brawl*: Inside Jackie Chan" (feature), Paul Maslak. Inside Kung Fu, August 1980.

"Jackie Chan: Kung-Fu Cinema's Newest Sensation" (feature), Neva Friedenn. *Martial Arts Movies*, August 1980, page 32.

JC holding an honorary deputy's badge that was awarded to him by the Las Vegas Sheriff's Department (above left)

In addition to his many awards and honors, JC is often the recipient of unusual presents from various fans, governments, and government agencies. Here fans in Moscow present him with a Russian marine uniform (above).

JC meets Grandmaster Jhoon Rhee (right), the Father of Taekwondo in America, at the presentation of the 1999 Asian-American Excellence 2000 Award in Washington, D.C. The award is given to Asian-Americans who are successful in business in the United States. It was created by the Asian-American Chamber of Commerce, whose founder and chairperson is Susan Allen (center).

Appendix 4

JACKIE CHAN'S AWARDS, HONORS, AND OFFICES HELD

Awards and Honors

2001

The City of Toronto

Award:

Jackie Chan received the key to the city of Toronto, and the mayor proclaimed November 18, 2001, "Jackie Chan Day" in Toronto.

2001 Montreal World Film Festival

Award:

Jackie Chan received the Grand Prix of the Americas Award for career achievements.

Blockbuster Entertainment Awards

Shanghai Noon

Nomination:

Jackie Chan and Owen Wilson for Favorite Action Team (per Internet votes only)

Harvard University

Jackie Chan presented with the 2001 Artist of the Year Award (March)

City of Los Angeles

Jackie Chan named an honorary Sheriff of Los Angeles

World Stunt Awards (U.S.)

Shanghai Noon

Nominations:

>Best Fight (Andy Cheng)
>
>Best Fight (collective stunt fighters for the barroom brawl)
>
>Best High Work (Andy Cheng)
>
>Best Specialty Stunt (Brent Woolsey)

2000

Hong Kong Film Awards

Shanghai Noon

Nomination:

>JC's Stuntman Association for Best Action Design

International Indian Film Awards (India)

Award:

>IIFA Board Achievement Award

Total Film Magazine (U.K.)

Award:

>Jackie Chan named One of the 30 Hollywood Men of All Time (He was ranked number two behind the late Steve McQueen.)

Excellence 2000 Award, Asian-American Chamber of Commerce

Award:

>Jackie Chan for Asian-American success in U.S. business.

1999

MTV Movie Awards

Rush Hour

>Jackie Chan and Chris Hunter for Best On-Screen Duo

Nomination:

>Jackie Chan and Chris Tucker for Best Fight

Blockbuster Entertainment Awards

Rush Hour

Award:

>Jackie Chan and Chris Tucker for Favorite Duo—Action/Adventure

Hollywood Film Festival

Award:

>Jackie Chan for Actor of the Year

1998

Cinequest San Jose Film Festival (U.S.)
Award:
   Jackie Chan for Maverick Tribute
   Award

1997

MTV Movie Awards
Mr. Nice Guy
Nomination:
   Jackie Chan for Best Fight

1996

Hong Kong Film Awards
Rumble in the Bronx
Award:
   Stanley Tong and Jackie Chan for Best
   Action Design
Nominations:
   Best Picture
   Jackie Chan for Best Actor
   Anita Mui for Best Actress
   Francoise Yip for Best Supporting
   Actress

Yiu-Chung Cheung for Best Editing
Stanley Tong and Jackie Chan for Best
Action Design
Thunderbolt
Nomination:
   JC's Stuntman Association and Sammo
   Hung's Stuntman Association for Best
   Action Design

MTV Movie Awards
Rumble in the Bronx
Nomination:
   Jackie Chan for Best Fight

Baptist University (Hong Kong)
Award:
   Jackie Chan received an Honorary
   Doctorate in Sciences for his
   contributions to Hong Kong society
   and filmmaking.

1995

MTV Movie Awards
Award:
   Jackie Chan for Lifetime Achievement

1994

Hong Kong Film Awards

Crime Story

Award:

Yiu-Chung Cheung for Best Editing

Nominations:

Jackie Chan for Best Actor

Kirk Wong for Best Director

JC's Stuntman Association for Best Action Design

Drunken Master II

Award:

Kar-Leung Lau and JC's Stuntman Association won for Best Action Design

Nomination:

Yiu-Chung Cheung for Best Editing

Golden Horse Awards (Taiwan)

Crime Story

Award:

Jackie Chan for Best Actor

Cine-Asia

Crime Story

Award:

Jackie Chan for Best Actor of the Year

Miss Universe Pageant (South Africa)

Judge

1993

Asia Pacific Film Festival (Asia)

Award:

Outstanding Contribution to Movies

1992

Hong Kong Film Awards

Police Story 3: Supercop

Nominations:

Jackie Chan for Best Actor

Stanley Tong for Best Action Design

Golden Horse Awards (Taiwan)

Police Story 3: Supercop

Award:

Jackie Chan for Best Actor

Taiwan Government

Award:

Jackie Chan named one of the Five Most Outstanding Young Chinese of the World

Hong Kong Radio & Television

Award:

Jackie Chan named one of the Ten Most Healthy Personalities of Hong Kong

1990

Hong Kong Film Awards
Armour of God II: Operation Condor
Nomination:
    JC's Stuntman Association for Best
    Action Design

Hong Kong Radio & Television
Award:
    Jackie Chan named one of the Ten
    Most Popular Performers in the 1980s

The Cinematheque Francaise (France)
Award:
    Jackie Chan for des Insignes de
    Chevalier des Arts et des Lettres

1989

Hong Kong Film Awards
Miracles: Mr. Canton and Lady Rose
Award:
    JC's Stuntman Association won for
    Best Action Design
Nominations:
    Jackie Chan for Best Actor
    Yiu-Chung Cheung for Best Editing
    Eddie Ma for Best Art Direction

Roadshow Magazine (Japan)
Miracles: Mr. Canton and Lady Rose
Award:
    Jackie Chan for Best Foreign Actor

Artists' Guild (Hong Kong)
Miracles: Mr. Canton and Lady Rose
Award:
    Jackie Chan for Best Actor

British Government (Hong Kong/ Commonwealth)
Award:
    Member of the Most Excellent Order of
    the British Empire

1988

Hong Kong Film Awards
Rouge
Awards:
    Best Picture
    Best Actress for Anita Mui
    Best Screenplay
    Best Editing
    Best Music
    Best Song

Dragons Forever
Nomination:
  Sammo Hung's Stuntman Association
  for Best Action Design
Police Story II
Award:
  JC's Stuntman Association for Best
  Action Design

Golden Horse Awards (Taiwan)
Rouge
Awards:
  Best Actress for Anita Mui
  Best Cinematography
  Best Art Direction

Roadshow Magazine (Japan)
Police Story II
Award:
  Jackie Chan for Best Foreign Actor and
  Best Foreign Action Director

Jaycees International (Japan)
Award:
  Jackie Chan named one of The
  Outstanding Young Persons of
  the World

1987

Hong Kong Film Awards
Project A II
Award:
  JC's Stuntman Association for Best
  Action Design
Nomination:
  Yiu-Chung Cheung for Best Editing
Armour of God
Nomination:
  JC's Stuntman Association for Best
  Action Design

Roadshow Magazine (Japan)
Project A II
Award:
  Jackie Chan for Best Foreign Actor

The City of San Francisco, California
Proclamation:
  Jackie Chan Day (September 6, 1986)

Hong Kong Junior Chamber of Commerce
Award:
  Ten Outstanding Young Persons of
  Hong Kong

1985

Hong Kong Film Awards

Police Story
Award:
>Best Picture, JC's Stuntman
>Association for Best Action Design

Nominations:
>JC for Best Actor and Best Director
>Brigitte Lin for Best Actress
>Yiu-Cho Cheung for Best
>Cinematography
>Yiu-Chung Cheung for Best Editing

Heart of Dragon
Award:
>Best Song

Nominations:
>Jackie Chan for Best Actor
>Sammo Hung's Stuntman Association
>for Best Action Design
>Man-Yi Lam for Best Music

My Lucky Stars
Nomination:
>Sammo Hung's Stuntman Association
>for Best Action Design

Roadshow Magazine (Japan)

Police Story
Award:
>Jackie Chan for Best Foreign Actor and
>Best Foreign Director

1984

Hong Kong Film Awards

Project A
Award:
>JC's Stuntman Association for Best
>Action Design

Nomination:
>Jackie Chan for Best Actor

Wheels on Meals
Nomination:
>JC's Stuntman Association for Best
>Action Design

Roadshow Magazine (Japan)

Wheels on Meals
Award:
>Jackie Chan for Best Foreign Actor

1983

Hong Kong Film Awards
Winners and Sinners
Award:
    Sammo Hung's Stuntman Association
    for Best Action Design
Nomination:
    Richard Ng for Best Actor

Roadshow Magazine (Japan)
Winners and Sinners
Award:
    Jackie Chan for Best Foreign Actor

1982

(This marked the inaugural year of the
    Hong Kong Film Awards.)

Hong Kong Film Awards
Dragon Lord
Nomination:
    Best Action Design

Offices Held

2001

Hong Kong Film Awards Association
Chairman

1994–present

Motion Picture Association, Hong Kong
President

1993–present

Hong Kong Performance Artiste Guild
Vice President

Hong Kong Society of Cinematographers
Honorary President

Hong Kong Directors' Guild
President

1992–present

Hong Kong Stuntmen Association
Member, Executive Committee

1991–1993

Hong Kong Director Guild

Vice President

1989–1991

Hong Kong Director Guild

Executive Committee Member

1988–present

Jackie Chan Charitable Foundation, Japan

Founder

1987–present

Jackie Chan Charitable Foundation, Hong Kong

Founder

JC and Hong Kong's famed kung-fu comic books maker Jademan Wong promote their new Taiwanese comic website, kingcomics.com.tw, in 2000 in Taipei.

Courtesy of Reuters NewMedia Inc./Corbis

Appendix 5

JACKIE CHAN OFFICIAL FAN CLUBS

Currently, there are only five official Jackie Chan Fan Clubs recognized by Chan's management group in Hong Kong.

Australia

Jackie Chan Fan Club—Australia
Christine Mullen, President
P.O. Box 795
Gladesville NSW1675
Australia
Local phone/fax: (02) 9817-5887
International phone/fax: 612-9817-5887
www.geocities.com/Hollywood/Set/8801
E-mail: jackiechanfans@dragon.net.au

Hong Kong

The Jackie Chan International Fan Club

Mr. Willie Chan, President and CEO
The J.C. Group
145 Waterloo Road
Kowloon-Tong
Kowloon
Hong Kong
Phone: 852-2794-4274
www.jackiechan.com or
    http://www.jackie-chan
    .com/member.html
E-mail: Mail2JChan@aol.com

Japan

The Jackie Chan International Fan
    Club—Japan Branch
B1 Ebisu St. Building
3-11-10 Higashi Shibuya-Ku

Tokyo 150-0011
Japan
Local phone: (03) 5485-1172
International phone: (81) 3-5485-1172

United Kingdom

Jackie Chan Fan Club—United
   Kingdom
Richard Cooper, President
P.O. Box 1989
Bath BA2 2YE
England
Phone/fax: 44-1225-420807
www.jackie-chan.co.uk
E-mail: 106412.71@compuserve.com

United States

Jackie Chan Fan Club—United States
Joy C. Al-Sofi, President
P.O. Box 2281
Portland, OR 97208
U.S.A.
Phone: (503) 299-4766
www.jackiechanfans.com *or*
   www.spiritone.com/~chanfans
E-mail: ChanFansUS@aol.com

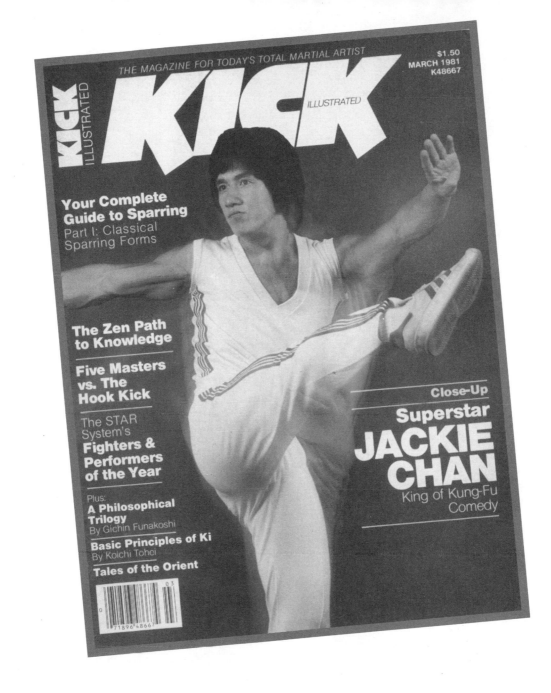

THE MAGAZINE FOR TODAY'S TOTAL MARTIAL ARTIST

$1.50
MARCH 1981
K48667

KICK ILLUSTRATED

KICK ILLUSTRATED

Your Complete Guide to Sparring
Part I: Classical Sparring Forms

The Zen Path to Knowledge

Five Masters vs. The Hook Kick

The STAR System's **Fighters & Performers of the Year**

Plus:
A Philosophical Trilogy
By Gichin Funakoshi

Basic Principles of Ki
By Koichi Tohei

Tales of the Orient

Close-Up
Superstar
JACKIE CHAN
King of Kung-Fu Comedy

0 71896 48667 03

Recording artist Jackie Chan

Courtesy of Reuters NewMedia Inc./Corbis

Appendix 6

JACKIE CHAN MUSICOGRAPHY

by Myra Bronstein

It may come as a surprise to those in the Western world that Jackie Chan is also a well-known pop singer in Asia with many hits to his credit. This musicography is an overview of his music. He has recorded many CDs (the only format included here), made a number of music/karaoke videos, has many soundtracks associated with his movies, and also records songs on other artist's albums.

Those recordings are detailed in the following five sections:

- Jackie Chan CDs
- Jackie Chan Music/Karaoke Videos
- Jackie Chan Movie Soundtracks
- Albums with Jackie Chan Songs
- Music Sources

One particular difficulty in obtaining JC's music and compiling this file is the language situation. With the exception of soundtracks for movies released in the West, his albums and videos are not recorded in English; generally, they are recorded in Mandarin or Cantonese. His albums, therefore, don't generally display English titles or song lists on the cover, though they might have English song names on the CD itself. As a solution, I've included brief descriptions in lieu of titles or to supplement titles.

Jackie Chan CDs

Jackie (1989)

Front of jewel case: Jackie in a yellow
  sweater reading *The Japan Times*.
Back of jewel case: Same as front
Insert: Lyric sheet
Language: Cantonese
Producer: Capital Records
ID#: CD-12-1006S
Length: 59:58 minutes
Number of songs: 16
Song titles:
1. "Before the Midnight Kiss"
2. "Giant Feelings"
3. "Film Cutting Machine of Life"
4. "This Night"
5. "New Diary"
6. "I Can Do It"
7. "Tender Hearts Sparkles"
8. "Thousand Times Chained in
  Feelings"
9. "I Try My Best"
10. Theme from Police Story, a.k.a.
  "Hero Story"
11. "My Little Girl"
12. "Life's Fulfillment"
13. "Stay With Me"
14. "Dare to Fight Against Bans"
15. "Just Want Tonight"
16. "OK, I Love You"
Notable song: number 10

First Time (a.k.a. *My First Time*) (1992)

Note: The title of this CD is reportedly
  First Time, but that title is not
  listed in English on the jewel case
  or the CD. The jewel case just reads
  "[Jackie] Chan" in English. The
  CD has English song titles.
Front of jewel case: Jackie in a red
  sweater
Back of jewel case: Jackie on a street,
  black-and-white photo
Insert: Lyric book with photos
Language: Mandarin with some
  Taiwanese
Producer: Rock Records
ID#: RD-1153
Length: 42:33
Number of songs: 10
Song titles:
1. "My Feeling"
2. "I Wish the Flowers Could Never
  Fade"
3. "The Reddish Face"
4. "Keep You Company Through
  Every Moment"
5. "So Transparent Is My Heart" (duet
  with Sara Chen)

6. "A Vigorous Aspiration in My Mind"
7. "The Betel Nuts Beauty"
8. "You Are a Lover in My Dream"
9. "Every Day in My Life" (duet with Tarcy Su)
10. "The End"
Notable song: number 6

Best of Jackie Chan (a.k.a. *The Best Songs for Jackie Chan's Super Motion Pictures & the Others*; *The Best of Jackie Chan's Soundtracks*) (1995)
Note: There is no English on the wrapper or album cover. The CD has English song titles.
Orange paper wrapper over jewel case
Front of jewel case: Five black-and-white photos of Jackie
Back of jewel case: Jackie with his arm covering his face
Insert: Lyric book, and great paperback photo book
Language: Cantonese, Mandarin, English
Producer: Rock Records
ID#: RD-1306
Length: 59:44
Number of songs: 13
Song titles:

1. "A Good Conscience"
2. "I Hope You Will Understand"
3. "A Vigorous Aspiration in My Mind"
4. "I Have My Way"
5. "You Give Me a New World"
6. "The Sincere Hero"
7. "I Did Not Let Myself Down"
8. "My Feeling"
9. "A Man Should Be of Self Help"
10. "The Drunken Master"
11. "You Are the One I Desire"
12. "Wedding Duet"
13. Selections from *Red Bronx*
Notable songs: Numbers 1, 3, 6, 11, 12, and 13

Jackie Chan (Japanese Release) (1995)
Note: Only actual song titles are enclosed in quotation marks.
Front of jewel case: Picture of Jackie and helicopter from *Supercop*
Number of songs: 18
Song titles:
1. "I Hope You'll Understand" (from *Supercop*)
2. "The Riddle" (from *Supercop*)
3. March from *Project A2*
4. Theme from *Project A2*

5. "Tribal Drums" (from *Armour of God*)
6. Theme from *Police Story*
7. Prelude from *The Protector*
8. "Power On" (from *Cannonball Run 2*)
9. Music from *Dragon Lord*
10. "Kungfusion" (from *Drunken Master*)
11. "Miracle Guy " (from *Shaolin Wooden Men*)
12. Theme from *Project A*
13. "Spartan X" (from *Wheels on Meals*)
14. "Dangerous Eyes" (from *Snake and Crane Arts of Shaolin*)
15. "The Cannonball" (from *Cannonball Run*)
16. Theme from *Young Master*
17. "Lesson of Kung Fu" (from *Snake in the Eagle's Shadow*)
18. "Crazy Monkey" (from *Fearless Hyena*)

Heartbeat of Jackie (a.k.a. *Heart of a/the Dragon*; *Dragon's Heart*) (1996)
Note: The front of the wrapper and the CD read *Jackie Chan*; the wrapper side reads *Heartbeat of Jackie*. The CD has English song titles.
Paper wrapper over jewel case
Front of wrapper: profile of Jackie
Back of wrapper: Jackie in front of a fish tank
Front of jewel case: profile of Jackie (same as wrapper front)
Back: Jackie sitting against a wall
Insert: Lyric/photo book, and fantastic hardback photo book entitled *Heartbeat of Jackie*
Language: Mandarin, Taiwanese
Producer: Rock Records
ID#: RD-1357
Length: 44:12 minutes
Number of songs: 10
Song titles:
1. "How Come"
2. "Would Rather Say Good-bye in Dreams"
3. "Know How You Feel"
4. Oddly, there is no title for this cut; it might have been lost in the translation.
5. "Cry with You Laugh with You"
6. "The Cold Rain"
7. "Let Me Be Your Man"
8. "I Would Start to Say but I Never Could"

9. "So Much Love"
10. "Love Hong Kong"
Notable song: number 1.

The Best of Jackie Chan (Japanese) (1999)
  Front of jewel case: Jackie in kung-fu
    stance
  Language: Cantonese, Mandarin
  Number of songs: 17
  Song titles:
  1. "Who Am I"
  2. "A Nice Guy"
  3. "How Come"
  4. "I Didn't Let Myself Down"
  5. "Drunken Boxing"
  6. "I Go My Own Way"
  7. "A Man Should Be of Self Help"
  8. "My Feeling"
  9. "So Transparent Is My Heart" (duet
    with Sarah Chen)
  10. "Keep Your Company Through
    Every Moment"
  11. "I Love Hong Kong"
  12. "I Know How You Feel"
  13. "Would Rather Say Good-bye in
    My Dreams"
  14. "If Love Should Fall Apart" (duet
    with Tarcy Su)
  15. "Midnight Shadow Dance"

16. "Hong Kong Is Coming Home"
17. "Who Am I" (reprise)

Asian Pops Gold Series 2000 (Japanese)
(2000)
  Front of jewel case: Hazy picture of
    Jackie in blue shirt
  Number of songs: 12
  Song titles:
  1. "Mystery"
  2. "Only You"
  3. "Ming Ming Bai Bai"
  4. "Hero Story"
  5. "End of Love"
  6. "Strong Rain"
  7. "Who Am I"
  8. Theme from *Drunken Master 2*
  9. "Nice Guy"
  10. "New Year"
  11. "Joy and Sadness"
  12. Theme from *Drunken Master 2*
    (Karaoke)

Jackie Chan Music/Karaoke Videos

I Wish the Flowers Could Never Fade
  (1992)

Album: *From Best of Jackie Chan*, song 1

Description: Jackie posing with a red sports car, the ocean, in a black jacket and blue scarf

So Transparent is My Heart (1992)

Description: Jackie in a duet with Sarah Chen, both in various wardrobe but often in black, sometimes singing back-to-back, which is the shot upon which it ends

Beauty and the Beast (1992)

Album: Presumably from *Beauty and the Beast* soundtrack

Description: Jackie in a beige suit singing a duet with Sarah Chen intercut with scenes from the movie

Every Day in My Life (1992)

Description: Jackie appears in this video courtesy of Tarcy Su's imagination. She is shown on a tropical vacation, and he is shown in her thoughts.

My Feeling (a.k.a. *Feeling*) (1992)

VCD: *Best of Karaoke, Volume 3*

VCD: *The Best of the Hot Songs (5) Karaoke*

Description: Jackie and actress Maggie Cheung in various wardrobe and scenes of domestic bliss and strife. It opens with an argument, and Jackie looks depressed.

A Vigorous Aspiration in My Mind (circa 1992)

VCD: *Best of Karaoke, Volume 6*

Description: Concert footage of Jackie on stage. A treat is a rare on-screen shot of Jackie's manager and business partner, Willie Chan, singing along in the audience.

You Give Me a New World (circa 1992)

VCD: *Best of Karaoke, Volume 1*

VCD: *The Best of the Hot Songs (3) Karaoke: Paradise*

Description: This video is cobbled together with scenes from *I Wish the Flowers Could Never Fade* and *My Feeling*, including some unused footage from the latter.

The Sincere Hero (1993)

Album: *From Best of Jackie Chan,* song 6

Description: Jackie in a purple and white-striped shirt, upstaging three other guys (Emil Chow, Anthony Wong, Tsung-Sheng Li), each taking turns singing, and sitting on a soundstage with TVs and spinning wheels.

How Come (1996)

Album: *From Heart of the Dragon,* song 1

VCD: *Best of Karaoke, Volume 5*

VCD: *The Greatest Hits of Rock, 1996* (Karaoke)

Description: Jackie in various wardrobe and shots including some *Police Story 4: First Strike* underwater footage, some shower beefcake playfully spitting water, and ending with him falling backward from a toy playground horse.

Red Sun (1996)

Description: Jackie is shown in various Australian settings used in the filming of his movie *Police Story 4: First Strike*.

As Long As I Loved (1997)

Description: A video with a dramatic arc wherein Tarcy Su is crying because Jackie is late for a date. He finally shows up with cute consolation gifts and they proceed to have an even cuter date. A notable aspect is that the crying scenes were filmed at Jackie's old corporate business office.

Man and Woman (1997)

Description: Jackie shown in a recording session with Sally Yeh, she in black, he in white.

The Accidental Spy Theme (2001)
   Description: Jackie shown in a
      recording session with Mavis Fan,
      mixed with scenes from the movie.

Disney's Mulan (1998)
Gorgeous (1999)
Shanghai Noon (2000)
The Accidental Spy (2001)

Jackie Chan Movie Soundtracks

Big Brawl (1980)
Young Master (1980)
Dragon Lord (1982)
Project A (1984)
Wheels on Meals (1984)
The Protector (1985)
Twinkle, Twinkle, Lucky Stars (1985)
My Lucky Stars (1985)
Armour of God (1986)
Police Story (1986)
Dragons Forever (1987)
Project A, Part II (1987)
Disney's Beauty and the Beast (1991)
Police Story 3: Supercop (a.k.a. *Supercop 3*)
   (1992)
Once Upon a Time in China (1992)
Drunken Master 2 (1994)
Thunderbolt (1995)
Mr. Nice Guy (1996)
Who Am I? (1997)
Rush Hour (1997)

Albums with Jackie Chan Songs

Various "Artists' Compilation" CDs reportedly have a song or two of Jackie's. Among them are:

Rock TV Theme Songs Collection (a.k.a.
   Hong Kong TV Soundtracks)
The Best of Hong Kong TV Soundtracks II
Perfect Match
Happy Forever
Best Radio Drama
Rock A Dance
Pairs + My Excitement
The King of Theme Songs
A New Pretty World
Yeung Pui Pui vs. Jin/Ching Yong
Rock & Roll's Theater (Vol. II) (a.k.a. *Rock
   Movie Soundtrack II*)
*Never Die Hero—Bruce Lee (Bruce Lee
   Tribute)*
The Classic of Jonathan Lee
Music Score of Rock's Greatest Love Songs

Music Score of Rock's Greatest Love Songs II

The Best Songs of Rock I & II

The Best Music of Disney, Volume 2

The Best of Hot Songs I

New Songs Every Night I & II, Friends

The Greatest Hits of Rock 1996

Rock Records' Best Male Artists II 1996

The Songs for Ordinary People

A Compilation of Stars

Holding Hand with Hand

The Best of Rock's Movie Soundtracks

Men Size Love

Rock Radio

The Best of the Pearl of East

The Eastern Pearl III

Compilation of Best of Rock's Artists

Hearts of Moving Men

Compilation of TV Soundtracks of Yang Pei Pei I & II

In the Name of Love

Compilation of Rock's Best Taiwanese Songs

Compilation of Rock's Best TV Soundtracks

Rock Record's TV and Movie Soundtrack

Music Sources

The following list of Web sites is not intended as an endorsement or advertisement. These Web sites are simply legitimate sources that sell CDs and might carry JC's music.

www.geocities.com/Hollywood/Set/8801/jccd.html

www.imarnet.com/rockEN/Artist.asp?artistID=81

www.yesasia.com

www.angelpop.com

www.jpophelp.com

www.cdjapan.co.jp

www.asianmall.com

The best online information I've found on the subject of JC's music is: http://www.jackiechanmusic.com/. Jewel, the webmaster, keeps it very current. You can see many of the CD covers, and even listen to song samples. It's a fantastic resource.

About the Author

Recognized as one of the world's premier martial arts authors and journalists, John Corcoran has been a prime force in taking modern martial arts literature into the major-league arena. In his twenty-nine-year literary career, he has written millions of words about the subject in an acclaimed body of work encompassing books, magazines, and screenplays. Overall, he has used the power of the media to bring thousands of martial artists to public attention, and a select handful—including superstar Jean-Claude Van Damme—to stardom.

Mr. Corcoran has authored ten books to date, which have collectively sold over 300,000 copies worldwide. He is perhaps best known for his masterwork, *The Original Martial Art Encyclopedia*, the definitive reference of the genre, which took ten years from concept to completion and has sold over 130,000 copies to date. His most recent book is *The Ultimate Martial Arts Q&A Book: 750 Expert Answers to Your Essential Questions* (McGraw-Hill/Contemporary Books).

In addition, over the past twenty-nine years, Mr. Corcoran has served as an editor or founding editor of almost every influential martial arts magazine in the industry, starting with *Black Belt* in 1973. Corcoran is currently editor of *Martial Arts Success*, the industry's foremost trade publication. In 1977, he pioneered multilanguage article syndication in his field and his stories have since appeared in six languages in over seventy countries.

Mr. Corcoran's writings on the martial arts have also extended into academia, motion pictures, and the mainstream media.

He was selected by the editors of both *The World Book Encyclopedia* in 1986 and Microsoft's electronic *Encarta Encyclopedia* in 1996 to write their inaugural entries for martial arts. His mainstream articles have appeared in *Parade*, the Sunday newspaper supplement, and *Daily Variety*, Hollywood's leading trade paper.

In 1993, he wrote the screenplay for *American Samurai*, the film in which Mark Dacascos ("The Crow: Stairway to Heaven" TV series) made his starring debut. He was a primary technical consultant for A&E's 1998 landmark TV documentary, "The Martial Arts," and served in that same capacity for "Modern Warriors" (2001), produced by Oscar-nominated documentarian Peter Spirer. He has also appeared as a stunt fighter in a dozen martial arts films.

In 1998, he coedited with John Graden *The ACMA Instructor Certification Manual*. Based on the contents of the book, Dr. Kenneth Cooper, the Father of Fitness, and his world-renowned Cooper Institute for Aerobics Research agreed to administrate the ACMA Instructor Certification Program. This endorsement provides unprecedented credibility for the martial arts with both the academic/scientific community and the health and fitness industry. Essentially, it elevates the martial arts from a "fringe" pastime to a mainstream fitness activity.

Mr. Corcoran's literary mentors are the late great Academy Award–winning screenwriter Stirling Silliphant (*In the Heat of the Night*), who was Bruce Lee's main Hollywood mentor, and bestselling author Joe Hyams (*Bogie, Zen in the Martial Arts*). Legendary Heavyweight Karate Champion Joe Lewis has been his chief martial arts mentor since 1977. A veteran black belt in karate, he began his training in 1967. He lives in Pittsburgh, Pennsylvania.

Photo by Gail O'Toole